ALSO BY BILL SCHNEIDER

The Confidence Gap: Business, Labor,
and Government in the Public Mind
(with Seymour Martin Lipset)

Standoff

How America Became Ungovernable

Bill Schneider

Simon & Schuster

NEW YORK   LONDON   TORONTO   SYDNEY   NEW DELHI

Simon & Schuster
1230 Avenue of the Americas
New York, NY 10020

First Simon & Schuster hardcover edition May 2018

SIMON & SCHUSTER and colophon are registered trademarks of Simon & Schuster, Inc.

For information about special discounts for bulk purchases, please contact Simon & Schuster Special Sales at 1-866-506-1949 or business@simonandschuster.com.

The Simon & Schuster Speakers Bureau can bring authors to your live event. For more information or to book an event, contact the Simon & Schuster Speakers Bureau at 1-866-248-3049 or visit our website at www.simonspeakers.com.

Interior design by Ruth Lee-Mui

Manufactured in the United States of America

1   3   5   7   9   10   8   6   4   2

Library of Congress Cataloging-in-Publication Data

Names: Schneider, William, 1941– author.
Title: Standoff : how America became ungovernable / Bill Schneider.
Description: First Simon & Schuster hardcover edition. | New York :
Simon & Schuster, 2018. | Includes bibliographical references and index.
Identifiers: LCCN 2017047840 (print) | LCCN 2018009500 (ebook) |
ISBN 9781451606249 (ebook) | ISBN 9781451606225 (hardback) |
ISBN 9781451606232 (trade paperback)
Subjects: LCSH: United States—Politics and government—1989– | Political
culture—United States. | Populism—United States. | Right and left
(Political science)—United States. | United States—Politics and
government—1945–1989. | BISAC: POLITICAL SCIENCE / Political Ideologies
/ Conservatism & Liberalism. | POLITICAL SCIENCE / Government / General. |
HISTORY / United States / 20th Century.
Classification: LCC E839.5 (ebook) | LCC E839.5 .S3325 2018 (print) | DDC
320.973/0904—dc23
LC record available at https://lccn.loc.gov/2017047840

ISBN 978-1-4516-0623-2
ISBN 978-1-4516-0624-9 (ebook)

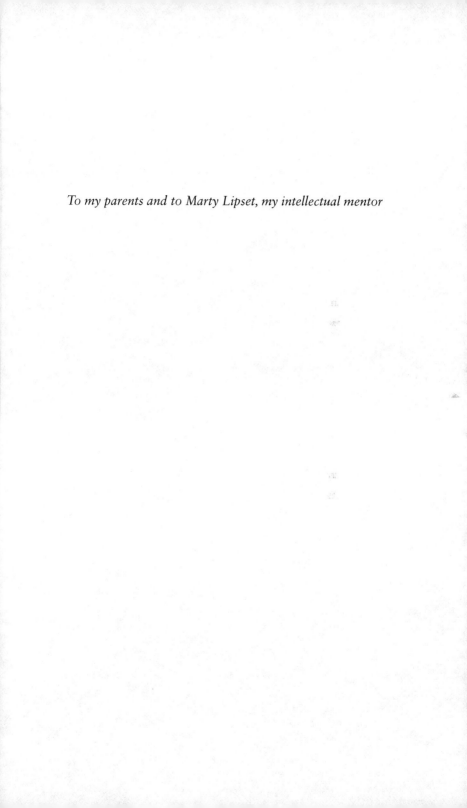

To my parents and to Marty Lipset, my intellectual mentor

Contents

Standoff

ONE

Old America Versus New America

On November 8, 2016, American voters did an astonishing thing. They elected a president of the United States who most voters—61 percent!—did not think was qualified to serve as president. How did that happen? How did we get from John F. Kennedy to Donald J. Trump?

A little more than fifty years ago, the United States started on a great political journey—in two opposite directions, part of the country to the right and part to the left. This is the story of where we are now and how we got here. It's the story of the country's journey and my own personal journey as I covered it.

It's the story of two political movements that first emerged in the 1960s. The New America is the progressive coalition of groups whose political consciousness was stirred in that decade: African Americans, young people, working women, gays, immigrants, educated professionals, and the nonreligious. What holds the coalition together is a commitment to diversity and inclusion. That commitment provoked a fierce backlash in 2016.

In fact, a conservative backlash has defied the New America for more than fifty years. The backlash came from the Old America— mostly white, mostly male, mostly older, mostly conservative, mostly religious, and mostly nonurban. In 2016 the Old America rallied to the theme "Make America Great Again." It was a call to restore the America they feared was being swept away by a tide of political correctness.

The two movements collided under President Barack Obama. Within weeks of Obama's inauguration on January 20, 2009, a right-wing opposition movement broke out in the form of the Tea Party. Republicans rode that anger to power in Congress, gaining control of the House of Representatives in 2010 and the Senate in 2014. Within one day of Trump's inauguration, a backlash broke out on the left with a massive spontaneous Women's March on Washington that drew throngs of supporters in cities across the United States. Using the Tea Party as a model, Democrats hope to ride anger on the left to power.

The right and the left started their journeys at the same place: 38 percent. That's the vote that Barry Goldwater got in 1964 and George McGovern got in 1972. The Republican presidential vote peaked with Richard Nixon in 1972 (61 percent) and Ronald Reagan in 1984 (59 percent). The Democratic presidential vote rose to a bare majority with Jimmy Carter in 1976 (50.1 percent) and then took thirty-two years to reach a majority again. Whereupon a new backlash quickly set in on the right. As of 2017, the Democratic Party had less clout in national and state governments than at any time since 1928.

Things started out pretty bad for Democrats. In 1972 a Democratic operative recounted the story of how George McGovern's campaign manager had called a Democratic congressional candidate in Ohio.

"I have wonderful news for you," the campaign manager said. "Senator McGovern is coming to campaign in your district."

"That is good news," the local candidate responded. "But I'm afraid I'm going to be in Florida, visiting my mother."

"Wait a minute," McGovern's campaign manager said. "I haven't told you when he's coming."

"It doesn't matter," the Democratic candidate replied. "Whenever he shows up, I'll be in Florida visiting my mother."

Democrats were forced to accommodate to the conservative ascendancy. Bill Clinton, who fashioned himself a "New Democrat" and a proponent of "the third way," got elected in 1992 with 43 percent of the vote. The presidential vote was split three ways that year, with Independent Ross Perot getting 19 percent. Clinton's coattails were unimpressive. Democrats lost seats in the House of Representatives in 1992. It was the first election following a census and redistricting. Redistricting always puts incumbents—mostly Democrats in 1992—at a disadvantage because they are forced to compete in an unfamiliar electorate.

The contours of Clinton's 1992 victory were different from anything Democrats had won with before. Democrats may have nominated two southern white Baptists for president and vice president in 1992, but the Clinton–Al Gore ticket fared worst in the South. It was the only region of the country where George H. W. Bush led Clinton (by 2 points). Among whites born in the South—the base of the pre-1960s Democratic coalition—Bush ran 19 points ahead of Clinton.

Clinton's vote—weakest in the South, strongest on the East and West Coasts—did not look like the Democratic votes that had elected

Franklin Roosevelt and John Kennedy and Jimmy Carter. It resembled the votes the Democrats got when they nominated liberals such as George McGovern in 1972 and Michael Dukakis in 1988. That's why 1992 was a breakthrough for Democrats: it was the first time they won with a vote that looked like the New America. But it was still not a majority.

Clinton narrowly missed a majority when he was reelected in 1996 with 49 percent. (Perot was on the ballot again.) Al Gore carried the popular vote in 2000, but it was not quite a majority (48 percent). John Kerry in 2004? Same thing: 48 percent and no victory. The breakthrough finally came in 2008 when Barack Obama won with a solid majority (53 percent), the highest percentage for a Democratic presidential candidate since Lyndon Johnson.

Even so, you could argue that the 2008 Democratic vote was inflated by the worst financial crisis since the Great Depression. What if there were no crisis? That's why Obama's reelection in 2012 came as such a shock. Obama was reelected with a majority (51 percent) despite a sluggish economic recovery. The New America came out to protect its president. And to prove that its coming to power was not a fluke.

However, 2016 was an even bigger shock because Trump's primary and general election victories were unexpected. First, he staged a hostile takeover of the Republican Party. The 2016 Republican primaries were expected to be a showdown between the party establishment (former Florida governor Jeb Bush) and Tea Party conservatives (Texas senator Ted Cruz). Trump beat them both. He did it by activating a populist following of working-class white voters who had been trending Republican since Richard Nixon but had never won control of the party.

Trump rallied his supporters with crude populism: anger at the political establishment and opposition to the global elite. The Trump movement and the conservative movement formed an alliance. Trump used conservatives to legitimize his rise to power. Conservatives wanted Trump in the White House to sign whatever legislation the Republican Congress passed (and keep his mouth shut, which he refused to do).

The Trump movement is the latest manifestation of resistance by the Old America. The gradual and halting rise of the New America faced resistance every step of the way. Two years after Bill Clinton was elected in 1992, Democrats lost their majority in the House of Representatives for the first time in forty years. Resistance sprang up in the 1995 government shutdown. A violent antigovernment backlash materialized in resistance to a search and arrest warrant by a religious sect in Waco, Texas, in 1993 and in the bombing of a federal building in Oklahoma City in 1995. The Clinton impeachment was an attempt to delegitimize the first president who embraced the liberal values of the 1960s.

The recount of Florida's votes in the 2000 presidential election between Governor George W. Bush and Vice President Al Gore is still seen by many Americans as a plot to steal the election by reversing the will of the voters. In 2009 President Obama faced a Tea Party rebellion within weeks of taking office. Obama also had to contend with a concerted effort to delegitimize him by challenging his birth, his religion, and his Americanism. The resistance showed no signs of slowing down after Obama was reelected. The most direct challenge to the New America came in 2016. Donald Trump's resistance movement spurned diversity and inclusion as "political correctness."

The conservative movement remains dug in largely as a result of de facto political segregation. In many red states and districts, Democrats are noncompetitive, and Trump supporters are a significant force in Republican primaries.

It's a standoff. Democrats try to reassure themselves that demographic trends are in their favor. The percentage of working-class whites is declining, while the country is seeing growing numbers of minorities, young people, working women, highly educated Americans, and people without a religious affiliation.

But there's a downside for Democrats. Demographics is long, politics is short. In 2016 politics clearly favored Republicans. So what happened? A Democratic resistance movement sprang up for the purpose of doing to President Trump the same thing the Tea Party did to President Obama: oppose everything the president tried to do. The result has become the new normal in the United States: gridlock and dysfunctional government.

Gridlock and Public Opinion

The potential for gridlock is built into the US constitution. The Founders set up a complex and ungainly system with two houses of Congress, three branches of government, and competing centers of power in the federal government and the states. The idea was to limit power. The result is a constitutional system that works exactly as intended. Which is to say, it doesn't work very well at all. As president after president has discovered, there are many ways opponents can stop measures from getting passed, even if the president's party holds a majority in Congress.

Today the New America has an advantage, though not a "lock," in presidential elections. Democrats carried the popular vote in six out of the last seven presidential elections (1992 to 2016, except for 2004). In two of those elections, 2000 and 2016, Republicans won the electoral vote because the Democratic vote was heavily concentrated in a few large states (California, New York, Illinois).

The Old America has the advantage in congressional elections. In the House of Representatives, Democrats have been the victims of gerrymandering—the drawing of district boundaries to benefit the Republican Party—as well as a "density" problem: too many Democratic votes concentrated in Democratic congressional districts. The Constitution guarantees two senators from every state, and there are a lot of small Republican states such as Idaho and Wyoming. California, with two Democratic senators, has sixty-seven times as many people as Wyoming, which has two Republican senators.

The Old America also has the advantage in elections for state governments. After the 2016 election, Republicans had total control of twenty-five state governments and Democrats only six. The Republican heartland is now the South and the interior West. Democrats dominate the Northeast and the West Coast.

So here we are: two political parties, entrenched in different institutions, at different levels of government, and in different places. The separation of powers has given rise to fortified bunkers. And gridlock.

In the British parliamentary system, gridlock is unconstitutional. A core principle of the British constitution is "Her majesty's government must be carried on." If the government is gridlocked and cannot act, the government falls, and new elections are held until the people elect a government that can govern decisively.

The United States has no queen. There is no constitutional necessity for the government to act decisively. Framers of the US Constitution had just waged a revolution against a king. To them, strong government meant despotism.

American government is set up to fail. The wonder is that it actually does work. It works when there is a crisis—when an overwhelming sense of urgency breaks through blockages and lubricates the system. Under the right conditions, barriers fall away, and things get done, sometimes with amazing speed and efficiency. That's where public opinion comes in.

The framers of the Constitution did everything they could to insulate government from public opinion with devices such as the electoral college, lifetime tenure for federal judges, and, until 1913, indirect election of senators. But public opinion has come to play a crucial role never envisioned by the Constitution. It can break gridlock and make government work. What's required is that overwhelming sense of urgency—the public's demand that the government do something, anything, to solve a pressing problem.

Politicians are always hyping issues to try to turn them into crises: an environmental crisis, an energy crisis, an education crisis, a moral crisis. Or they declare "wars" on things: a war on poverty, a war on crime, a war on inflation, a war on drugs, a war on terror. (Senator Daniel Patrick Moynihan of New York once said sardonically, "We declared war on poverty, and poverty won.") Without a crisis or war to rally public opinion, the system doesn't work at all. It was not designed to.

When Barack Obama took office in the midst of a financial disaster, his chief of staff, Rahm Emanuel, remarked, "You never want a serious crisis to go to waste. And what I mean by that is an opportunity to do things you think you could not do before."[1] Emanuel got a lot of criticism for saying that. It sounded as if he were trying to exploit the nation's troubles. But he was right.

What distinguishes a real crisis from a phony crisis? Public urgency.

8

If the public urgency is not real, opponents won't have much trouble blocking government action—as they did repeatedly on measures to combat climate change, a long-term threat but not an immediate crisis for most Americans.

We've had plenty of real crises: the launching of Sputnik by the Soviet Union in 1957; civil rights in the 1960s; ten years of war in Vietnam, the Watergate scandal, a tax revolt, inflation, and energy shortages in the 1970s; a wave of violent crime in the 1980s; recession in the early 1990s; 9/11 in 2001, the war in Iraq, the 2008 financial crisis. They all resulted in decisive breakthroughs in public policy: the National Defense Education Act in 1958, the Civil Rights Act, campaign finance reform, the War Powers Act, tax reform, energy efficiency standards, the Patriot Act, a ban on torture by the US military, the economic stimulus plan. What happens if the sense of urgency isn't real? Then the system of limited government locks into place. Nothing much gets done. We get gridlock. It's in the Constitution.

The default setting in the United States is limited government.[2] Almost every state has some sort of balanced-budget requirement. Franklin Roosevelt and Barack Obama, each of whom presided over huge expansions of federal spending, both proclaimed their commitment to deficit reduction.

So why do we have such high levels of government spending? Because Americans are pragmatists. Pragmatists believe that whatever works is right. Ideologues believe that if something is wrong, it can't possibly work—even if it does work. That's how Republicans always felt about the Affordable Care Act: it could never work because it was wrong, even if there was evidence that it was working (by shrinking the number of uninsured Americans by 20 million).

President Trump represents an extreme version of pragmatism.

Conservatives have long distrusted him because he has never shown much interest in ideology. With Trump, it's not about right and wrong, it's about winning and losing. If you are a winner, then everything you say must be right.

Americans may not believe in big government, but they are willing to support government spending if it solves a problem. Progressives have to rely on pragmatism, not ideology, to make the case for their agenda. President Obama's economic program got into trouble in 2010 because the recovery was weak and fitful. People did not believe stimulus spending was working, so it was difficult to make the case for more spending. The public fell back to its default position: limited government.

Showdowns

The 2012 and 2016 campaigns were showdowns between the Old America and the New America. The Old America's rallying cry at the 2012 Republican National Convention in Tampa was "Restore Our Future." Take us back to the days when America was rich, great, and powerful—the undisputed leader of the world. Mitt Romney declared, "You might have asked yourself if these last years are really the America we want; the America won for us by the Greatest Generation." That same sentiment was appropriated by Trump in 2016: "Make America Great Again!" The Hollywood celebrity who spoke at the 2012 Republican convention was Clint Eastwood, age eighty-two.

The New America's rallying cry at the 2012 Democratic Convention in Charlotte, North Carolina, was "Forward, Not Back." President Obama declared, "When Governor Romney finally had a chance to reveal the secret sauce, he did not offer a single new idea. It was just retreads of the same old policies we've been hearing for decades."

The New America celebrates diversity in age, race, sexual orientation, and lifestyles. (The Old America doesn't have lifestyles; they have lives.) The Hollywood celebrity who spoke at the 2012 Democratic Convention was twenty-seven-year-old Scarlett Johansson.

After nearly fifty years, the two Americas have fought each other to a standoff. A college student of mine once asked me, "Is this the most divided we have ever been as a country?" I reminded him, "We did, once, have a Civil War. Three-quarters of a million Americans died in that war." But I acknowledged that this was probably the most divided the country had been since that terrible time. We will see evidence for that argument in chapter 3.

Knowing the Times

You can't talk about public opinion for long without using the word *fickle*. Former British prime minister Harold Wilson once said, "A week is a long time in politics." Look at how quickly public opinion turned against Bill Clinton after he took office in 1993. And how quickly he recovered after the shattering setback of the 1994 midterm election.

An Oxford University student once wrote a letter to British prime minister Benjamin Disraeli asking him what he should know to prepare for a career in public life. "Young man, there are only two things you must know to succeed in public life," the politician responded. "You must know yourself. And you must know the times."

Knowing the times is a challenge. What was true yesterday may not be true tomorrow. In 2006 the war in Iraq was the all-consuming issue that drove American politics. By 2008, Iraq had nearly disappeared from the political agenda, despite the fact that more than 180,000 US troops were still deployed in Iraq—some 44,000 more than in 2006.

If you understand public opinion—not just polls, but public opinion—you can solve many mysteries about American politics. Like how John McCain won the Republican nomination in 2008. (It was a personal vote.) And how he lost the general election. (It was an issues vote.) And how a candidate can win an election and still look like a loser (by having fared "worse than expected").

And what happened to the so-called Bradley Effect, where white voters tell poll takers they will vote for an African American candidate and then don't do it. I covered the 1982 race when Los Angeles mayor Tom Bradley narrowly lost the election for California governor that he was expected to win. The polls were more reliable when Barack Obama ran for president in 2008. There are still racist voters out there, but they don't lie about it as much as they used to.

I am not usually surprised by the direction public opinion takes, but sometimes the logic of public thinking escapes me.

One of those times was in the recount following the disputed 2000 presidential election. A week before Election Day, I had written, "If Gore became president after more people vote for Bush, the electoral college will be history." The premise turned out to be backward. George W. Bush became president despite more people having voted for Al Gore.

The electoral college did not become history. There was no wave of public outrage over an "undemocratic" electoral system. People did complain loudly about the unfair outcome of the presidential election. By and large, however, the electoral college was not the principal complaint. Why not?

Some reporting and a careful reading of the polls revealed the answer: Florida. For five weeks after Election Day, the media focus stayed on Florida. Public anger was directed at the state's chaotic voting procedures, not at the electoral college. The final count showed Gore winning the national popular vote by a substantial margin: nearly 540,000 votes. But the figure most Americans complained about was Bush's disputed margin in Florida: 537 votes.

What if Bush had won the popular vote and lost the electoral college? Then the situation might have been different. Outraged Republicans would have called Gore an illegitimate president. Republicans, who were desperate to win after eight years of Bill Clinton, would probably have balked at Gore's becoming president because of a "quirk in the rules." If Gore had become president after more people had voted for Bush, chances are the electoral college would be gone. And Hillary Clinton would have beaten Donald Trump in 2016.

Some political mysteries are difficult to explain. Like why liberals can't do talk radio. Liberals prefer satire such as Jon Stewart, Stephen Colbert, and *Saturday Night Live.* You could argue that liberal talk radio is NPR, with its flagship show *All Things Considered.* Conservative firebrands don't consider all things. They consider what they damn well want to consider.

And why, if Hollywood is a nest of liberals and Democrats, have so many Hollywood celebrities who've run for political office been Republicans (Ronald Reagan, George Murphy, Fred Thompson, Sonny Bono, Fred Grandy, Clint Eastwood, Arnold Schwarzenegger)?

An observer of public opinion has to distinguish between public attitudes that are resistant to change, such as the American public's distrust of government; views that shift over time, such as opinions on racial segregation and same-sex marriage; and opinions that can turn in a moment.

My initial experience of live television news coverage came during Supreme Court confirmation hearings for Clarence Thomas in 1991. Until Anita Hill gave her testimony, men regarded sexual harassment as something of a joke. They thought of it as "flirting." They failed to comprehend women's anger and humiliation. Professor Hill's testimony about her degrading experiences turned out to be one of those rare moments when public consciousness changed, transforming sexual harassment from a joke to a crime.

I grew up in the segregated South, where I witnessed firsthand the transformation of a society. In 1955, when Rosa Parks refused to give up her seat on a bus to a white man in Montgomery, Alabama, her action released the pent-up anger and frustration of millions. Southern whites, who had allowed themselves to believe that segregation worked, suddenly saw how outraged black people were to live under Jim Crow laws. Consciousness changed. And eventually a social order was overturned.

I was teaching at Harvard University during the student strike of 1969. At first, most students saw the antiwar protesters as crazy radicals acting out. Then in the early morning of April 10, university authorities called in the police to remove students occupying the administration building. The resulting bloody confrontation roused student consciousness. What had been something of a joke on April 9 turned into a deadly serious cause on April 11. I could see it in my classes: career-minded students were transformed overnight into political activists.

When Matthew Shepard was brutally beaten, tortured, and left to die tied to a fence post in 1998, the public began to understand the violence and hatred gay people face. Previously, many Americans saw gay rights as a solution for which there was no known problem. But consciousness changed. Now same-sex couples have a constitutional right to marry.

All Politics Is National

Presidential elections are the markers the United States uses to define itself every four years. President and vice president are the only elected officeholders whose constituency is the entire country.

It may have been the case long ago that presidential elections involved separate campaigns for each state's electoral votes, as the authors of the Constitution intended. But especially since the rise of television coverage in the 1960s, presidential campaigns have become nationalized. National swings toward one party or the other are the rule, with smaller local variations. Congressional and state elections are also becoming more nationalized. The 2006 midterm election was a nationwide referendum on the war in Iraq. The 2014 midterm was the "Nobama election."

The issues and alignments that define American politics tend to appear first at the national level. State and local elections often take awhile to catch up to national trends because voters feel personal attachments to state and local candidates, even if they are in a different party. House Speaker Thomas P. "Tip" O'Neill Jr.'s famous dictum "All politics is local" is outdated. Today presidential elections lead; state and local elections follow.

White southern voters driven by racial backlash started abandoning the Democratic Party in presidential elections in the 1960s. It took decades for white southerners to acquire the habit of voting Republican in state and local elections. A lot of southern Democrats held on to

Standoff

their seats in Congress through the 1970s and 1980s because of deeply entrenched personal and local loyalties. But then many of those Democrats suddenly got swept away in the 1994 midterm election, which became a negative referendum on President Bill Clinton. Popular Texas representative Jack Brooks, for example, had served in Congress for forty-two years. The Democrat lost his seat in 1994 because of his support for Clinton.

The Power of Public Opinion

It is a core popular belief that ordinary people don't have any power. Time and time again, however, I have seen public opinion prevail over the political elite. I saw it in the Elian Gonzalez case in 2000. The American public saw the story as a terrible human tragedy that politicians were trying to exploit for political advantage. The polls sent out a strong signal: anyone who tried to politicize the issue would pay a price. Public opinion thwarted efforts by conservatives to keep the child, who had survived a shipwreck and lost his mother, in the United States as a political refugee.

Public opinion prevailed again in the Terri Schiavo case in 2005. Americans saw this story, too, as a personal tragedy that politicians were trying to exploit for political gain. Once again, the polls sent a powerful signal that politicians should not interfere. Public opinion thwarted efforts by conservatives to keep Ms. Schiavo, who had been in a persistent vegetative state for fifteen years, on life support. In a Gallup poll, three-quarters of Americans disapproved of Congress's involvement in a private family matter.[3] But the Republican-led Congress did interfere. And Republicans paid a price in the next election.

In January 1998, shortly after the Monica Lewinsky story broke,

I received a late-night telephone call from Barbra Streisand, a well-known Clinton supporter. She asked me whether I believed President Clinton could survive the scandal.

Washington insiders were declaring the Clinton presidency over. The president's fellow Democrats weren't rushing to his defense. They felt betrayed. At CNN, we had trouble finding Democrats who would go on the air to defend Clinton. The public's response was shock and dismay. Pundits started talking about how Clinton's days were numbered, what Al Gore would do as president, and whom he would choose as his vice president. (The consensus in the chattering class was that he would pick Senator Dianne Feinstein of California.)

I told Ms. Streisand that I seriously doubted the president could survive. He was a married man accused of having a sexual relationship with a woman less than half his age. Lewinsky was a White House intern and therefore someone under the president's supervision. And the sexual encounters had occurred in the Oval Office.

"I don't know," Ms. Streisand replied. "I think he can get through this. After all, it's just about sex. People make allowances when it's just about sex." The House of Representatives impeached Clinton for perjury and obstruction of justice. But the core of the matter was sex.

The polls saved Clinton—literally. There were no public demonstrations in support of the president. No rallies. No phone banks. Just the polls, which astonished Washington and the world when they showed the president's public support *rising*. Conventional wisdom shifted 180 degrees. Congressional Democrats rallied to defend the president—once they saw whose side the public was on.

Bill Clinton knew and understood the American public better than any president since Ronald Reagan. He was just as skillful a communicator, too. How Bill Clinton survived impeachment remains one of the great feats of political dexterity in US history. His feel for public opinion played a key role. If there had been no polls, Clinton would have been finished. We will examine that amazing story of redemption in chapter 4.

Public opinion is often misunderstood. Its importance is typically either overestimated or underestimated. Overestimated because its importance seems obvious. The United States is a democracy. Of course public opinion matters. Politicians have to pay attention to it. At least they are supposed to. But do they? Politicians are frequently uncomprehending, or heedless, of public opinion. When that happens, there are painful consequences. Democrats failed to grasp the centrality of the terrorism issue in the 2002 and 2004 elections. Republicans refused to acknowledge the public's opposition to the impeachment of President Clinton in 1998, until their election losses drove home the point.

The power of public opinion is also underestimated by the public. Since the 1960s, growing numbers of Americans have come to believe they don't have much say in what the government does.[4] Why not? Because distrust of elites is a core populist belief. Populism creates a wall of cynicism between "us" and "them," the people and the political insiders. The people believe political leaders are hostile or indifferent to their concerns. Leaders often assume that the people are ignorant or passive or easy to manipulate.

Americans root for the underdog and stand up for the little guy. They vent their anger at insiders, big shots, experts, Washington, Wall Street—anyone in a position of power who is seen as disdainful of ordinary people or remote from their concerns. It's the Howard Beale outcry from the 1976 movie *Network*, a satire of television news: "We're mad as hell, and we're not going to take it anymore!" No political figure embodied that view more than Donald Trump, who has the traits of a populist demagogue.

Ordinary Americans don't believe they have much power. But they do. They have the power to stop wars (Vietnam and Iraq). They have the power to keep a president in office (Bill Clinton). They have the power to slash taxes (Proposition 13 in California). They have the power to defy the political establishment (Trump). They even have the power to stop themselves from reelecting the same people over and over again (popular referendums to impose term limits on elected officials).

To argue that the people rule is not to argue that government always does what the people want. Clearly it doesn't. It is to argue that US political leaders are far more attentive to public opinion than most Americans suspect. And when leaders fail to act, or act in defiance of what the public wants, they pay a price.

I first grasped the power, and complexity, of public opinion in 1968 when, as a graduate student, I studied the New Hampshire Democratic presidential primary. Antiwar candidate Senator Eugene McCarthy of Minnesota nearly defeated incumbent president Lyndon Johnson in his own party. But there was another surprise: polls revealed that many Vietnam "hawks" voted for McCarthy, the "dove." Why? Because they were furious with LBJ for the way the war was being conducted.

A little reporting revealed that a lot of New Hampshire voters could not be classified in the conventional Washington categories as either hawks or doves. They were both. What did they want the United States to do in Vietnam? "We should win or get out" was the answer I heard over and over again. It was perfectly rational for them to vote for McCarthy because that was the easiest way to send a message of dissatisfaction with LBJ's war policy.[5]

Johnson got the message and withdrew from the race two weeks later. But the antiwar movement never quite grasped what had happened: the consensus in the country had become antiwar but not dovish. As a result, the McGovern campaign crashed and burned in 1972, and the war went on.

Not a lot has changed since 1968 in the way Americans think about military intervention. The public hates political wars. People believe the military should be used to win military victories, not to win the hearts and minds of foreigners. As a candidate for the White House in 2000, George W. Bush appeared to understand that lesson. He declared that the US military should never be used for "nation building." But as commander in chief, that is exactly what he did in Iraq, and Republicans paid the price in the 2006 midterm. When President Bush responded by defying public opinion and sending more troops—the "surge" of 2007—he triggered an outpouring of public rage.

Public opinion polls are common in every democratic country. But they are far more pervasive in the United States. In other countries, polls assess the popularity of the government and its chances of survival in the next election. In the United States, polls assess the popularity of every policy and every politician. All the time.

The United States does not have a tradition of party government. When Bill Clinton took office in 1993, Democrats were in control of both the House and Senate. But the president was unable to hold his party together to pass health care reform. In America, you have to poll on every individual issue. Simply gauging public support for the president and the president's party doesn't tell you much about how an issue is likely to fare.

Question: If public opinion is such a powerful force, why is it that the majority often does not rule?

After the horrifying school shootings in Newtown, Connecticut, in December 2012, when 20-year-old Adam Lanza killed 20 six- and seven-year-old schoolchildren and six adult staff members as well as his mother and himself, close to 90 percent of the public favored expanded background checks for gun purchasers. But the measure could not get through the US Senate. Likewise, polls show that a solid majority of Americans favors a path to citizenship for illegal immigrants. But immigration reform with citizenship provisions has been impossible to get through Congress. The public has long favored a budget deal that balances spending cuts and tax increases. But balanced deals are difficult to pass. A majority of Americans support abortion rights, yet more and more abortion restrictions have been imposed.

The reason is that *intensity* of opinion matters, not just numbers. Politicians don't just pay attention to how many people are on each side of an issue. They also need to know how much people on each side of the issue see it as an overriding priority. How many votes will be driven by those who feel one way or the other? An intensely committed minority—gun owners, for instance—can have a bigger impact than a casually committed majority for whom the issue does not determine their vote. I will take up the intensity factor in chapter 6. But it is not inconsistent with the idea of populism. Public opinion matters. Loud opinions matter more.

Coalitions and Movements

American political parties have always been coalitions: diverse interests that join together to pursue a shared objective. When I started covering politics, the dominant coalition was the Franklin D. Roosevelt coalition. That coalition reached its peak strength in President Lyndon Johnson's 1964 landslide victory. It proceeded to fall apart during LBJ's second term. FDR brought together a coalition of groups that had one thing in common: they all wanted something from the federal government. The Roosevelt coalition included working-class voters, first- and second-generation immigrants, African Americans, Jews, southern whites, labor unionists, seniors, and farmers.

In 1980 a new coalition emerged: the Reagan coalition. Ronald Reagan brought together diverse interests that also had one thing in common: they all had a grievance with the federal government. It included suburban taxpayers, business interests, white voters motivated by racial backlash to civil rights and affirmative action, religious conservatives, gun owners, anti-Communist intellectuals, and men. They were hostile to the federal government for different reasons: taxes, government regulations, activist federal judges, civil rights laws, and gun restrictions. They agreed with Ronald Reagan when he said at his first inaugural, in 1981, "Government is not the solution to our problem. Government is the problem."

The New America is also a coalition. It can trace its roots back at least as far as the George McGovern campaign of 1972. The New America came to power in 2008, defeated a conservative backlash in 2012, and continued to outnumber the backlash in 2016. It includes African Americans, Latinos, Asian Americans, Jews, gays, working women, single mothers, educated professionals, young people, and the unchurched (the nearly one-fifth of Americans who claim no religious affiliation).

Members of a coalition are expected to agree on one common objective: "If you support our candidate—for whatever reason—you're one of us. No further questions." Supporters of a movement are expected to agree on everything. For conservatives, that means the entire conservative agenda: from tax cuts, to outlawing abortion, curbing immigration, and loosening environmental regulations. Disagree on anything, and you can be declared a heretic and expelled from the movement. Movement politics is out of line with the American political tradition. But its influence has been growing in both major parties.

In 2010 the Tea Party tried to act as the enforcement arm of the conservative movement. Tea Party activists threatened Republican waverers with primary opposition if they deviated from the conservative line. Their triumph came in 2014, when Tea Party voters defeated House Majority Leader Eric Cantor in his Virginia district's Republican primary.

But the Tea Party was not the only backlash to Obama. In 2016 Donald Trump led a right-wing populist movement that overwhelmed both the establishment Republican candidate (Jeb Bush) and the Tea Party favorite (Ted Cruz). The Trump movement and the conservative movement became allies in the 2016 campaign. It's an uneasy alliance. Tea Party conservatives are intensely ideological. Trump is not driven by devotion to conservative principles. Sooner or later, Republicans are bound to split over President Trump.

Hillary Clinton tried to hold together Obama's winning coalition in 2016, but she was not able to revive the enthusiasm Obama had generated in 2008 and 2012. After surviving a populist challenge by Senator Bernie Sanders, Clinton became the candidate of the Washington establishment and the status quo. Support from blue-collar white voters in midwestern battleground states, egged on by Russian interference, gave Trump the edge he needed to win the electoral college.

As noted earlier, Democrats have carried the popular vote in six out of the last seven presidential elections. You could say that after forty long years in the wilderness, the McGovern coalition finally emerged as a contender for power. But it continues to face determined opposition from the Old America.

After Trump took office in 2017, a powerful backlash broke out on the left. The New America was enraged by Trump's assault on their most cherished values, diversity and inclusion. That enthusiasm had been missing from the Clinton campaign, most likely because she was so widely predicted to win. During the campaign, Democrats were described as taking Trump "literally but not seriously."[6] Once they were forced to take him seriously, progressive forces were galvanized into opposition, and the prospect of a Tea Party of the left emerged suddenly. Movements beget countermovements.

Interests and Values

Two forces drive people's political behavior: interests and values. They are often in conflict. When that happens, values usually prevail over interests.

Barack Obama got in trouble during the 2008 campaign when he talked about blue-collar voters in Pennsylvania's small towns, telling a group of supporters in San Francisco: "They get bitter, they cling to guns or religion or antipathy to people who aren't like them or anti-immigrant sentiment or antitrade sentiment as a way to explain their frustrations." Obama seemed to be depicting those sentiments as irrational—in other words, contrary to the voters' economic interests. But to many of those voters, their values are just as important as their economic interests, if not more so.

During the 2004 presidential campaign, I met with a group of voters in West Virginia. In addition to being one of the poorest states in the country, it is also one of the whitest. West Virginia, a coal mining state, was strongly prolabor and Democratic since Franklin D. Roosevelt's New Deal, voting for the Democrat in fourteen out of seventeen presidential elections from 1932 to 1996. The former Democratic Senate leader Robert Byrd was the embodiment of that tradition. But in the last five presidential elections, West Virginia has gone Republican by increasing margins (52 percent in 2000, 56 percent in 2004 and 2008, 62 percent in 2012, 69 percent in 2016).

I asked the voters in the room how many of them had health insurance. Only three out of ten did. I asked them which candidate they thought would be more likely to help the uninsured. Most of them said the Democrat, Senator John Kerry. So were they planning to vote for Kerry? Almost all said no. "Why not?" I asked.

"We hear he wants to take our guns away," one participant said.

"Are your guns more important than your health insurance?" I asked.

A woman replied, "Mister, our guns *are* our health insurance."

The ideological politics that emerged in the 1960s is not class based. It crosses class lines. "Limousine liberalism" is often characterized as a top-bottom coalition of the guilt-ridden rich and the dependent poor. The poor vote their interests, while the rich vote their values. The conservative coalition is also a top-bottom one, allying "country-club" conservatives with less sophisticated "rednecks" and religious fundamentalists. In this case, the rich vote their interests, and the poor vote their values.

Liberals are sometimes shocked to learn that working-class voters often vote their values over their interests. But so do a lot of educated upper-middle-class liberals. Jewish voters, for instance, are disproportionately well educated and high income. Their economic interests ought to lead them to vote Republican. Many Jews are also staunch supporters of Israel, and Israelis such as Prime Minister Benjamin Netanyahu have signaled that Republicans today are more reliable supporters of Israel than Democrats are. Nevertheless, Jews voted strongly for Obama in 2008 and 2012 and for Hillary Clinton in 2016. They were voting their liberal values, not their conservative interests. As the late Milton Himmelfarb, research director of the American Jewish Committee, once wrote, "Jews have the wealth and status of Episcopalians and vote like Puerto Ricans."

The values divide in the nation's upper-middle class first became visible in California in the 1960s among upper-middle-class voters. What is distinctive about the upper-middle class is its sense of security and self-satisfaction for having achieved the good life.

In 1967 political scientist James Q. Wilson, who grew up in what he called "Reagan country," wrote an article in *Commentary* magazine in which he tried to explain "the political culture of Southern California" to Eastern intellectuals.[7] The Goldwater and Reagan movements were protest movements, Wilson argued, but they were not expressions of personal unhappiness, frustration, or despair. Just the opposite, in fact. In describing Goldwater and Reagan supporters, Wilson pointed out that "it is not with their lot that they are discontent, it is with the lot of the nation. The very virtues they have and practice are, in their eyes, conspicuously absent from society as a whole."

The same year, author and editor Richard Todd, wrote an article in *Harper's* magazine in which he tried to explain "the Berkeley phenomenon" to puzzled outsiders.[8] Why had that University of California campus become the focal point of student unrest? Was it true, as many commentators suggested, that UC Berkeley students were frustrated and dehumanized by the "mega-university" and that their political protest was an expression of personal anger and discontent? Todd found little evidence of despair or alienation at Berkeley. What he found instead was "a sense of rightness . . . the peculiar kind of joy that is the result of self-absorption." Berkeley students lived by a code of tolerance, openness, free expression, nonviolence, and permissiveness. They were angry because the country was not being governed in accordance with their code.

Both the right and the left draw support from people who feel certain about their own values and resentful that the rest of society does not embrace them. Each has captured a political party.

The two parties are led by upper-middle-class elites, but they are bitterly competitive elites. In 2012 Mitt Romney was the prince of wealth. Republicans prefer to call it "success." Romney said at the 2012 Republican convention, "The centerpiece of President Obama's entire reelection campaign is attacking success . . . In America, we celebrate success; we don't apologize for it." Barack Obama was the prince of education. He told Democrats at their convention, "Education was the gateway of opportunity for me. It was the gateway for [First Lady] Michelle. It was the gateway for most of you." (Columnist David Brooks once observed that President Obama "governs like a visitor from a morally superior civilization."[9])The two elites have been competing for power since the 1960s. The showdown was 2012: two elites, two elitists, both posing as men of the people. And neither with a populist bone in his body.

The presidential race of 2016 saw a populist backlash in both parties. Bernie Sanders led a left-wing populist challenge to the Democratic Party establishment that garnered 43 percent of the Democratic primary vote. Donald Trump led a right-wing populist challenge to the Republican Party establishment. He won 45 percent of the Republican primary vote.

TWO

Populism

The United States is the most populist country in the world. Next to America, the rest of the world is Saudi Arabia.

That's because public opinion is a key player in US politics all the time, not just at election time. In the United States, more than anywhere else, public opinion shapes events. It does so despite the fact that the framers of the Constitution tried to restrain the impact of public opinion.

American politicians are independent political entrepreneurs. They're all in business for themselves. They are not foot soldiers in a party army. American politics, like the American economy, is highly entrepreneurial. If there is a market, there will be a product. If there is an unpopular war, there will be an antiwar candidate. If voters are angry about taxes, there will be an antitax candidate. If they are fed up with Washington, outsiders will suddenly spring up—Ross Perot in 1992 and 1996; Donald Trump in 2016—to carry the antiestablishment banner.

Like every ideology, populism sees the world as us versus them. In populist terms, the people are us. The elites are them. There are many different elites, of course, and they can be targeted in different ways. The left goes after country-club conservatives. The right attacks limousine liberals. Outsiders rail against the political establishment, Washington insiders, and special interests.

The opposite of populism is elitism: the belief that the people in charge know what they are doing and can be trusted. Elitism does surface occasionally in US politics—think former mayor Michael Bloomberg of New York City, whose governing principle seemed to be "Trust us. We know what we're doing. And we know what's good for you." Like banning smoking in bars and restaurants and limiting the size of sugary soft drinks. But elitism is not the norm. The norm is distrust of elites, a deep-seated value that runs throughout US history. Resentment of elites infuses American popular culture. Ever notice how rich and powerful people—business executives, politicians, bureaucrats—are portrayed on television? Usually as incompetent, corrupt, or worse.

Populism has been a driving force for both the left and the right. Left-wing populism is typically economic, targeted at "the 1 percent," Wall Street, and big business. Right-wing populism is typically cultural, targeted at educated elites who seem out of touch with the values of ordinary Americans. Antiestablishment populism is neither left nor right, just antielite. ("Throw the bums out!")

You can see the influence of populism in many small ways. The federal government has minted several versions of the dollar coin, but Americans refuse to use them (to the despair of vending machine operators). Elites in other countries have imposed the metric system because it is scientific and rational. Good luck trying to get Americans to go metric. In 2015 Lincoln Chafee, the former US senator and governor of Rhode Island, ran for the 2016 Democratic nomination for president. One of Chafee's key proposals was adoption of the metric system. He left the race after one primary debate.

Americans refuse to leave legal judgment to the experts. US courts rely far more on jury trials than courts in any other country do, including Great Britain, where the modern jury system was devised. The United States is the only nation in the world that elects judges, for goodness' sake (state and local judges, not federal judges).

In Europe, the people may favor the death penalty, but elites tell them that capital punishment is cruel and barbaric and must be outlawed. In order to join the European Union, a country has to abolish the death penalty. When George W. Bush made his first presidential visit to Europe in 2001, he faced protests against the death penalty in the United States (Oklahoma City terrorist bomber Timothy McVeigh had just been executed). At a press conference in Madrid, President Bush explained, "Democracies represent the will of the people. The death penalty is the will of the people in the United States."

The Two Faces of Populism

Populism has two faces: economically progressive and socially conservative. Elites tend to be rich and well educated; hence, economically conservative and culturally progressive. Liberal Democrats are vulnerable to attack as cultural elitists, and conservative Republicans, as economic elitists. True populists do not feel entirely comfortable in either party.

Voters often have to decide which is the greater threat; economic insecurity or cultural anxiety. In the 1968 and 1972 elections, cultural anxiety prevailed. The country was torn by racial violence, student protests, and anti-Vietnam war agitation. That's when Republicans first discovered the power of social issues: racial backlash, law and order, and support for the military. Richard Nixon built his "silent majority" on the social issue (the Southern Strategy, branding Democrats as the party of "acid, amnesty, and abortion"). In the 1980s, the social issue became "values." In 1988 George H. W. Bush used the Pledge of Allegiance, the death penalty, and criminal furloughs to portray Michael Dukakis as outside the mainstream.

Each time they won, Republicans had something else going for them as well: the fact that economic populism was neutralized. The economy was booming in the 1960s and early 1970s, right up until the 1973 Arab oil embargo, imposed in retaliation for US support for Israel in the 1973 Arab-Israeli war. Economic insecurity was not a driving force in the elections of 1968 and 1972.

Democrats had a different problem in the 1980s: they lost the economic issue. Under Jimmy Carter, Democrats failed to fulfill the mandate of economic populism. They did not protect people against economic adversity. Under Ronald Reagan, the country enjoyed a long economic boom. In 1988, with no economic issue to help them and the values issue going against them, Democrats faced disaster.

In 1992 Democrats got the economic issue back, just as they did in 1976, when the economy faltered under a Republican administration. Something else stands out about the 1976 election: the GOP failed to rally voters around social issues. The Gerald Ford–Bob Dole ticket had little appeal to racial-backlash voters. Jimmy Carter, a born-again Christian, carried the evangelical vote. 1992 was another election where Republicans could not win on the economic issue. But in 1992, the GOP showcased "family values." George H. W. Bush did not want to be another Gerald Ford. He still lost.

The 1992 election was a straight fight between the Democrats' economic populism and the Republicans' social populism. It was no contest. Voters were obsessed with economic issues. Other concerns, such as foreign policy and family values, barely registered. Moreover, Democrats protected themselves on the social issue by nominating a moderate ticket. Governor Clinton supported welfare reform. He enforced the death penalty in Arkansas. He supported the Gulf War. He insulted Jesse Jackson by criticizing rap artist Sistah Souljah at an event sponsored by Jackson's Rainbow Coalition after she had expressed antiwhite sentiment. He endorsed the North American Free Trade Agreement (NAFTA). The attitude among liberals was "We can live with that." Right-wing political correctness was, and continues to be, a problem for Republicans. From George H. W. Bush, to John McCain, to Mitt Romney, conservatives have demanded that Republican candidates pay fealty to their issues. They even tried to pressure Donald Trump, who set his own agenda.

Class Politics, American Style

Since the 1930s, Democrats have laid claim to the tradition of economic populism. President Franklin Roosevelt's New Deal drew the support of economic populists in the Huey Long tradition. Long agitated against the rich. Theodore Roosevelt advocated a more activist federal government to counter the power of special interests. Democrats are the party of the poor, "the common man," and the average American—the party that protects the economically vulnerable against adversity. From the 1930s to the 1980s, the principal barrier to the Republicans' becoming a majority party was their persistent identification as the party of the rich, big business, the country club, and the boardroom.

Since the civil rights revolution, Republicans have moved in the direction of social and cultural populism. The Democratic Party's endorsement of the values of the educated upper-middle class—racial liberalism, feminism, gay rights—has driven away white working-class Democrats. President Reagan's moral traditionalism, his defense of religion in the public space, and his foreign-policy toughness all had an undeniably populist appeal. A lot of white working-class voters felt comfortable with the Democrats economically but not culturally. Upper-middle-class suburbanites liked Reagan's fiscal conservatism but were turned off by his appeal to racial backlash voters and the religious right.

The nation's upper-middle class has been divided left and right since the 1960s. Working-class voters have also been divided left and right. In 1968 we saw a split between Democratic Vice President Hubert Humphrey, who appealed to workers' economic interests, and Independent candidate Governor George Wallace, the leading defender of racial segregation. Both had an appeal to white working-class voters. After Senator Robert F. Kennedy's assassination, there were indications that some of his white working-class supporters went for Wallace.[1] In 2016 some white working-class voters came out for Bernie Sanders in the Democratic primaries. Others rallied behind Donald Trump in the Republican primaries.

Who could heal the division? Bill Clinton tried. As president, Clinton blurred party differences on economic policy while creating a deeper division over values. Clinton made it safe for tax-sensitive suburbanites to vote Democratic. He also provoked economic progressives such as New Jersey senator Bill Bradley and Vermont representative Bernie Sanders, a self-described socialist who founded the Congressional Progressive Caucus, to denounce Clintonism as a sellout. Take California and New Jersey, two heavily suburban, culturally liberal coastal states. Both states voted Republican in every presidential election from 1968 through 1988, but both have voted for the Democrat in every election since then. At the same time, Clinton reduced the Democrats' appeal in culturally conservative areas of the country such as West Virginia, Tennessee, and his own Arkansas.

We do have class politics in the United States, but these days, the class division is mostly inside the two parties rather than between them. Most Democratic presidential contests in recent decades have come down to a choice between a progressive and a populist. In the 1950s, it was Adlai Stevenson the progressive versus Estes Kefauver the populist. In 1968 it was Eugene McCarthy the progressive versus Robert Kennedy the populist. In 1972, George McGovern (progressive) versus Hubert Humphrey (populist). In 1984, Gary Hart (progressive) versus Walter Mondale (populist). Michael Dukakis (progressive) versus Richard Gephardt (populist) in 1988. Paul Tsongas (progressive) versus Bill Clinton (populist) in 1992. Bill Bradley (progressive) versus Al Gore (populist) in 2000.

In the 2008 Democratic primaries, Barack Obama was the progressive candidate, and Hillary Clinton was the populist. The difference? Social class. Progressives appeal to upscale Democrats: well-educated, upper-middle-class, Prius-driving liberals. Populists appeal to working-class

Democrats who look to government for protection from economic adversity: single working women, racial minorities, pickup truck drivers.

Populist Democrats nodded in agreement when Walter Mondale asked Gary Hart in 1984, "Where's the beef?" (a quote from a popular ad for a hamburger chain). And when Hillary Clinton said in 2008, "If I tell you I will fight for you, that is exactly what I intend to do." Barack Obama's strongest support in the 2008 Democratic primaries came from African Americans and educated upper-middle-class white voters. Hillary Clinton carried the white working-class vote in state after state. She demolished Obama in West Virginia, Kentucky, Arkansas, and Tennessee. When Clinton recalled her grandfather teaching her to shoot as a child in Scranton, Pennsylvania, Obama mocked her for "talking like she's Annie Oakley." Obama disparaged economically stressed small-town Pennsylvania voters who "cling to guns or religion." Clinton beat Obama by 10 points in Pennsylvania.

Class differences were diminished in the 2016 Democratic primaries. Bernie Sanders was a progressive who turned out huge crowds in college towns. But his message was that of an economic populist: "We will no longer tolerate an economy to benefit the wealthiest Americans in this country at the expense of everyone else."

The big differences in the 2016 Democratic primaries were by age (Sanders crushed Hillary Clinton among young voters) and partisanship (Clinton won Democrats, Sanders won Independents).[2]

In 1968 Hubert Humphrey proved that populists can't win without progressives. George McGovern proved in 1972 that progressives can't win without populists. The Democratic Party is a great cross-class coalition that wins when it sticks together: upper-middle-class progressives and working-class populists. In recent years, Democrats have been gaining ground in the first category but losing ground in the second.

The Republican Party is also a great cross-class coalition: country-club conservatives and self-described "values voters." On the one side, Mitt Romney, whose conservative social values were always in doubt. Romney could be elected president of any country club in Greenwich, Connecticut. On the other side, Sarah Palin, former governor of Alaska, and John McCain's running mate in 2008, who would probably not be admitted to any country club in Greenwich, Connecticut.

In the 2012 Republican primaries, conservatives tried to stop Romney. Values voters, the populist wing of the Republican Party, rallied behind one conservative candidate after another: Michele Bachmann, Herman Cain, Rick Perry, Newt Gingrich, Rick Santorum. But social issues were not high on the agenda in 2012. As a result, we had the odd spectacle of Gingrich and Perry lobbing attacks at Romney as an economic elitist. Perry called Romney a "vulture capitalist." Gingrich said, "Show me somebody who has consistently made money while losing money for workers, and I'll show you someone who has undermined capitalism."

Those attacks drew counterattacks from conservatives who believed, correctly, that economic populism is the preserve of the left. Republican candidate Mike Huckabee said, "It's surprising to see so many Republicans embrace that left-wing argument against capitalism." Romney complained that "free enterprise" was on trial. "I thought it was going to come from the president, from the Democrats on the left, but instead it's coming from Speaker Gingrich and apparently others," he said.

The attacks failed. Economic populism has never had much resonance on the right. What the attacks did was spare Romney from having to defend his wavering positions on social issues.

Meanwhile, President Obama's December 2011 speech in Osawatomie, Kansas, signaled his own turn toward economic populism: "the breathtaking greed of a few" . . . "on-your-own economics" . . . "a level of inequality we haven't seen since the Great Depression hurts us all."[3] It was a deliberate echo of Theodore Roosevelt's 1910 "New Nationalism" speech in Osawatomie, when he, too, embraced populist economic themes.

Neither Obama nor Romney was a very convincing populist. President Obama continued to sound like a college professor speaking from a lectern (actually, a teleprompter). Mitt Romney was Mr. 1 Percent. At a time of populist outrage, populists had no authentic champion. Think of it this way: in Obama's first term, we saw a populist eruption on the right (the Tea Party movement) and a populist eruption on the left (the Occupy movement). Neither had a strong candidate for president in 2012.

The result was the populist backlash in 2016 that produced Donald Trump. The real estate mogul and reality TV celebrity is the whole populist package. He's conservative on many social issues (immigration), liberal on some economic issues (trade), and isolationist on foreign policy ("America First"). He is despised by the liberal cultural elite and distrusted by the conservative economic elite.

Populist Eruptions

The United States has experienced a sequence of right-wing populist surges over the past fifty years. The first came as the result of white racial backlash to civil rights in the 1960s. Racists were one of the earliest constituencies in the new Republican coalition. They were almost all Barry Goldwater had in 1964, and they were the target of the

Richard Nixon–Spiro Agnew strategy to win the South in 1972. Richard Nixon's worst state in 1968 was Mississippi (14 percent for Nixon, 64 percent for George Wallace). Nixon's best state in 1972, when Wallace did not run, was Mississippi (78 percent for Nixon). It was a simple additive strategy: Nixon '68 plus Wallace '68 equaled Nixon '72—and beyond.

But Goldwater, Nixon, Ronald Reagan, and George H. W. Bush did not have to run overtly racist campaigns in order to take advantage of racial resentment. Backlash voters are attracted to the GOP's antigovernment agenda. They oppose an activist- and reform-minded federal government in part because they want to protect their interests against what they regard as minority encroachment.

Ronald Reagan expanded the party's support among religious conservatives, even though he was not a particularly religious man. In his speech to an evangelical prayer breakfast at the 1984 Republican National Convention, he argued that traditionally in the United States, "the state was tolerant of religious belief, expression, and practice . . . but in the 1960s, this began to change." [4]

As the president explained it, "We began to make great steps toward secularizing our nation and removing religion from its honored place. The frustrating thing is that those who are attacking religion claim they are doing it in the name of tolerance, freedom, and openmindedness. Question: Isn't the real truth that they are intolerant of religion?"

Beginning with the civil rights revolution of the 1960s, Democrats and liberals came to support a wide variety of reformist social causes, including women's rights, affirmative action, busing, gay rights, immigration rights, reproductive rights, sex education, contraception, required teaching of evolution, tolerance of pornography, opposition to prayer in public schools, and legalization of marijuana and same-sex marriage. Liberals defend these measures as enhancements of individual rights. Conservatives see them as enhancements of state power.

Christian conservative leader Pat Robertson once argued to me that every item on the religious right's social agenda started as a reaction to a liberal initiative such as those just listed. Many originated in federal court cases, often in Supreme Court decisions.[5] The courts are the least democratic institution of American government. That's why the religious right sees itself as a populist force protesting government encroachments on personal morality and religious freedom.

Liberals see the religious right as culturally aggressive and themselves as culturally defensive. To conservatives such as Robertson and Ted Cruz, it's the other way around. They see liberals trying to give official status to their "antireligious" moral and social values, while conservatives defend pluralism and tolerance. That conflict came to a head with the Supreme Court's 2014 Hobby Lobby decision (*Burwell v. Hobby Lobby Stores, Inc.*). The case pitted women's rights against religious rights, with the court ruling that religious employers had the right to refuse to pay for insurance coverage of contraception. This time the court sided with the right. Conservative blogger Erick Erickson wrote, "My religion trumps your 'right' to employer-subsidized, consequence-free sex."[6]

The Family Research Council, the leading political organization of the religious right, hosts a conference every year in Washington for social conservative activists and elected officials. They call it the Values Voter Summit. It is a source of irritation to liberals that social conservatives have appropriated the label "values voters." After all, liberals contend, they have values, too. But the religious right has created a movement that rallies to the banner of traditional values, with other issues regarded as secondary.

The influence of the religious right reached a peak in the 1994 mid-term election. Religious right voters were the key to the Republican takeover of Congress. Speaker Newt Gingrich acknowledged that fact shortly after the election, when he said, "The activity engaged in by the Christian Coalition to educate and make sure people back home knew what was happening was a vital part of why we had a revolution at the polls." The Christian Coalition was founded by Pat Robertson in 1989, the year after he ran for the Republican nomination for president.

One in five voters nationwide in 1994 were white evangelical Christians, and just over three-quarters of them voted Republican for Congress. Anger at President Clinton rallied them. They stormed the polls to repudiate the president. Four years earlier, in the 1990 mid-term, Republican House candidates got just over 27.6 million votes nationwide. In 1994 the Republicans' national vote total shot up to nearly 36.6 million—a record increase for the party from one midterm to the next.

Where did all those new Republican votes come from? They didn't come from the Democrats. The total Democratic House vote slipped from 32.5 million in 1990 to 31.7 million in 1994. Democrats lost less than 1 million votes.

House Speaker Gingrich knew the answer. He gave it when the Christian Coalition unveiled its "Contract with the American Family" in 1995. It was an effort to put a religious spin on the "Contract with America" that many Republicans believed brought them to power in Congress in 1994. Gingrich said, "[1994] was the first time since 1934 that the vote for a party went up dramatically, and it's well worth studying. Our vote went up by almost nine million. The Democrats lost a million votes."

Those 9 million voters were the Republican Party's new base. A lot of them were Christian conservatives and gun owners—the kinds of people who, in previous midterm elections, had rarely bothered to vote. In the 1994 House election, the entire country voted 52 percent Republican. The figure among gun owners, who composed a quarter of the electorate, was 69 percent. Among Christian conservatives, 76 percent. Gun owners and the religious right were more loyal to the GOP than rich people were. Voters with incomes over $100,000 a year voted 63 percent Republican.[7]

Ralph Reed, executive director of the Christian Coalition in 1994, insisted after the election that the religious right was not threatening anybody. "We have no intention of doing to this Congress what the unions, the feminists, and the gay lobby did to Bill Clinton when he took office," Reed said. "They made unreasonable demands, presented an extremist agenda, and forced his administration way out of the mainstream." That's exactly what a lot of Republicans feared the religious right would do.

Christian conservatives claimed they were not trying to impose their ideas on anybody. Just the reverse. According to their "Contract with the American Family," "With each passing year, people of faith grow increasingly distressed by the hostility of public institutions toward religious expression." They saw themselves not as aggressors but as defenders of religious liberty against those who wanted to eliminate religion from public life.

The 1998 midterm election was a low point for the religious right. It was the Great Impeachment Referendum. In every midterm election since 1934, the president's party had suffered a net loss of House seats.

Not in 1998. That year, an amazing 82 percent of voters said the nation's economy was in good shape. When Clinton first got elected in 1992, only 19 percent felt that way. In 1996, when things were good enough to get both the Democratic president and the Republican Congress reelected, 55 percent thought the economy was good. The 1998 figure—82 percent—could be described only as euphoric.

The impeachment saga was a shock for social conservatives. The problem wasn't Congress—the House of Representatives delivered impeachment. The shock was that the country wasn't with them. It wasn't that something was wrong with American government. It was that something was wrong with American culture if the public wanted to keep President Clinton in office.

The religious right retains a powerful influence in the Republican Party, but it does not control the party. Christian conservatives resisted the nomination of John McCain in 2008 and Mitt Romney in 2012, even though both candidates adapted their positions to match those of religious conservatives. McCain had labeled leaders of the religious right "agents of intolerance" in 2000, and Romney had supported some gay rights and abortion rights as a candidate for governor of Massachusetts in 2002, though as governor his views "evolved," as he put it, in a more conservative direction.

Donald Trump was not supposed to be the favorite candidate of the religious right in the 2016 Republican race. With his often coarse language, his impulsive and casually observant lifestyle, and his three marriages, Trump hardly exemplified Christian conservative values. The Christian conservative favorite was expected to be Rick Santorum, a former US senator from Pennsylvania who had come in second in the 2012 GOP primaries. After losing badly to Ted Cruz among evangelical voters in the Iowa Republican caucuses, however, Santorum dropped out. Cruz, who ultimately came in second in the 2016 Republican race, lasted until the May 3 Indiana primary. A majority of Indiana Republican primary voters were evangelicals. Yet they favored Trump over Cruz, 50 percent to 44 percent, forcing Cruz to drop out of the race.

In 2016 the religious right proved its loyalty to the Republican Party. White born-again Christians voted 80 percent for Trump.

The Tea Party

Within weeks of Barack Obama's taking office in January 2009, a new Republican faction suddenly burst upon the scene: the Tea Party. This movement was driven by political fundamentalism, not religious fundamentalism.

Tea Party supporters and religious fundamentalists share many of the same characteristics. They do not tolerate waverers (such as former Utah senator Bob Bennett, who was denied renomination by Utah Republicans in 2010 because he, like former president George W. Bush, supported a federal bank bailout). They drive out "heretics" (like former Florida governor Charlie Crist, whose photo hugging President Obama in 2009 enraged conservatives). They punish "unbelievers" (like former Delaware senator Mike Castle, who ran in the Republican primary as a moderate who could win the general election). Tea Party conservatives believe in the total inerrancy of Scripture—for the Tea Party, that would be the United States Constitution as written in 1787. And they had an antichrist: President Obama. Their mission was to stop President Obama's policies and reverse them wherever possible. To root out sin, as it were.

President Obama's original sin was the economic stimulus plan, which entailed a nearly $1 trillion increase in federal spending. In March 2013, Tea Party activists pressured Congress to allow budget sequesters to go into effect, cutting federal spending by $1.2 trillion over ten years. The sequesters could be seen as an act of revenge for Obama's original sin.

A CNN poll taken in 2011 found Republicans split down the middle. Half called themselves Tea Party supporters. Half did not.[8] The big difference was ideological. Nearly 80 percent of Tea Party Republicans were conservatives. Almost half of non–Tea Party Republicans did not call themselves conservatives. It was a split between a rising ideological movement that was deeply conservative and the moderately conservative traditional Republican establishment.

Tea Party voters share the same obsession with opposing big government as establishment Republicans. But the Tea Party has a moralistic approach to politics that refuses to play by the rules of the political establishment. No deal making, no compromises. In a 2011 CNN poll, a notable difference between Tea Party and establishment factions of the Republican Party was the level of anger. Fifty percent of Tea Party Republicans polled by CNN said they were "very angry" about the way things were going in the country; 29 percent of non–Tea Party Republicans felt the same way.

Tea Party Republicans saw the 2010 midterm election as giving them a mandate to obstruct. The political right had long trafficked in obstruction. When Republicans took control of Congress after the 1994 election, they tried the path of obstruction for a year. The Republican Congress refused to pass a budget President Clinton would sign, instead proposing spending cuts in Medicare, Medicaid, education, and other popular government programs. It led to a train wreck: the government shutdown. Eventually President Clinton and the Republican Congress figured out a way to work together. Clinton triangulated. Newt Gingrich cooperated.

In the 1990s, even before the Tea Party existed, conservatives were mobilized by Clinton hatred. What drove it wasn't so much disagreement on policy. Republicans supported many of Clinton's policies, such as welfare reform, free trade, the "three strikes" crime bill, Wall Street deregulation, and a balanced budget. Conservatives hated Clinton because of his values.

In 1998 I asked Tom Roeser, a leading conservative broadcaster in Chicago, why he hated President Clinton so much. His answer? It was because Clinton was, in his words, "a womanizing, Elvis-loving, truth-shading, noninhaling, draft-dodging, war-protesting, abortion-protecting, gay-promoting, gun-hating baby boomer." In other words, a child of the 1960s. It wasn't the policies. It was the values. Republicans supported many of Clinton's policies and then impeached him.

In Obama's case, you could say that conservatives hated his free-spending, high-taxing, overregulating, bailout-pandering, health-care-reforming, government-enhancing, freedom-diminishing, enterprise-killing ideas. With Obama, it was the policies, stupid.

To Tea Party activists, collaboration with Obama's policies meant selling out. They pressured Republican leaders in Congress to stand on principle, to reject deals with the antichrist. Professional politicians are in the business of making deals. Deals mean compromise. When the Tea Party movement said it wanted to change Washington, what it meant was that it wanted to get rid of politics.

NASCAR Nation

In April 2004 I saw American populism at close range when I spent a weekend with President George W. Bush's hard-core base. It was not a political rally. It was a NASCAR race at the Talladega Superspeedway in Alabama. A NASCAR official told me that he would guess about 85 percent of the fans at the speedway would be voting to reelect President Bush. They called themselves "NASCAR nation."

Stock car racing was at the time one of the fastest growing spectator sports in the United States. (That ended after the 2008 recession.) From what I saw, it had broken out of its stereotypical southern base and was drawing fans from all over the country. Spectators came from Minnesota and Washington State and even "Bronx, New York," one of them told me. A considerable number of them—some 40 percent, according to official estimates—were women. Still, the race drew only a handful of African American spectators, even in Alabama. The fans included a lot of business and professional people. They were Middle America, not predominantly poor or working class. High ticket prices ensured that.

The NASCAR staff was more than welcoming. They offered my cameraman and me a ride around the steeply banked track in the pace car—at ninety miles per hour. ("If we go any slower, the car will flip over," the driver explained.) We got all the chicken-fried steak we could eat. We were allowed to tour the infield on Saturday night in a golf cart—but no cameras. Fans pay a lot of money to park their recreational vehicles and trailers in the infield, and there are some pretty raunchy activities there on Saturday night before a big race. As a NASCAR staffer put it, "We want to maintain our image as a family sport."

What did NASCAR nation like about President Bush? One word:

security. "If you're not strong enough on security and you let another 9/11 happen, all the other things John Kerry talks about are not going to happen," one fan told me. Their philosophy for keeping the country secure? "Go get 'em." They admired aggressiveness in their drivers and in their president. "I believe in a firm, aggressive, give-'em-hell kind of an attitude," one said. Another put it this way: "Hey, we're NASCAR fans and Americans. Don't jack with us."

The political values of NASCAR nation are culturally conservative. No surprise there. An organizer told me, "These guys go hunting, and they go fishing, and they come to watch NASCAR racing." There was also a tinge of economic populism. A fan said, "One of the things that I am definitely against is farming out all the overseas work and taking away from Americans and their families."

At the same time, NASCAR has to be one of the most procorporate environments in America. Corporate logos are everywhere. On the haulers that bring the cars to the track, on the racing suits, and all over the cars. There was even a Viagra car. (And a "Jesus car.") The drivers see themselves as salesmen. "I have two jobs," a driver told me. "One is to drive the Tide Monte Carlo to the victory lane. The other is to help sell Tide." They admire salesmanship. One of them said, "Bill Clinton was a great salesman. I'd like to have him working for my company, selling."

NASCAR fans are intensely loyal. First and foremost, they are loyal to the drivers. "Once they're your fan, they're always your fan," a NASCAR staffer explained. "You do wrong, you do right, they're right there with you. You don't lose fans." That came home to me when I interviewed a NASCAR driver in his impressive two-level hauler. When I walked out, I was besieged by fans asking me for *my* autograph. Were they TV news junkies? Not exactly. As I signed my name, I noticed people writing underneath it, "Interviewed Jimmie Johnson."

They are also loyal to the sponsors. "We find the NASCAR fan to be by far the most loyal fan in terms of a brand, from a purchasing power standpoint, than any other sport," one sponsor's representative told me. That's why it was so valuable for a politician to hear NASCAR fans say, as many of them said to me in 2004, "I'm a Bush fan."

Trumpism

President Trump's dream is to put together a populist coalition of working-class Democrats, Republicans, and Independents against the political establishment. He even fantasizes about attracting Bernie Sanders supporters. But the values that divide those voters left and right are more powerful than the antiestablishment resentment they share.

Trump touted the Brexit vote in Britain as the model for what he is trying to do. He issued a statement in 2016 saying that British voters "have declared their independence from the European Union and have voted to reassert control over their own politics, border, and economy. Come November, the American people will have the chance to redeclare their independence . . . They will have the chance to reject today's rule by the global elite." [9]

When the populist Andrew Jackson became president in 1829, voters began to divide between Jacksonians and anti-Jacksonians. The Jacksonians became the Democratic Party, and the anti-Jacksonians turned into the Whig Party. It's not hard to imagine a Trump party and an anti-Trump party emerging in the wake of the Trump presidency.

But what would they stand for? Who knows? No one knew what

Donald Trump would actually do as president. Not even Trump, who said in January 2016, "When I'm president, I'm a different person. I can be the most politically correct person you've ever seen." Trump surprised everyone by toning down his harsh, divisive rhetoric when he delivered his first address to Congress in February 2017. Skeptics called it "Trump's bar mitzvah speech." [10]

Trump's white working-class followers felt threatened by the changes happening in the country: globalization, job loss, immigration, and political correctness. His supporters were thrilled by Trump's show of defiance toward Washington, the media, the Republican establishment, and received wisdom. He has even defied science on climate change.

Trump's slogan—"Make America Great Again!"—resonated with them because they want to restore the Old America where wages were high, immigrants were few, white men ran things, and US power in the world was unchallenged. When Trump came out to claim victory on election night, his followers chanted in triumph, "USA! USA!"

Trump's victory was pure populism—antielitist to the core. He carried noncollege whites by better than two to one (67 percent to 28 percent according to the exit poll). [11] Let Hillary Clinton denounce Trump supporters as "a basket of deplorables." They rose up and gave her the collective finger. They made a similar gesture to the rest of the world, much of which regarded Trump's victory as shocking. Asked to describe his countrymen's view of Donald Trump, a British radio commentator said, "Disgust."

What drove Trump supporters was an intense desire for change. More voters said they wanted a candidate who "can bring about change" (39 percent) than said they were looking for "experience" (22 percent), "judgment" (20 percent), or a candidate who "cares about me" (15 percent). Voters who wanted change voted 82 percent for Trump. [12]

Democrats are defined by a commitment to diversity and inclusion—the very things that Trump and his supporters detest. White men do not contribute to diversity. And the idea of inclusion usually excludes them.

Steve Schmidt, a senior adviser to Senator John McCain's 2008 Republican presidential campaign, said in 2015, "We have reached a moment where conservatism isn't defined by issues anymore." What Trump has is attitude—bombastic, bullying, crude, and insulting—like a right-wing radio talk show host. Trump was himself the host of a reality TV show where his signature line was "You're fired!"

Way back in 1896, it was the Democrats who nominated a pure populist: William Jennings Bryan, an economic radical, religious fundamentalist, and foreign-policy isolationist. Bryan is remembered for his attack on the nation's economic elite: "You shall not crucify mankind upon a cross of gold." Bryan was also the defender of the fundamentalist faith at the Scopes trial in 1925. He resigned as secretary of state in 1915, when President Woodrow Wilson protested a German submarine's sinking of the British cruiser *Lusitania* in which 128 Americans died. Bryan, an ardent isolationist, was concerned that President Wilson was leading the country into a world war. Isolationism is pure populism.

In his presidential campaigns, Bryan alienated cosmopolitan America. He did well in rural America and the South but lost the fast-growing, urbanizing, and industrializing states that were attracting immigrants. Democrats nominated Bryan three times (1896, 1900, and 1908), and each time, he did worse. Democrats became the nation's minority party for thirty-six years.

With Trump as their standard-bearer, Republicans are inviting a similar fate. They are becoming what the Democrats once were: the party of declining America. Democrats are becoming the educated cosmopolitan party: the party of the New America.

Trump led a resistance movement against President Obama. Now Democrats are leading a counterresistance movement against President Trump. Adam Jentleson, a top aide to former Senate Democratic leader Harry Reid, said, "There's not going to be a grace period this time because everybody on our side thinks [Trump] is illegitimate and poses a massive threat." It's a partisan fight to the death.

THREE

Polarization

How It All Started

In the 1960s, the United States experienced the Great American Cultural Revolution. In 2004 Bill Clinton offered this defining explanation of American politics: "If you look back on the sixties, and, on balance, you think there was more good than harm in it, you're probably a Democrat. And if you think there's more harm than good, you're probably a Republican."[1] It's a split between two baby boomer presidents who came of age in the sixties: Bill Clinton, who sees more good than harm, and George W. Bush, who sees more harm than good.

In 1964, when I was a sophomore at Brandeis University in Massachusetts, a remarkable thing happened. The student body held a mock

Republican National Convention. It was not especially remarkable at the time. A group of political junkies, including me, organized the event. Hundreds of students participated, mostly for the fun of it. The keynote speaker was Leonard Hall, then chairman of the Republican National Committee.

Two years later, when I graduated, such an event would have been difficult to organize. The Brandeis student body has always been strongly liberal and Jewish. The university was a refuge for many black-listed intellectuals from the Joe McCarthy period, when many scholars were targeted for having radical and "un-American" affiliations. One of my classmates was political activist Angela Davis. One of my advisers was New Left philosopher Herbert Marcuse. Brandeis students were certainly not attuned to the revolution going on in the Republican Party. The actual Republican convention that year nominated Barry Goldwater for president. We chose Nelson Rockefeller. After all, much of the student body was from New York, where Rockefeller was governor.

When I asked Chairman Hall how Goldwater won the nomination, he offered a memorable answer: "Goldwater's supporters are the kind of people who stay until the ends of meetings."

A revolution in political consciousness was taking place, not only on the right but also on the left. My first recollection of freshman orientation in 1962 was being urged by student activists to sign up for freedom rides to liberate African Americans in the segregated South, where I grew up. Our incoming class was greeted by political organizers recruiting volunteers to work in the Massachusetts campaign of H. Stuart Hughes, a peace activist running as an Independent for President John F. Kennedy's vacated Senate seat. Hughes lost (badly) to a young Democratic upstart named Edward M. Kennedy.

One event that doomed Hughes's peace campaign was the Cuban Missile Crisis of October 1962. The crisis produced its own controversy on campus, as two anthropology professors (David Aberle and his wife, Kathleen Gough) defended Fidel Castro's Cuba. Four years later, at our graduation ceremony, many students stood and turned their backs on the commencement speaker, Supreme Court Justice Arthur Goldberg, because he had been a cabinet member in the hated Lyndon Johnson administration (and therefore, presumably, bore culpability for the war in Vietnam). By 1969, Brandeis, like many other campuses, was in turmoil. A mock Republican convention could never have happened that year.

Like many universities, Brandeis was caught up in the political revolution of the 1960s. The year 1964 marks the dividing line between the old politics of consensus and the new politics of tribal warfare. Goldwater's nomination defined a more aggressive conservatism and occasioned a sharp break with the Republican past. Democrats, under the leadership of John Kennedy, Robert Kennedy, Lyndon Johnson, and Hubert Humphrey, also broke with their party's past by making the courageous decision to embrace the civil rights movement.

The roots of America's political deadlock go back to the great civil war of the 1960s: a cultural civil war in which a New Left and a New Right emerged to challenge the country's post–World War II consensus. The center emptied out, especially in the 1970s, after two centrist presidents, Republican Gerald Ford and Democrat Jimmy Carter, failed to govern effectively.

The dominant political figures of the late twentieth century were Ronald Reagan and Bill Clinton, two presidents whose political identities were forged by the conflicts of the 1960s. The 2000 election was a showdown between Reaganism and Clintonism. The result? A near tie.

Europeans are often perplexed by the failure of Americans to get over the sixties. After all, they, too, were convulsed by great cultural changes during that turbulent decade. But the United States experienced a fierce and enduring backlash against those changes, based partly on America's uniquely religious culture.

Religion has lost influence everywhere in the industrial world. But in the United States, more than elsewhere, it has continued to thrive. The reason goes back to the fact that a lot of immigrants came to America seeking religious freedom, starting with the Puritans in the seventeenth century. People seeking religious freedom are, by definition, deeply religious, and many of them preserved their religious commitment over the generations.[2]

The United States is not the only predominantly Protestant country in the world. But it is the only country where the dominant religion is what Europeans call "dissenting churches." Dissenting churches in Europe rejected the authority of established churches. And they often embraced a more pietistic style of religion that values personal faith over ritual observance.

In the early 1990s, I held a post as visiting professor of American politics at a leading Jesuit university. One of the perquisites of that position was an invitation to tea with the cardinal. After we exchanged pleasantries, the cardinal asked, "Is there anything happening in American politics that I should be aware of?"

"As a matter of fact, there is," I answered. "Since 1980, religious Americans of all faiths—fundamentalist Protestants, observant Catholics, even Orthodox Jews—have been moving toward the Republican Party. At the same time, secular Americans have found a home in the Democratic Party.

"This is something new in American politics," I observed. Then I went a fateful step further, adding, "I'm a little uncomfortable with the idea of a religious party in this country." The cardinal pounced: "Well, I'm a little uncomfortable with an irreligious party in this country."

To which I replied, "Your eminence, I think I'll have more tea."

Today church attendance is one of the best ways to identify a person's partisanship. In 2016, regular churchgoers voted 55 percent for Trump. Nonchurchgoers went 62 percent for Clinton. In the 1930s, the question that defined the partisan divide would have been "In disputes between business and labor, which side do you sympathize with more?"[3]

As noted in chapter 1, the values divide between the Old America and the New America first emerged in the 1960s, when cultural divisions were breaking out all over the world. What made the divide deeper and more enduring in the United States than elsewhere? The fact that the political backlash to the social changes of the 1960s was grounded in America's deeply religious culture. For many Americans, religion is the core of their identity.

Identity is the basis of partisanship. Which party you identify with is a function of who you are. An older southern white man is almost certain to be a Republican today. Minorities and young single women are overwhelmingly Democrats. The whole point of a campaign today is to rally party supporters. So identity always becomes sharper and clearer in a presidential campaign.

How people vote is a little more complicated. Sure, voting is influenced heavily by identity, but other, more powerful forces can determine an election outcome—forces that sweep voters across the board in one direction or the other. Political scientists call them "valence issues":

issues with a positive valence, such as prosperity, and issues with a negative valence, like corruption. They are issues that move everybody in the same direction, regardless of identity.

If voting were determined wholly by identity, then an election would just be a census: how many African Americans, how many young single women, how many southern white men, and so on. The United States has not reached that extreme, although we certainly came close in 2000.

In 2015, when the Supreme Court ruled in favor of same-sex marriage, Justice Antonin Scalia offered this scathing dissent: "If I ever joined an opinion for the court that began: 'The Constitution promises liberty to all within its reach, a liberty that includes certain specific rights that allow persons . . . to define and express their identity,' I would hide my head in a bag." Scalia was expressing contempt for identity politics. Identity politics is at the core of the New America.

But it's also at the core of the Old America. Donald Trump's rallies are a celebration of white male identity politics. The difference is that white men don't think in terms of identity politics. That would open them up to charges of racism and sexism. The identity white men rally to is "American." They see themselves as "real Americans." And they responded to Trump's call to "Make America great again." That's identity politics disguised as patriotism.

The Big Tents Get Smaller

In the 1950s, it was possible to talk about a Democratic Party establishment and a Republican Party establishment that were more or less in control of their parties' policies and organizations. While divided on economic issues—Democrats supported an expansive view of government, Republicans were the party of fiscal discipline—neither social issues nor foreign policy figured prominently as partisan issues. Both parties endorsed the Cold War consensus. The most pressing social issue, race, was confused. Democrats still had a large contingent of southern white racists, while it was a Republican chief justice, Earl Warren, who wrote the 1954 Supreme Court decision *Brown v. Board of Education* mandating school integration and a Republican president, Dwight Eisenhower who sent troops to Little Rock to enforce it.

Both party establishments were the targets of protest movements in the 1960s and 1970s. One came from the right in 1964, when the Goldwater movement mobilized conservative activists to wrest control of the Republican Party from "the Eastern establishment." The left protest movement emerged with the antiwar candidacy of Eugene McCarthy in 1968. Four years later, liberal activists mobilized in the Democratic primaries and caucuses to nominate George McGovern and defeat the party establishment that they believed had stolen the nomination from them four years earlier.

The presidential nominations of Barry Goldwater in 1964 and George McGovern in 1972 signaled the initial victories of these protest movements. Although both candidates were defeated soundly in the ensuing general elections, their followers moved into positions of prominence in the two parties, either displacing the party regulars or forcing them to accommodate.

The protest movements introduced new ideological issues into party politics. New Right conservatives attacked the Republican establishment for making too many compromises with big government and for being too willing to accept peaceful coexistence with Communism.

For Democrats, it was more complicated. The Democratic coalition that emerged under Franklin D. Roosevelt and reached its peak under Lyndon Johnson was committed to three core principles: the social welfare liberalism of the New Deal, the Truman Doctrine of anti-Communist containment, and civil rights under JFK and LBJ. All three came under attack.

By the mid-1960s, Democrats had already taken a giant step to the left when the party establishment embraced civil rights. The New Left went one step further in the late 1960s and challenged the party leadership's commitment to military intervention to contain communism, which had led to the war in Vietnam.

What held the Democratic Party together was its continuing commitment to social welfare. That commitment came under attack from the Reagan Revolution. Since the 1930s, Democrats had defined themselves as the party that protected ordinary Americans against economic adversity. That's what kept white working-class voters in the party despite their mistrust of its racial and foreign-policy liberalism. If the Democrats could not offer people economic security, what reason was there to stay in the party?

As a result, Democrats became less a populist party and more a liberal party. As the party lost moderate and conservative Catholics and southern whites, it strengthened its appeal to African Americans and educated upper-middle-class liberals—constituencies that eventually became the core of Barack Obama's coalition.

Party leaders like to say that a political party is a big tent, with room inside for all kinds of people. That certainly used to be true. Democrats ran the gamut from southern white racists to African Americans and liberal intellectuals. The old GOP included right-wingers like Barry Goldwater and left-wingers such as John Lindsay, the former mayor of New York City. In recent years, however, the tents have gotten smaller. Racists and right-wingers are no longer welcome in the Democratic tent. Liberal Republicans face a choice of either losing (like New York senator Jacob Javits, New Jersey senator Clifford Case, and Massachusetts senator Edward Brooke) or abandoning the party (like Lindsay, Illinois congressman John Anderson, Connecticut senator and governor Lowell Weicker, Vermont senator Jim Jeffords, and Lincoln Chafee).

Antiestablishment populism was the key to the success of both the New Right in the Republican Party and the New Left on the Democratic side. Kevin Phillips saw it in 1969, when he published *The Emerging Republican Majority*.[4] To Phillips, the energy behind the Goldwater and Reagan movements came more from antiestablishment resentment than from conservative ideology.

Meanwhile, the Democratic Party establishment came under attack not from one side but two. First, George Wallace ran against Lyndon Johnson in the 1964 Democratic presidential primaries and carried the politics of racial backlash from South to North. A second front opened up in 1968, when the party establishment was challenged from the left by the anti–Vietnam War movement.

During this tumultuous period in the Democratic Party's history, the battle was not between the party's left and right; it was the left and the right against the center. What made Lyndon Johnson, Hubert Humphrey, Chicago mayor Richard Daley, and the labor unions such inviting targets was that they epitomized the entrenched power of an establishment that thrived on bosses and deals and froze out "the people." Humphrey won the Democratic nomination in 1968 without running in a single primary. You didn't have to in those days. The nominee was chosen by party insiders who were loyal to the vice president.

The same forces mobilized in 1972, with former Independent candidate Wallace on the right and Senator George McGovern leading the antiwar left. McGovern's pollster, Patrick Caddell, came up with an interesting idea. If a good populist theme could be found—possibly tax reform—then maybe the right and the left could join forces and defeat the Democratic Party establishment. That turned out to be impossible in 1972 because the issues on which Wallace and McGovern voters disagreed—civil rights, Vietnam—were far more salient than the views they shared. To his credit, however, Caddell stuck with his "alienated voter" theory and made it work for Jimmy Carter in 1976.

Carter was the perfect antiestablishment candidate: an outsider with no clear ideological identification. He defeated the party's ideological factions one at a time, each on its own turf: the right (Wallace) in the Florida Democratic primary, the left (Morris Udall) in the Wisconsin primary, and the center (Henry "Scoop" Jackson) in the Pennsylvania primary. In the general election, Carter was able to pull together enough regular Democrats, Wallace voters, and McGovernites to win. It helped that his opponent, Gerald Ford, had already been softened up by a primary challenge from Ronald Reagan.

Bill Clinton was the first president to come out of the liberal cultural world of the sixties: sex, drugs ("I didn't inhale"), and rock 'n' roll. Clinton was a hero to African Americans, Hollywood liberals, and women's rights supporters because of his liberal values, not his centrist policies.

Barack Obama, born in 1961, was not a child of the sixties. In his book *The Audacity of Hope: Thoughts on Reclaiming the American Dream*, Obama wrote that as he reflected on the 2000 and 2004 elections, "I sometimes felt as if I were watching the psychodrama of the baby boom generation—a tale rooted in old grudges and revenge plots hatched on a handful of college campuses long ago." [5]

In 2008, Republicans tried to make an issue out of Obama's association with former sixties radical Bill Ayers and with inflammatory preacher Jeremiah Wright. It didn't work. Nevertheless, President

Obama remained a symbol of the transformation wrought by the sixties. He was the nation's first African American president. He came to prominence as an antiwar Democrat. His enemies branded him a socialist and an illegitimate president because he embodied cultural changes they have never accepted. Obama's values were the elite liberal values of the sixties. What's different now is that many of those values (like gay rights) have become more mainstream.

From Reagan to Trump

The political alignment that emerged after the 1960s is essentially two-dimensional. The system of class politics associated with the New Deal remains strong and, in fact, has been revitalized by the focus on economic issues following the 2008 financial crash and the Great Recession. Overlying it are the cultural divisions of the past fifty years.

When Republicans won a sweeping victory in the states in the 2010 midterm, one of the first things they did was pass antilabor legislation. Their aim was to roll back collective bargaining rights that had been in place since the 1930s. That was the old conservatism, not the new.

In the 2016 campaign, Trump embraced populist positions on both dimensions. Obama's elitist positions—specifically on immigration reform and free trade—alienated white working-class voters. Trump's hostility to foreign trade, immigration, and military intervention were pure populism. Hillary Clinton supported immigration reform. She favored foreign trade (though in the 2016 campaign, she shifted her position on the pending Trans-Pacific Partnership (TPP) and opposed what she once called the "gold standard" of trade deals). And she had a record of supporting military interventions. Pure elitism.

In 2016 Clinton was in the awkward position of defending Washington, the political establishment, and the status quo. Her handling of government emails, her paydays from Wall Street speeches, and her hobnobbing with ultrarich donors reinforced the impression of privilege and remoteness from ordinary Americans. It made her vulnerable to a surprisingly strong primary challenge from Bernie Sanders, an economic populist. And it created a wave of white working-class support for Trump, a social populist who scandalized the Republican establishment by embracing economic and foreign-policy populism.

Conservative intellectuals had favored Senator Ted Cruz in the 2016 Republican primaries. Cruz was completely committed to principle. Unlike Trump. The conservative magazine *National Review* called Trump "a confidence man." He was ideologically incoherent. He had no problem with big government—walls on the border, mass deportations, entitlements, and infrastructure spending—as long as he was in charge. The only thing Trump truly believed in was himself.

In chapter 1, Trump's supporters were described as a coalition of conservatives and economic populists. As soon as Trump took office in 2017, congressional conservatives appeared to have the upper hand. The new president's appointments included a lot of billionaires and Wall Street executives. The administration's initial budget proposed massive cuts in programs vital to working-class Americans such as Medicaid, after-school programs, housing initiatives, job training programs, and regional assistance programs for rust belt states, where Trump won his crucial margin of victory. Hal Rogers, a Republican congressman from Kentucky and former chairman of the House Appropriations Committee, told the *New York Times*, "Many of the reductions and eliminations proposed in the president's skinny budget are draconian, careless, and counterproductive."

The first priority of the Republican-controlled Congress was to repeal Obamacare, not President Trump's call for $1 trillion in new infrastructure spending. About the only concession to economic populism was something Trump did not propose: cuts in spending for Social Security and Medicare. The test for economic populists will be the president's ability to deliver their number one priority. Not a border wall with Mexico. Jobs.

Tribal Politics

Political polarization has been institutionalized. New media—cable TV, the internet, talk radio, bloggers—thrive on harsh confrontation. Moreover, there's evidence that Americans are becoming increasingly segregated by politics, living among others who share their lifestyle and their political views.[6]

Political parties have become tribal. Compromise has come to mean selling out. Reaching across party lines is tantamount to collaboration with the enemy. Moderates are attacked as unprincipled. When Senator Richard Lugar ran for the Republican presidential nomination in 1996, I described him as a "moderate." I was quickly chewed out by his spokesperson, who insisted that the senator was no such thing. Even then, *moderate* was a curse word in the Republican lexicon. Lugar was eventually defeated for renomination to the Senate by a conservative in the 2012 Indiana Republican primary. His own party considered him too moderate.

The term "political correctness" originated on the left, but it has become a problem for Republicans as well. In 2009 a group of conservative members of the Republican National Committee planned to propose a resolution that would establish a sequence of tests candidates would have to pass in order to win the Republican Party's official endorsement. They would be required to oppose President Obama's economic stimulus and health care plans, "amnesty" for illegal immigrants, government funding of abortions, and government restrictions on gun ownership. Republican candidates would also be expected to oppose same-sex marriage and support "military-recommended troop surges" in Iraq and Afghanistan. Candidates would be allowed to deviate on no more than two of the ten tests.

When it was pointed out that Ronald Reagan would probably not have passed, the resolution was watered down to a statement urging Republican candidates to support "the core principles" of the party platform. But the thinking behind it captures the tribal spirit of American politics. Deviate, and you're cast out of the tribe.

Party Bases Harden

The most dramatic change in American politics since World War II has been the hardening of party lines. You can see it in the public's presidential job ratings.

Gallup uses a simple index of polarization: the difference between the job ratings given to presidents by supporters of their own party and the ratings given by supporters of the opposition party. For the six presidents before Ronald Reagan (Dwight Eisenhower through Jimmy Carter), the partisan gap averaged 34 points. From Reagan through George W. Bush, the average difference between Democrats and Republicans jumped to 55 points.[7]

Gallup reports, "Prior to Ronald Reagan, no president averaged more than a 40-point gap in approval ratings by party during his term; since then, only the elder George Bush has averaged less than a 50-point gap."[8] The average gap between Democrats and Republicans under Bill Clinton was 55 points. Under George W. Bush, 61 points. Under Barack Obama, 70 points. After his first six months in office, the gap between Republicans and Democrats in President Trump's approval rating was 78 points.

It used to be the case that when a president got in trouble, he got in trouble with everybody. Public opinion turned against him. He even lost support in his own party.

- When Lyndon Johnson was deeply unpopular in August 1968—at the time of the tumultuous Chicago Democratic National Convention where antiwar protesters clashed with police—he was drawing only 48 percent approval from Democrats and 21 from Republicans, a 27-point difference.
- Just before Richard Nixon resigned in August 1974, he was drawing 13 percent support from Democrats and 50 percent from his fellow Republicans, a 37-point gap.
- During the so-called malaise crisis of 1979 when energy shortages led to gasoline rationing, Jimmy Carter was getting only 41 percent support from Democrats and 19 percent from Republicans, a 22-point difference.

Things began to change with Ronald Reagan.

- When the Iran-contra scandal broke in 1986 over the diversion of illegal profits from arms sales to Iran to guerrillas in Nicaragua, Reagan had 24 percent approval among Democrats. But Republicans stood by him: 74 percent. The partisan gap was 50 points.

- When Bill Clinton was at a low point in 1994, only 14 percent of Republicans approved of the way he was handling his job. But 75 percent of Democrats supported him. The difference was 61 points.
- Just before George W. Bush left office during the 2008–09 financial crash, his rating from Democrats was exactly 5 percent. But his fellow Republicans still supported him (61 percent). The gap was 56 points.
- In February 2017, after a month filled with controversy, Trump was getting just 8 percent support from Democrats. But he was getting 87 percent support from his fellow Republicans.

A politician once said, "In politics, you have to have a base. Your base is the people who are with you when you're wrong." Ronald Reagan held his base during the Iran-contra scandal. Bill Clinton held his base during the Monica Lewinsky scandal. Today partisan bases are stronger than they've ever been, at least in modern times. During the 2016 campaign, Republican nominee Donald Trump sometimes defied his party's conservative base yet still ended up with 88 percent of the Republican vote.

Polarization has been going on for nearly fifty years. Liberal Republicans have gone the way of the dodo bird. Some became Democrats (former senator Arlen Specter of Pennsylvania, former governor Lincoln Chafee of Rhode Island). Some became Independents (former senator Jim Jeffords of Vermont, former governor Lowell Weicker of Connecticut). The number of moderate Republicans in the Senate is nearing the vanishing point. As of 2017, there were only a few left: Susan Collins of

Maine and, arguably, Lisa Murkowski of Alaska and Rob Portman of Ohio. None of them endorsed Trump for president in 2016.

Conservative Democrats used to thrive in the South. But they, too, became an endangered species after their habitat turned Republican. One of the last truly conservative Democrats was former Georgia governor and senator Zell Miller. Miller, who had delivered the keynote speech at the 1992 Democratic convention that nominated Bill Clinton, was last sighted delivering the keynote speech—a fiery denunciation of the Democratic Party—at the 2004 Republican convention. The leading moderate Democrat in the Senate, Joe Lieberman of Connecticut, was the party's vice presidential candidate in 2000. But his support for the war in Iraq drew intense opposition from his own party. Lieberman lost the 2006 Connecticut Democratic primary and was reelected and served his last term as an Independent.

Beginning in 1968, social issues paid off for Republicans for many decades. In 1968, Democrats lost votes because of the Vietnam War, civil rights, and the law-and-order issue. In 1972 Republicans attacked Democrat George McGovern as the candidate of "acid, amnesty, and abortion." In 1980 and 1984 the religious right rallied voters for Reagan. In 1988 it was criminal furloughs, the death penalty, and the Pledge of Allegiance. In 1994 it was the gun issue. In 2004 it was same-sex marriage.

In 2012, however, every time a social issue came up, it exploded in the Republican Party's face. When conservatives tried to define access to contraception as an affront to religious liberty, it made them look out of touch with reality. Even same-sex marriage was not the wedge issue it had been in 2004, as public attitudes toward gays shifted with breathtaking speed.

Democrats have learned through bitter experience that Americans do not want to glorify single mothers, homosexuals, illegal immigrants, and other unconventional groups. But Americans don't want to stigmatize them, either. Conservative rhetoric on social issues has become harshly stigmatizing. It has acquired a tone of meanness—too much harsh denunciation, too much smug self-righteousness, too many issues posed as "us" versus "them."

Ronald Reagan was not a hater. He shared none of the malice that we have seen in many recent Republican campaigns. Reagan never veered from his conservative faith, but he never stigmatized those who disagreed with him. He made it clear that they were welcome in his party.

Four presidents before Trump all got elected on a pledge to end the bitter division in American politics. The first President Bush offered "a kinder, gentler" politics. He lasted one term. Bill Clinton, who called himself a "New Democrat" and a believer in the third way, a political philosophy that borrows from both left and right, pulled the Democratic Party back to the center. He got impeached for his behavior, not his policies. The second President Bush said he would be "a uniter, not a divider." He took a divided country and intensified the division. Barack Obama created a sensation when he said in 2004, "There's not a liberal America and a conservative America—there's the United States of America." He got a Tea Party revolt.

After fifty years of cultural civil war, the American public appears ready to move on. What will it take to end the division? A new trauma? 9/11 did bring the country together, but for only one year. In September 2002, after the Bush administration began to roll out plans for the invasion of Iraq, the old divisions reemerged with even greater ferocity. A charismatic leader? Obama, like his three predecessors, got caught up in the old divisions. Under each of the four presidents be-fore Trump—two Democrats and two Republicans—a divided coun-try ended up even more divided. Then in 2016, American voters faced a choice between two highly divisive candidates. Hillary Clinton and Donald Trump were the two least popular presidential nominees on record. The winner promised to exploit the country's divide, not heal it.

The great disconnect in American politics today is between public opinion, which longs for unity, and politics, which thrives on division.

FOUR

Political Separation

Tribalism is evident in the trend of growing political separation. Democrats and Republicans increasingly live apart, among others like themselves. The pattern was first noticed by Bill Bishop, who wrote a series of articles in the *Austin American-Statesman* in 2004 noting a trend that had been going on for nearly thirty years. Bishop called it, in his 2008 book, *The Big Sort: Why the Clustering of Like-Minded America Is Tearing Us Apart.*" [1]

People choose where to live primarily because of their jobs. But occupation has a lot to do with lifestyle. And the choice of location within a general area is a lifestyle choice as well. As Bishop explained it, "People seem to know where to move through some sixth sense that tells them, this place is comfortable for me socially. Which these days means politically, too." The implication is that politics followed values and lifestyle, not just interests.

In 2014 the Pew Research Center released a study of "Political Polarization in the American Public." The key finding: "Republicans and Democrats are more divided along ideological lines—and partisan antipathy is deeper and more extensive—than at any point in the last two decades." The percentage of partisans with an intensely negative view of the opposing party (their policies are "so misguided that they threaten the nation's well-being") had doubled since 1994.[2]

Americans on the right and the left said that it was important to them to live where people shared their political views. Liberals were far more likely to value racial and ethnic diversity. Conservatives were more likely to say it was important to live among people who shared their religious faith. Three-quarters of conservatives said they preferred to live in a community where "the houses are larger and farther apart" (suburbs and rural areas). Three-quarters of liberals wanted to live where "the houses are smaller and closer to each other" (urban areas). Politics reflected lifestyle.

A study by the *Guardian* found that in 1992, just 51 percent of House Democrats represented congressional districts that voted at least 5 points more Democratic for president than the country as a whole. In 2012, 88 percent of Democrats came from districts where Obama did at least 5 points better than his national popular vote.[3] In 2017 nearly 30 percent of House Democrats came from just two states: California and New York.

The number of battleground states has been shrinking. In the 1960 presidential election, there were twenty-four swing states where the margin of victory was 5 percentage points or less. In the 2016 election, using the same criterion, there were eleven swing states.

In 2017 California, the nation's largest state, did not have a single statewide elected Republican officeholder. Neither did New York, the nation's fourth largest state. The second largest state, Texas, has not elected a Democrat statewide since 1994.

In 2017 thirty-one state governments were "trifectas" controlled by one party (governor and both chambers of the state legislature). All six Democratic trifecta states voted for Hillary Clinton in 2016. All but one of the twenty-five Republican trifecta states had voted for Trump. (The exception: New Hampshire voted for Clinton.)[4]

Split-ticket voting is becoming a thing of the past. Out of 435 congressional districts, the number that voted for different parties for president and Congress dropped from 83 in 2008 to 35 in 2016.[5] From 1956 to 1996, more than 100 districts had regularly split their tickets. As party lines have hardened, political separation has become the rule in American politics.[6]

Disappearing Moderates

There are still plenty of moderates in the electorate. In the 2016 exit poll, 39 percent of voters described themselves as moderate, a larger number than either conservatives (35 percent) or liberals (26 percent).

One reason moderates have lost influence is that we have had a sequence of "wave elections": a Democratic wave in 2006 and 2008; a Republican wave in 2010 and 2014. Whenever a wave hits, the first incumbents to get swept away are those who represent marginal districts or states. Republicans in marginal constituencies got swept away in '06 and '08. Democrats in marginal constituencies got swept away in '10 and '14.

The *New York Times* estimated that the number of swing House districts, where the presidential vote margin was within 5 points of the nationwide vote, dwindled from 103 in 1992 to 35 in 2012. Statistician and political journalist Nate Silver wrote, "Most members of the House now come from hyperpartisan districts where they face essentially no threat of losing their seat to the other party. Instead, primary challenges, especially for Republicans, may be the more serious risk."[7]

Redistricting does not affect the Senate, but Senate moderates have been declining as well. A major reason is the shrinking number of battleground states, as noted above. The *Guardian* study found that, after the 1992 election, 49 percent of Democratic senators came from states that voted more Republican than the country as a whole. After the 2012 elections, only 25 percent came from relatively Republican states.[8]

In the 2010 midterm, moderate House Democrats got it in the neck. Membership in the moderate Democratic "Blue Dog" caucus fell from fifty-four seats in 2009 to fourteen in 2013. Meanwhile, the Tea Party continued to threaten Republicans who dared to make deals with President Obama or the Democrats. Back in the 1980s, there were a lot of "Reagan Democrats" that Republicans could make deals with. There were never any "Obama Republicans." And we are unlikely to see "Trump Democrats."

Party lines are getting firmer. In 1964, 20 percent of Republicans voted for Lyndon Johnson. In 1984, 21 percent of Democrats voted for Ronald Reagan. But when Bill Clinton was reelected in 1996, only 10 percent of Republicans voted for him. In 2004, only 7 percent of Democrats voted for George W. Bush. In 2012 Obama drew only 6 percent of the Republican vote. The number was only slightly higher in 2016, when 8 percent of Republicans voted for Hillary Clinton and 8 percent of Democrats voted for Donald Trump.

Major policy achievements used to be bipartisan. That gave them enduring political legitimacy. Look at the congressional votes to establish Social Security in 1935. The measure got almost unanimous support from Democrats: 95 percent of House Democrats and 98 percent of Senate Democrats voted for the new program. But Republican support was also overwhelming: 84 percent of House Republicans and 76 percent of Senate Republicans.

Look at the passage of Medicare in 1965. Once again, Democrats were nearly unanimous (83 percent in the House, 89 percent in the Senate). On Medicare, Republicans were more closely divided, but they still delivered significant support: seventy Republican representatives (51 percent) and thirteen Republican senators (43 percent) voted for Medicare.

Now look at the votes on health care reform in 2010. The final House measure passed with 85 percent support from Democrats and no Republican votes. The Senate vote on health care reform was totally polarized: all 60 Democrats voted yea; all 39 Republicans voted nay.

The health care debate in 2009 and 2010 was a low point (to date) in bipartisanship. Representative Joe Wilson of South Carolina committed a rare breach of protocol when he shouted "You lie!" at President Obama as the president was addressing a joint session of Congress. Wilson later apologized for the outburst and was reprimanded by the House. Representative Trent Franks called the president an "enemy of humanity" because of his views on abortion rights. Democratic congressman Alan Grayson said the Republican health care plan was for sick people to "die quickly."

Both parties concentrate on rallying their own forces: the true believers, whom they can reach quickly and cheaply with new media. "It leads to an ideological escalation in both parties," veteran California political consultant Dan Schnur said. "If you only hear one side of the story, from your favorite blog or your favorite talk show host, you're not engaging in the broader discussion about the future of government." No one is talking to the broader audience. In war, there is no broader audience. There is only us and them.

Books have become weapons in the tribal war. The Clintons spawned an entire industry of anti-Clinton books with titles such as Ann Coulter's *High Crimes and Misdemeanors: The Case Against Bill Clinton* and *No One Left to Lie To: The Triangulations of William Jefferson Clinton*, by Christopher Hitchens. But the Clintons got their revenge when Hillary Clinton's *Living History* became a worldwide best seller. Bill Clinton's autobiography, *My Life*, also became a bestseller, as did *What Happened*, Hillary Clinton's account of the 2016 campaign.

Later there was a thriving market in anti-Bush books with titles like Molly Ivins's *Bushwhacked: Life in George W. Bush's America* and *Weapons of Mass Deception: The Uses of Propaganda in Bush's War on Iraq*, by Sheldon Rampton and John Stauber. The 2004 campaign produced a market for pro-Bush books such as *Deliver Us from Evil: Defeating Terrorism, Despotism, and Liberalism*, by Sean Hannity and Stephen Mansfield's *The Faith of George W. Bush*.

Online booksellers such as Amazon and Barnes & Noble tell you, "Customers who bought this book also bought" certain other books. One scholar used that information to map out books that shared the same readers. Sure enough, he found two distinct markets. There was a network of conservative readers who purchased books like *The O'Reilly Factor*, by the former Fox News host. And a network of liberal readers who purchased books like Peter Hart's *The Oh Really? Factor: Unspinning Fox News Channel's Bill O'Reilly*. Amazon reported in 2012 that sales of conservative books outnumbered sales of liberal titles by 56 percent to 44 percent, most likely because the number of self-described conservatives in the United States is greater than the number of self-described liberals.[9] Shortly after the 2016 election, Michael J. Knowles self-published *Reasons to Vote for Democrats: A Comprehensive Guide*. The book quickly became an Amazon bestseller. It contains a table of contents, a bibliography—and 266 blank pages. "It took a very long time to research this book," Knowles said. "I've been observing the Democratic Party for at least ten years now, and when I observed their record and reasons to vote for them—on reasons of economics or foreign policy or homeland security or civil rights and so on—I realized it was probably best to just leave all the pages blank."[10]

Blue readers and red readers rarely read each other's books. And there are very few books that both sides read. "A lot of things in our politics and our book buying are driven by anger and fear," Rich Lowry of *National Review* said in a television interview. Who needs neutrality when there's a war on?

Parallel Universes

In 2003 I spent some time in those parallel universes for CNN. I visited the conservative universe in Kennesaw, Georgia. Kennesaw, once a small town, is now a fast-growing suburb twenty-five miles outside Atlanta. It was described to me by several locals as "a two-Walmart town." And it has a powerful sense of history—southern history. Kennesaw was a Confederate stronghold, and the Confederate battle flag still flew proudly.

Kennesaw made national news in March 1982, when the city council unanimously approved an ordinance requiring every household to maintain a firearm, together with ammunition, in good working order. People in Kennesaw are comfortable with guns. "I truly don't know what percentage of people would actually have a gun in their home, but you can assume that everyone does," one citizen told me. "And if the assumption is there, it makes everyone feel comfortable being here."

And safe. Another citizen said, "Actually, over the years, I think the notoriety of that story probably did allow Kennesaw to enjoy a real, almost-crime-free atmosphere." Don't people in Kennesaw worry about gun safety? I was told, "You can keep it loaded, and you can still put a lock on it because you might trust your own children but you can't always trust their friends." Kennesaw's gun law made a statement: this is not Atlanta. "It was, more or less, we were going to keep the crime of Atlanta away from our door," a resident explained.

If Kennesaw has a lifestyle, you could describe it in one word: faith. As the mayor at the time told me, "We have a very churchgoing base. We're in the Bible Belt." Churches are everywhere in Kennesaw. They're a big part of life. "The churches have given people a sense of community," a Republican activist said. "It's a gathering place of people who feel the right way about life in the country. This is a very patriotic area."

In 2003 the Kennesaw City Council passed a resolution supporting the official recognition of God in government. It was sponsored by the mayor in solidarity with Chief Justice Roy Moore of the Alabama Supreme Court. Moore had refused to comply with a federal court order to remove a granite monument of the Ten Commandments from the state judicial building. "We're not talking about religion," the mayor said. "We're talking about God. Don't tell me I can't talk about it. You can talk about who you want. That's fine if that's what you want to do. But don't tell me I can't. Don't suck me into your unbelief."

Compare that with the parallel universe of Bethesda, Maryland, where Al Gore got 64 percent of the vote in 2000. In 2016 Hillary Clinton carried Montgomery County, Maryland, which includes Bethesda, with 76 percent of the vote.

Bethesda is deepest blue America. It's just outside Washington, DC. Bethesdans seem to feel more connected to Washington than Kennesaw residents do to Atlanta, according to a longtime civic activist. "It is a good place to raise children because of our proximity to Washington, DC, and all the monuments and museums and learning opportunities there," she explained.

Bethesdans certainly have a different view of government. "I have lived here for twenty-five years," one resident told me. "I have never heard people complain about the taxes. And our taxes are high." They also have a different view of guns. "The gun issue here is whether we should hire sharpshooters to try to cull the deer herds," a civic leader explained. "There are people who don't want guns used by sharpshooters even in controlled situations. We don't want guns doing anything."

Religion has a different meaning in Bethesda than it does in Kennesaw. Less a matter of faith, more a matter of justice. "It manifests itself in ways that you would see in the attitudes toward poor people, toward people without medical insurance, toward social issues," I was told. "It's a social justice orientation toward religion."

Bethesdans have a deep and abiding faith in one thing: education. "You are in a place where most everybody has a college degree," columnist David Brooks, who lived in Bethesda, observed. Bethesda, site of the US National Institutes of Health, is one of the best educated communities in the United States in terms of residents with graduate degrees. Education informs everything, including politics.

Bethesda is a highly involved community with no shortage of experts. On everything. A Bethesda resident said, "There will be an initiative to do something, and, invariably, the world's leading expert on that subject lives here and has an opinion." Bethesdans have an obsessive interest in education. "The schools are wonderful," one resident said. "People are prepared to pay whatever it costs to have their schools first-rate. People move here because of the schools."

If education is the local faith, its central doctrine is meritocracy. People who live in Bethesda feel they have earned their success. "Because this is an area where meritocracy has brought success to parents, they believe in education," the resident noted. "They know what it's done for them."

When did faith in meritocracy emerge? The sixties, of course. Brooks explained, "What the sixties were all about was a rise in the meritocratic class: a class of newly educated people who wanted to displace the old establishment, which was a Protestant WASP establishment. Bill Clinton was part of that meritocratic class. He embodied it in every respect—culturally and in his own background and attitudes. George W. Bush, on the other hand, was part of that old class." Nobody epitomized the triumph of meritocracy more than Barack Obama.

What we are seeing is the cultural conflicts of the 1960s increasingly politicized. Two Americas, red and blue. The country split nearly evenly. And bitterly. Kennesaw values versus Bethesda values. People in Kennesaw worry about their children getting into heaven. People in Bethesda worry about their children getting into Yale.

A Case Study of the Values Divide

The values divide reached peak intensity in 1998 over the issue of President Bill Clinton's impeachment. The impeachment debate dramatized and personalized the division, although the trauma was much more intense for voters on the right than on the left. Following a year of frustration and outrage over the public's reaction to the Monica Lewinsky scandal, conservatives were ready to declare defeat in the culture war.

After all, President Clinton didn't just lie under oath. He lied bald-faced to the American people when he said in January 1998, "I want you to listen to me. I'm not going to say this again. I did not have sexual relations with that woman, Ms. Lewinsky." Seven months later, he finally told the truth: he did have what most people would consider sexual relations with her. Depending on the legal definition of "sexual relations," of course.

Throughout the controversy, most Americans believed the president was at least guilty of lying under oath. But by two to one, the public consistently opposed impeaching and convicting him. Why? Because the more evidence they saw—*The Starr Report*, the president's videotaped testimony—the more they became convinced that this was just about sex. A private matter.

The electorate consistently endorsed the view that "Bill Clinton's personal life doesn't matter as long as he does a good job of running the country." Americans respect the boundary between public and private lives. They resented it when, in their view, the independent counsel, the press, and the Congress crossed that line. Especially when Republicans attacking Clinton's character could be portrayed as hypocrites. Running on the character issue is a high-risk proposition. The voters may be looking for character in their leaders, but they are not looking for character police.

What clinched the president's victory was the insane decision by House Republican leaders to release prosecutor Kenneth Starr's lurid report and the president's videotaped testimony, thinking the scandalous details were sure to finish him off. What they did instead was confirm the suspicion that this was "just about sex" and therefore nobody's business. Not the independent counsel's business. Not the Congress's business. And not the press's business. It was a colossal political blunder, and it ended up forcing House Speaker Newt Gingrich out of office.

When *The Starr Report* was released in September 1998, it spelled out all the salacious details of President Clinton's relationship with Monica Lewinsky. The juiciest parts (the cigars, the stained blue dress) were reprinted in newspapers all over the country. I decided to call my eightysomething-year-old mother in Virginia to ask her what she made of it all.

My mother said that, since I was in the press, people were asking her about the Clinton scandal. So she decided she had better find out more about it. Excerpts of *The Starr Report* had been printed in her local newspaper a few days before. She told me that she locked the door, pulled down the shades, and read what was reported in the paper.

"What do you think?" I asked.

My mother remained silent for a moment. Then she said, "You want to know what I think?"

"Of course," I said. "That's why I'm calling you."

"Well, here's what I think," she said in a lowered voice. "I think . . . men are dogs."

That's when I realized the president was going to survive.

Public opinion is supposed to be fickle. But on the impeachment issue, the American public appeared to have rock-solid convictions. Did people want to see President Clinton convicted and removed from office? By two to one, the answer was always no. It was that way before the president was impeached and after the president was impeached. One-third of Americans wanted him out. Twice as many wanted him to stay.[11]

The polls drove Republicans crazy. Every time one came out, Republicans claimed that the poll takers were not interviewing them, or that Republicans didn't trust polls and were not talking to the interviewers. That was nonsense, of course. Republicans were included in the polling. They were the persistent one-third of the country who wanted Clinton removed from office.

Why, then, did the House of Representatives defy public opinion and vote to impeach the president? The answer is partisanship. When the issue came to a vote in the House of Representatives in December 1998, only 36 percent of Americans favored impeachment, according to a Gallup poll. Among Republicans, however, the number was twice as high: 72 percent.

At the same time, the polls showed consistently that the public believed President Clinton was guilty of lying under oath. So why didn't the American people want to convict him? That, too, drove Republicans crazy. The reason was that the only penalty available was the political equivalent of the death penalty, and most Americans didn't think the Lewinsky scandal was a capital case. It was consensual sex. Not murder. Nevertheless, the public did want to see the president punished in some way for what he did, if only because he'd embarrassed the country.

In the end, the public got more or less what it wanted. President Clinton stayed in office. But he had to live with a kind of disgrace.

Impeachment has gone down on Clinton's permanent record. He is one of only two presidents to be impeached, even if he, like Andrew Johnson before him, managed to stay in office. Was there any remote similarity between the impeachment of Clinton in 1998 and that of Johnson 130 years earlier? Actually, there was.

This country went through a terrible Civil War in the 1860s. The bitter division of that war, North versus South, infected partisan politics for decades afterward. Andrew Johnson's impeachment was a direct product of those hatreds.

Johnson was a Union Democrat from Tennessee and the only southern senator to retain his seat in the US Senate after his state seceded. President Abraham Lincoln put Johnson on the ticket in 1864 as a gesture to unify the country. Six weeks after his second inauguration in 1865, Lincoln was assassinated and Johnson became president. The Radical Republicans who controlled Congress were vehemently anti-Southern and deeply resented Johnson's conciliatory policy toward the conquered South.

In a straight party-line vote, the House of Representatives impeached President Johnson on bogus charges of violating congressional prerogatives. Johnson was charged with illegally removing Secretary of War Edwin Stanton from office without Senate approval, in violation of the Tenure of Office Act (which was eventually repealed). After a three-month trial in 1867, the Senate came one vote shy of convicting the president and removing him from office. Johnson's impeachment was an act of pure political revenge.

A century later, in the 1960s, the United States went through a cultural civil war. At the heart of the conflict were the tens of thousands of Americans killed in Vietnam. The bitter divisions created by that war and the other conflicts of the 1960s—not North versus South but liberal versus conservative—have poisoned American politics for more than fifty years. The effort to impeach Clinton was a direct product of those hatreds.

The puzzle throughout Clinton's presidency was why he was hated by so many Americans. After all, Clinton fashioned himself a New Democrat who led his party back to the center. Nevertheless, liberals were powerfully loyal to Clinton—as loyal as conservatives were to Ronald Reagan during the Iran-contra scandal of the mid-1980s. Why? It was not because of his policies. Clinton was a hero to liberals because of his values. They were the values of the sixties. Tolerance of alternative lifestyles (gays in the military). A deep commitment to the African American struggle for equality. Support for women's rights, including abortion rights.

Clinton haters hated the president because they hated the sixties, which they believed corrupted American culture with an ethic of self-indulgence. (See any book by conservative commentator and broadcaster Bill Bennett.) Clinton was the first president to come out of the elite liberal culture of the sixties. Conservatives began by reviling Clinton the draft dodger. Eventually they reviled Clinton the sex fiend. (See *The Starr report.*)

During the impeachment hearings in 1998, I interviewed conservative activists in suburban Chicago (the congressional district then represented by Republican representative Henry Hyde, chairman of the House Judiciary Committee). One activist referred to Clinton contemptuously as "the first rock star president." Another said, "A president is with us today who is a child of the sixties. He is the adolescent in chief."

The culture wars also explain the astonishing outpouring of support for Clinton among African Americans, feminists, and Hollywood liberals, despite the president's faithlessness to many liberal causes.

I visited inner-city Detroit, the congressional district formerly represented by John Conyers, the ranking Democrat on the House Judiciary Committee during the impeachment hearings. I was puzzled by the fact that many African Americans I spoke to—radio talk-show hosts, ministers, community leaders—told me they thought the campaign to impeach President Clinton was driven by racial backlash.

An African American minister said, "On the grass-roots level, many blacks think impeachment is really about them."

"About blacks? Really?" I asked. "What's race got to do with it?"

He explained, "When you talk to people in barber shops and bus terminals, they think the president's enemies are after him because he likes black people. His enemies are our enemies."

Clinton's liberal values helped him keep the support of his political base. But the thing that saved the president was not his liberalism, which was often challenged. It was his populism. To many Americans, Clinton was "one of us," a leader with whom ordinary people could identify. His strengths were "our strengths." And that may be why so many Americans were willing to forgive him. They saw his weaknesses as "our weaknesses."

One more thing contributed to the president's survival: the economy, stupid. In a January 1999 Gallup poll, just before the Senate voted on whether to convict Clinton, more than 70 percent of Americans said the US economy was the best it had ever been in their lifetime. That was a phenomenal figure. The people who said things were great opposed convicting the president by three to one. They were okay, so he was okay.

Voters conveyed that message very clearly in the 1998 midterm election, when, for the first time in sixty-four years, a sitting president's party gained House seats in a midterm. In the exit poll that year,

82 percent of voters thought the nation's economy was in excellent or good shape. Those who thought the economy was in excellent shape voted 77 percent Democratic in the House election. Those who said it was in good shape voted 50 percent Democratic. Democratic support dropped to 29 percent among the small number who thought things were bad.[12]

President Clinton and the Democrats were saved by middle-class voters, who, under Clinton, began to feel economically secure and even prosperous. They were the people who, just a few years earlier, had been victims of the middle-class squeeze. They had trouble buying a home, educating their children, saving for retirement. They lived under the constant threat of downsizing and unaffordable health care. They were the angry voters of 1992, and that year, many of them gravitated to Ross Perot.

In 1998 they were making it. Their jobs and health care were more secure. They were among the eighty million Americans invested in the stock market. They could breathe easier about the future. They could even afford a few luxuries, like vacations, dining out, and a $3 cup of coffee. Most important, they credited Clinton. They understood him, just as he understood them. Clinton was their president. After Republicans defined the midterm election as a referendum on impeachment, those "new rich" voters came out in large numbers to protect their president.

No issue in recent years has so clearly demonstrated the populist character of American democracy. As noted in chapter 1, once the polls started coming out, conservatives were helpless to defy the will of the people. If there had been no polls, President Clinton never could have survived.

FIVE

The Great Reversal

"Preserving our individual freedoms ultimately requires collective action."

With that bloodless, analytical sentence from his second inaugural address on January 21, 2013, President Obama set off a firestorm of protest among conservatives. Senate Republican leader Mitch McConnell called the speech "unabashedly far-left-of-center." House Speaker John Boehner said the president's mission was to "annihilate the Republican Party."

Obama was framing a response to the Reagan Revolution. The rallying cry of that revolution, delivered in President Reagan's 1981 inaugural address, was: "Government is not the solution to our problem. Government is the problem." That was the reigning principle of

American politics for thirty-two years after 1980. Even President Clinton affirmed it when he said in 1996, "The era of big government is over."

President Obama was issuing a ringing defense of the essential functions of government. He had just defeated a Republican ticket that tried to sell smaller government. The Republican message in 2012 was shaped by the Tea Party, which challenged the most consensual functions of government, such as securing the safety net. The president dared to call for collective action. The term "collective action" gives Republicans a nosebleed. It sounds like collectivism.

The United States has been debating strong government versus weak government for more than two hundred years. The bias has always been in favor of weak government. Most people came to America seeking either religious freedom or economic freedom. Sociologist Seymour Martin Lipset wrote that the United States was settled by "runaways from authority"—not just oppressive governments but also economic monopolies and established churches. The country's first governing document, the Articles of Confederation (1781), set up a central government that was so weak it was unworkable. It had to be thrown out and replaced by the Constitution in 1788.

The power of government is the eternal issue in American politics. That power has been challenged in two different spheres: economics and culture.

An economically activist federal government is one that manages, guides, and regulates the economy. Is that liberal or conservative? In the nineteenth century, government was associated with the aristocracy of wealth and privilege. Out-groups in society favored a laissez-faire state. Thomas Jefferson and Andrew Jackson were intensely antigovernment. Jacksonian Democrats, as the party of the "left," opposed many forms of government economic intervention: currency controls, a national bank, incorporation by legislative charter, and protective tariffs. As president, Jackson became hostile to the idea of federal spending for internal improvements: local roads, canals, and bridges, which were desperately needed in an undeveloped country. He believed it invited corruption and gave the federal government too much power.

Throughout the nineteenth century, the Democratic Party was the antigovernment party. As the party of the left, Democrats appealed to the out-groups of society: working people, immigrants, the nonreligious. Even southern slaveholders—hardly an out-group—who suspected, correctly, that the federal government would take away their property without compensation. The Federalists (1790–1816), the Whigs (1834–1854), and later the Republicans (1854–) were more comfortable with a strong national government, which they defended in the name of nationalism. Whig Party leader Henry Clay—a Kentucky senator and representative who became Speaker of the House of Representatives, secretary of state, and three-time candidate for president— advocated the "American System," a plan for government promotion of economic growth.

Those were the days before the federal income tax, which was not authorized until the Sixteenth Amendment in 1913. Before that, the principal source of revenue for the federal government was not "internal revenue" (taxes) but "external revenue" (tariffs). The debate over tariffs was the defining partisan issue. Democratic Party platforms in the nineteenth century called for "tariffs for purposes of revenue only." Meaning, don't spend government money for purposes other than the essential functions of government. Low tariffs meant limited government.

It's the same debate we have today over taxes, with the party positions reversed. In his first speech to Congress in February 1981, President Reagan said, "The taxing power of government must be used to provide revenues for legitimate government purposes. It must not be used to regulate the economy or bring about social change." In other words, taxes for purposes of revenue only. Low taxes mean limited government.

The debate over the role of government in endorsing cultural values was even more divisive. Should the federal government favor certain social values, such as abolitionism, temperance, racial equality, sexual freedom, or religious observance? Those who favor a culturally activist federal government usually do so in the name of promoting morality ("good values"). Those who resist say they are defending pluralism: we are a country with no official religion, ideology, or culture, and so the state must be scrupulously neutral in such matters.

In the nineteenth century, the conservative parties were the parties of the cultural establishment; namely, the Protestant elite that wanted to use government to reform and control society. The Jeffersonian Democrats were the party of dissenters and the disestablished. Democrats supported religious freedom, states' rights, and cultural laissez-faire.

These historic party positions—weak-government Democrats and strong-government Republicans—were reversed in the twentieth century for a simple reason: the role of government changed. Around the turn of the twentieth century, progressives discovered something radically new: that the power of government could be used to curb abusive economic power, which was rampant in the era of trusts and monopolies. Former Republican president Theodore Roosevelt articulated the progressive doctrine in a speech he gave in 1910 in Osawatomie, Kansas (to be discussed in chapter 7). In order to curb the power of wealth and special interests, Roosevelt called for "a far more active governmental interference with social and economic conditions in this country than we have yet had."

One hundred one years later, President Obama echoed the same themes at Osawatomie. Obama said in 2011, "As a nation, we've always come together, through our government, to help create the conditions where both workers and businesses can succeed." In his second inaugural address, in 2013, Obama said, "A modern economy requires railroads and highways to speed travel and commerce." So much for Andrew Jackson's hostility to internal improvements.

Twentieth-century progressives discovered that the power of the state could be used to attack private concentrations of wealth and power. Government became the enemy of economic privilege, or what Franklin D. Roosevelt called "the economic royalists." Economic out-groups began to look to the federal government for protection: for jobs, relief, unemployment compensation, old-age pensions, and the safeguarding of labor rights. Government power became associated with the economic left. In the 1930s, many voters who supported the Progressive movement, including economically radical progressive Republicans in the Theodore Roosevelt mold, were folded into FDR's Democratic Party (once they got over their discomfort with organized labor and urban political machines).[1]

Government, which was once seen as a bastion of privilege, came to be viewed in the twentieth century as a force for social and economic egalitarianism. That would appear to give the Democrats a populist appeal. As noted earlier, populism is ideologically ambiguous: left wing on economic issues, right wing on cultural issues. Conservatives have often been able to disguise a regressive economic agenda with culturally populist rhetoric, while authentic economic reformers have, time and again, been bought off by the right on social issues. To take an extreme case, Communist regimes have used both economic radicalism and social traditionalism (but never religion) to rally the masses.

The agrarian protest movement of the 1890s, when organized populism reached its greatest strength in the United States, illustrates this ideological dualism. The platforms of the People's Party regularly called for government ownership of railroads and telegraph systems, a graduated income tax, currency expansion, regulation of banking and "money power," and, in some instances, a "war on capital." At the same time, the populism of the 1890s was deeply imbued with the values of evangelical Protestantism. ("You shall not crucify mankind upon a cross of gold.")

Sociologists Lipset and Earl Raab found evidence of nativism, anti-Catholicism, and anti-Semitism associated with various populist leaders.[2] The cultural gulf between Populist farmers and the heavily immigrant and urban labor movement made coalition difficult. Farmer-labor politics did not emerge until twenty years later, with the Progressive movement. In 2016 Donald Trump embodied the dual values of populism. On the one hand, Trump criticized big business, denounced free trade, and defended entitlement programs. On the other hand, he attacked illegal immigrants and Muslims. And his views on foreign policy bore more than a hint of isolationism ("America First").

Democrats discovered in the 1930s that the power of the federal government could be used to promote economic justice: the New Deal. Democrats discovered in the 1960s that the power of the federal government could be used to promote social justice: the civil rights movement. Those were the two great formative experiences of the modern Democratic Party. To be a progressive today is to be supportive of federal power as an instrument of justice.

While the Democratic Party changed its ideology from antigovernment to progovernment, the party never changed its social base. The Democratic Party remained the party of the underprivileged, the disadvantaged, and victims of discrimination: out-groups. The party of "losers," as Republicans sometimes say at intemperate moments. Except only now, those out-groups see the federal government more as an ally than an enemy.

Antistatist Democrats—economic conservatives and racists, who often claim a continuity with the Jeffersonian states' rights and laissez-faire traditions—were made to feel distinctly unwelcome. The progressive vision that animated Obama's agenda (collective action) was the same progressive vision that had animated Theodore Roosevelt and Franklin Roosevelt. "Progress does not compel us to settle centuries-long debates about the role of government for all time," President Obama said at his second inaugural. "But it does require us to act in our time."

Health Care Reform: A Case Study of the Debate over Government

More than any other issue, health care reform symbolizes the Obama legacy and the New America's coming to power. The New America's core political commitment is to diversity and inclusion. Obamacare was designed to include everybody.

To conservatives, however, the Affordable Care Act of 2010 is the embodiment of big government: a "radical" change that they regard as out of line with traditional American values. Specifically, with the principle of limited government. The Affordable Care Act did not pass because of a deal. It passed because Democrats relied on a practice considered normal in parliamentary democracies but unusual in the United States: party government. That continues to have consequences for the political legitimacy of the new law.

Democrats had been trying to pass universal health care since Harry Truman was president in the 1940s. It represents the third major leg of the Democratic legacy of the last century: Social Security in the 1930s, Medicare in the 1960s, and universal health care, which was supposed to arrive in the 1990s under President Clinton. It got delayed until 2010.

Why did Obama succeed where Clinton failed? The simple answer is that the Democratic Party did something in 2009–10 that it did not do in 1993–94, which was the last time it controlled all three branches of government: Democrats governed. They had a majority and used it to pass their program. That is rare in the United States and has the taint of being somehow "un-American."

Democrats did pay a price. They lost their majority in the House of Representatives in 2010 (just as they did in 1994). Americans remained sharply divided over the Affordable Care Act long after it was signed into law. It became "Obamacare"—an intensely partisan policy.

First Try: Clinton

President Bill Clinton had a deep understanding of the American middle class. He got elected in 1992 as a champion of the middle class, "people who work hard and play by the rules." He designed his health care reform plan to meet the needs of the middle class. But the plan failed in 1994 because it lost the support of the middle class. How did that happen?

President Clinton deliberately modeled his health care plan on

Social Security. During his speech to a joint session of Congress in September 1993, he held up a card and said, "Under our plan, every American will receive a health security card that will guarantee a comprehensive package of benefits over the course of an entire lifetime . . . that can never be taken away." It looked just like a Social Security card. Clinton figured that his dogged insistence on universal coverage was the key to winning the middle class.

When Americans call themselves "middle class," what they mean is "neither rich nor poor." Middle-class people know that there are people poorer than they are. They know that government programs based on "need" will help poor people because their needs are the greatest. At the same time, the middle class tends to go along with policies that tax the rich. To the middle class, both the rich and the poor mean "not me."

In his 1994 State of the Union speech, Clinton turned his offer of health care security into a threat. This time he held up a pen: "If you send me legislation that does not guarantee every American private health insurance that can never be taken away, you will force me to take this pen, veto the legislation, and we'll come right back here and start all over again."

The problem with the Clinton health care plan was that it collided with an inescapable reality: most Americans were happy with their health care and their health insurance. In a 1994 *USA Today*–CNN–Gallup poll taken at the peak of the debate, 80 percent of Americans said they were satisfied with the quality of their health care. And 69 percent said they were satisfied with their health insurance.[3] People wanted to be assured that they could keep what they had and liked. Not change it. Keep it.

There was also a moral issue. The growing number of uninsured Americans was a source of national shame and outrage as it approached forty million. (By 2010, it was nearing fifty million.) Voters wanted something done about the uninsured. As long as they didn't have to give up what they had and liked.

Republicans discovered another middle-class concern: that the federal government would have too much control over the nation's health care system. Senate minority leader Bob Dole said the Clinton health care bill was based on "the principle that government knows best." If the bill passed, Dole warned, "the federal government will have broad and sweeping new powers in almost every aspect of health care."

A 1994 Gallup poll tested those two fears. Which concerned Americans more: that Congress would pass a plan that gave the federal government too much control over health care? Or that Congress would pass a plan that failed to guarantee health insurance for every American? Too much government was a bigger concern than too little health insurance, by 53 percent to 40 percent.[4] The public came to see the Clinton administration's plan as a typical Democratic social welfare program: one that would help the poor, hurt the middle class, and create bigger government. That was exactly the perception that President Clinton, as a self-styled New Democrat, was trying to avoid.

What went wrong? Three things.

First, the recession ended. By 1994, the recovery was not yet strong enough for anyone to call it a Clinton boom. But it was robust enough for the middle-class panic over health care to subside. That, plus the fact that health care providers, fearful of reform, began to reorganize. As a result, the rapid inflation of health care costs slowed considerably. Between 1990 and 1994, the annual rate of increase in health care costs dropped from 11.0 percent to 5.4 percent. At the same time, the economic growth rate rose from 1.9 percent to 4.0 percent.[5]

Second, the Clinton administration displayed poor political judgment. It turned health care reform over to a five-hundred-person task force, meeting for months in secret, chaired by liberal activist Ira Magaziner and a hard-charging First Lady. Who elected them? The task force came up with a document that could not have been better designed to scare the wits out of the American people. It looked like a blueprint for big government—or Big Brother: 1,300 pages of new government regulations telling you what you could and could not do with your health care. "What's in there?" people asked. The Health Insurance Association of America started running TV ads featuring a fictional husband and wife, Harry and Louise, to give scary answers.

Third, the administration miscalculated by assuming it could sell health care reform to the middle class as the logical extension of Social Security and Medicare—part of what President Clinton called "the unfinished business of our country." Opponents of health care reform, Senate Majority Leader George Mitchell said, "will find themselves on the wrong side of history, just as the opponents of Social Security did, just as the opponents of Medicare did."

But the analogy didn't hold. When Social Security came up in the 1930s, most people didn't have retirement income security. Pension plans were often meager or nonexistent. Most of the elderly had to rely on the tender mercies of their relatives. Social Security gave them something they didn't have. When Medicare came up in the 1960s, most seniors didn't have adequate health insurance. Most Americans get their health insurance from their employers, and the vast majority of the elderly are not employed. Seniors, who had the greatest need for health care, faced prohibitive costs. Medicare gave them something they didn't have.

By the 1990s, however, the vast majority of middle-class Americans did have health insurance. And they were satisfied with it. So what were they worried about? Mainly, losing their health insurance if they lost their jobs. And being able to afford it if the rates went up. Those were the problems they wanted health care reform to fix. They were limited and specific problems.

They saw the Clinton administration's health care plan as doing far more than that. People's biggest concern was that it would take what they already had and make it worse. Members of Congress reported that they were getting more calls and letters from constituents asking, "What's going to happen to me if this bill passes?" than from people asking, "What's going to happen to me if this bill doesn't pass?"

The Gallup poll put that issue to the test. "Thinking about just your own health care situation," the poll asked, "which worries you more: that you could end up without health insurance if Congress doesn't pass a bill, or that you could end up worse off than you are now if Congress does pass a bill?" By a solid margin, 54 percent to 30 percent, Americans were more worried about what would happen to them if health care reform passed.[6]

Second Try: Obama

For fourteen years after the demise of the Clinton plan, health care reform was virtually a taboo subject in American politics. But Democrats refused to let it die. A month after he first got elected, President Barack Obama said at a press conference, "The time has come, this year, in this new administration, to modernize our health care system."

The issue had been debated during the 2008 campaign, especially in the Democratic primary race between Obama and Hillary Clinton. "I did try in 1993 and 1994, and I like to say that I have the scars to show for it," Clinton said at a Democratic primary debate. "But I learned a lot about what we have to do." Like what? Like you can't do it with a closed process that produces a scary 1,300-page plan. You'll frighten Harry and Louise. Obama seemed to understand that. "My goal is to make sure that we have everybody involved—doctors, nurses, patient advocates, businesses, labor, everybody—sitting around the table, Republicans and Democrats," Obama said. "This is going to be an open, transparent process."

There was one big difference between 1994 and 2009: the economy. In 1994 the economy was clearly in recovery. The middle class was no longer in a panic over health care. In 2009 economic anxiety had risen to a new peak. The public's biggest concerns were job losses, mortgage security, business failures, and the credit squeeze. All bigger than health care.

One thing, however, had not changed since 1994: a solid majority of Americans continued to say they were satisfied with their health care (83 percent in a 2009 CNN poll) and with their health insurance (74 percent).[7] A solid 71 percent of Americans were satisfied with both. President Obama addressed the satisfied majority at his July 2009 press conference. "Many Americans are wondering, 'What's in this for me? How does my family stand to benefit from health insurance reform?' " The president's answer: "If we do not act to bring down costs, everybody's health care will be in jeopardy."

Democrats had to convince the satisfied majority that they had nothing to fear from health care reform but that they did have something to fear if reform failed. In a 2009 *New York Times*–CBS News poll, more than three in four Americans said they were concerned that, if health care reform passed, their health care costs would go up. And if health care reform did not pass? More than three in four said they were concerned their health care costs would still go up.[8]

The Obama plan was never popular, even after it was signed into law in 2010.[9] It was not until 2017, when the Republican Congress threatened to repeal it, that a majority of Americans began to favor Obamacare. The process was part of the problem. President Obama did not make the same mistake as President Clinton and turn the bill-writing process over to a secretive commission. Instead, he made a different mistake. Promising that the process would be open and transparent, he turned it over to Congress. There is nothing less edifying to Americans than witnessing the process of bill writing in Congress—the deal making, the influence peddling, the horse trading. Deals like the "Cornhusker kickback" to get the support of Nebraska senator Ben Nelson and the "Louisiana purchase" to bring Senator Mary Landrieu into the fold. The public's disgust was captured perfectly by an uninsured eighteen-year-old waitress in New Hampshire who explained her opposition this way to the *New York Times*: "If you have to bribe people to vote for it, it can't be good."

What intensified the opposition was everything else the Obama administration did in its first two years. For Tea Party supporters, the Obama administration epitomized their worst nightmare of big government. Huge increases in federal spending. A federal takeover of major corporations on the verge of bankruptcy. Wall Street bailouts. The mortgage rescue plan. And on top of all that, more government control of health care. The fact that President Obama did it with the support of the New America—minorities and young people—just made it seem more alien. But the core of the complaint was not bigotry. It was fear of the abusive power of big government.

"There's no fixing the government health care takeover Democrats forced through," South Carolina senator Jim DeMint told the *New York Times*. "Freedom dies a little bit today," Representative Marsha Blackburn of Tennessee warned. A Tea Party activist told a rally in Iowa, "Every single person's body in this whole country belongs to the government now."

Party Government

In 2009 and 2010, Democrats had solid majorities in the House and Senate. Democrats held 257 House seats (59 percent of the House) when health care reform first came up for a vote in 2009. That was about the same number of seats they held during Clinton's first two years (258 Democratic seats in 1993–94). In 1994 Democrats held 57 seats in the US Senate. In 2009 Democrats had 60 votes in the Senate (including two Independents), just enough to end a filibuster. The Senate Democratic caucus slipped to 59 members when Senator Edward Kennedy died in 2009 and his successor, Republican Scott Brown, was chosen to succeed him in a special election.

But Democrats succeeded this time by hanging together to a degree that Democrats rarely do. House Democrats voted 219 to 39 for the Obama plan in 2009, enabling the measure to pass the House by 5 votes. Senate Democrats voted 54 to 3 for the plan in 2010. (Two Independent senators also voted for the plan.) Not a single Republican voted for the plan when it came up for final passage in 2010. In 1994, when Democrats had comparable majorities, the Clinton health care plan never made it to the floor of either chamber for a vote.

What united Democrats in 2009 and 2010? Answer: Republicans. It's Sir Isaac Newton's third law of motion: for every action, there is an equal and opposite reaction. It applies to politics just as it does to physics. Case in point: Representative Joe Wilson's "You lie!" outburst during President Obama's speech to a joint session of Congress. Action: Wilson's apparently spontaneous gesture of contempt. Reaction: outraged Democrats rallied to the cause of health care reform.

Which is exactly what Barack Obama needed to happen. In his speech, the president carefully tried to carve out a middle way between two objectives: building a consensus on health care reform ("I will continue to seek common ground in the weeks ahead") and standing up to his opponents ("If you misrepresent what's in the plan, we will call you out"). He got nowhere with Republicans. Their resolve had been strengthened over the previous summer by Tea Party activists, who laid out a path of defiance.

The Democratic Congressional Campaign Committee sent a message to backers that said, "Calling the president of the United States a liar in front of the nation is a new low even for House Republicans." Americans United for Change charged in a web video, "It's official: the Party of No has become the Party of No Shame."

The loss of Ted Kennedy's seat in January 2010 came very close to killing the health care bill. The crush of press coverage of the Massachusetts race caused Bay State voters to see the election as a national event: a referendum on health care reform in a state that already had it. Polls showed no great enthusiasm for the federal health care bill among Massachusetts voters—in some cases, because they didn't think they needed it, and, in many cases, because they didn't like it any more than voters in other states did. The special Senate election invited Massachusetts voters to send a message to Washington: "Stop."

The only option left for Democrats was to try to pass the bill with a purely partisan majority. In his response to President Obama's weekly radio address in February 2010, Republican senator Tom Coburn of

Oklahoma charged that congressional Democrats "want to use procedural tricks and backroom deals to ram through a new bill that combines the worst aspects of the bills the Senate and House passed last year." Coburn was referring to the reconciliation process whereby the bill could pass the Senate with 51 votes without being subject to a filibuster. After Kennedy's death, Democrats were one vote short of the supermajority needed to end a filibuster. Questioned about reconciliation at her news conference, House Speaker Nancy Pelosi replied, "What you call a complicated process is called a simple majority."

The health care bill did pass the Senate by a simple majority, 56 to 43. It was an unusual experience for the United States. Most major legislation in American history has been passed with bipartisan support: Social security, Medicare, the civil rights and voting rights laws, the Reagan tax cuts, the Bush tax cuts, the Patriot Act. But not the Obama health care law. It was owned exclusively by Democrats, and Republicans have never ceased campaigning for repeal. Even after the defeat of Mitt Romney, who promised to repeal the law even though it was similar to the health care law that he had signed as governor of Massachusetts. The new law became Obamacare, a term the president ultimately embraced.

When the Affordable Care Act finally passed in March 2010, the public was divided over the new law, with 46 percent favorable and 40 percent unfavorable in the Kaiser Health Tracking Poll. A year later, the public was still divided: 41 percent to 41 percent. In 2012? 41 percent favorable, 40 percent unfavorable. Opposition increased after the disastrous website rollout in October 2013, with 50 percent to 34 percent opposed in January 2014. After the website was fixed, opinion settled back to a closer split: 45 percent opposed, 38 percent in favor in May 2014. Then a barrage of anti-Obamacare ads began running as the 2014 midterm campaign got under way, and opposition peaked at 53 percent in July 2014, with only 37 percent in favor. In January 2016 the public remained divided: 44 percent opposed to the new health care law and 41 percent in favor.[10]

A Tax?

Public opposition to the law has always focused on the individual mandate requiring people to purchase health insurance or pay a fine. In fact, Barack Obama was against an individual mandate before he was for it. During the 2008 campaign, he said his opposition to a mandate without making health care affordable for all was "a genuine difference between myself and Senator Clinton." Once he became president, however, Obama was persuaded to accept an individual mandate because it was the only way health insurance companies would support the new law. (A mandate guaranteed them more customers.) No wonder so many voters thought the policy had been imposed on them. They didn't vote for an individual mandate when they elected Obama.

In 2012 the Kaiser Family Foundation poll gauged public support for twelve specific provisions of the new law. Eleven of the twelve provisions had majority support, ranging from 80 percent who favored "tax credits to small businesses that offer health insurance to their employees," to 51 percent who favored requiring insurance plans to offer "a minimum package of health insurance benefits to be defined by the government." Only one provision did not garner majority support: the one requiring "nearly all Americans to have health insurance by 2014 or else pay a fine." The public opposed the individual mandate by more than two to one (66 percent to 32 percent).[11]

President Obama reversed himself again on whether to label the penalty a tax. He objected strongly when Republicans called it a tax. But here too, the administration shifted arguments, eventually accepting the idea that the mandate could be called a tax. That reversal proved crucial to the law's survival.

"The mandate is not a legal command to buy insurance," Chief Justice John Roberts wrote in his June 2012 health care ruling. It's not? Really? It sure sounds like it. No, Roberts insisted, "It makes going without insurance just another thing the government taxes, like buying gasoline or earning income." With that bit of sophistry, the Supreme Court upheld the health care law and refrained from throwing millions of Americans off the health insurance rolls. Democrats were thrilled. They didn't care how the court got there as long as the court got there.

But it *does* make a difference how it got there. Because what the court did was to deny that health care is a right. In the court's view, the right to health care has no constitutionally protected status, such as abortion rights or gun rights. It's just a benefit. Rights can't be taken away. Benefits can. If universal health care is simply a tax, it's dispensable. Taxes can be raised or lowered or abolished. We do that all the time. "Those decisions are entrusted to our nation's elected leaders, who can be thrown out of office if the people disagree with them," the court said. Could that have been a partisan recommendation? It sure sounded like it. "It is not our job to protect the people from the consequences of their political choices," Roberts wrote.

The Supreme Court's ruling amounted to a challenge to the Obama administration: if you want to keep the health care law, you're going to have to sell it to the American public. That's something the administration never really did. Speaking on CNN, former White House chief of staff Jack Lew said, "We have a Supreme Court, and when it rules, we have a final judgment." In the case of health care reform, however, the court left the final judgment to the American people.

The Debate Goes On . . . and On

I once interviewed an elderly Russian woman who had immigrated to the United States. I asked her what she thought of the US health care system. She said she didn't like her American doctor. I asked her why not.

"He is *nekulturny*," she replied.

"Uncultured?" I suggested.

"Yes," she said. "My Russian doctor read Balzac. My American doctor has never heard of Balzac."

"So do you think medicine in Russia is better?" I asked.

She thought about the question for a moment. Finally, she said, "I don't think so. You see, my American doctor knows where my liver is."

In 2013, Republican senators shut down the federal government for sixteen days rather than pass a budget that included funding for Obamacare. "If you pay for a budget that includes Obamacare . . . you have voted for Obamacare," Senator Marco Rubio of Florida announced. "Some will say, 'That is crazy. You are going to shut down the government over Obamacare.' No. What is crazy is moving forward with [Obamacare]." By the end of 2015, the House of Representatives had voted more than sixty times to roll back all or part of Obamacare, only to see the votes ignored by the Senate. Finally, at the beginning of 2016, a repeal measure made it through both the House and Senate and reached the president's desk. President Obama vetoed the repeal within two days. Neither House nor Senate Republicans had the votes to override the president's veto.

As the law moved toward implementation in 2014, President Obama remained optimistic. "If it works, it will be pretty darn popular," he said in a *New York Times* interview. The danger was that not enough young and healthy people would sign up. Without those new customers, the insurance rolls would be overwhelmed by older and sicker Americans who couldn't get coverage otherwise—and who would drive up costs. And insurance premiums.

The problem was that many healthy young people might opt to pay the penalty—up to 1 percent of their income—rather than purchase insurance, which could be far more costly. After all, young people, particularly young men, believe they are immortal. They might prefer to take their chances with health care and use the cash to buy a car or go to Cancun, Mexico, for spring break.

Former Montana senator Max Baucus, one of the architects of the Affordable Care Act, warned of "a train wreck" if preparations for the new law were inadequate. Meanwhile, Republicans were doing everything they could to derail the train. GOP House members withheld funds for the campaign. Congress provided less money than it did for the rollout of President Bush's prescription drug program in 2004. That program had a constituency of seniors who were eager to participate.

Republicans were determined to resist. Republican governors were uncooperative. A spokesman for the National Republican Senatorial Committee said Republicans intended to make the 2014 midterm a referendum on Obamacare "in a more tangible way than it was in 2010." Democrats were worried. Senator Ron Wyden of Oregon said "There is reason to be very concerned about what's going to happen with young people. If their premiums shoot up, I can tell you, that is going to wash into the United States Senate in a hurry."

The fate of Obamacare remains uncertain as of November 2017. Congressional Republicans continue to plot strategies to defund the law and eliminate the tax penalty for the uninsured. The Supreme Court continues to hear challenges to the law. For Republicans, opposition to Obamacare has become a defining issue. It's like antiwar sentiment was for Democrats in 2006. In Iraq, of course, people were being killed. But look at what Minnesota representative Michele Bachmann said about Obamacare: "Let's repeal this failure before it literally kills women, kills children, kills senior citizens." Senator Coburn, a physician, said the message to seniors was: "You're going to die sooner. When you restrict the ability of primary caregivers in this country to do what is best for their senior patients, what you're doing is limiting their life expectancy."

The Obama administration estimated that more than fifteen million Americans had gained health insurance by the end of 2015 because of Obamacare. "This thing is working," the president said. The October 2014 Kaiser poll reported that most Americans wanted Congress to work to improve the law (64 percent) rather than repeal it and replace it with something else (33 percent).[12] But conservatives will never agree that Obamacare is working. They're ideologues, and ideologues believe that if something is wrong, it can't possibly work. Even if it does work.

Obamacare is supposed to be an entitlement program, like Social Security and Medicare. Both of those programs are universal: everyone who pays into the system is entitled to a benefit whether or not he or she actually needs the money. We bribe the middle class to support entitlements. That's why they're so expensive. And so popular.

A social welfare program targets benefits by need. Only people who can show they actually need the benefit get it. Under Obamacare, some people who have to purchase health insurance can't afford it and have to be subsidized. Those subsidies are being paid for with fines, new taxes, and higher premiums for people who can afford it. That's a transfer of wealth.

Programs targeted by need have always been controversial. How can we be sure people don't take advantage of the system? That the benefits go only to the "truly needy"? "I think [Obamacare] is viewed more as a social welfare program than a social insurance program," longtime Obama adviser David Axelrod told the *New York Times*.

Obama promised several times in 2009, "If you like your health care plan, you'll be able to keep your health care plan, period." It was politically devastating when the Affordable Care Act went into effect in 2013, and people started losing their insurance plans because the plans didn't meet Obamacare standards. They believed the president lied to them. "The way I put that forward unequivocally ended up not being accurate," Obama acknowledged in November 2013.

True, only a small number of people with individual policies were affected by the cancellations. But as a congressional Democrat put it, "There was an ability to exploit the unknown, to exploit the fear of people losing something that they have. That wasn't true with Social Security and Medicare."

Democrats had used a routine parliamentary principle—party government—to pass the health care law. It passed, narrowly, at the cost of forever defining the Affordable Care Act as a partisan policy. Seven years later, Republicans were making the same mistake as they took up the effort to repeal and replace Obamacare. In July 2017 the ailing

Senator John McCain made that point when he returned to Washington to cast the decisive vote to open debate on the issue.

"We keep trying to find a way to win without help from across the aisle," McCain said in a dramatic floor speech. "That's an approach that's been employed by both sides, mandating legislation from the top down without any support from the other side, with all the parliamentary maneuvers that requires."[13]

He accused his fellow Republicans of making precisely the same political mistakes that Democrats did. "We've tried to [amend the Affordable Care Act] by coming up with a proposal behind closed doors in consultation with the [Trump] administration, then spring it on skeptical members, trying to convince them it's better than nothing and force it past a unified opposition. I don't think that's going to work in the end, and it probably shouldn't."

The bill to replace Obamacare with the American Health Care Act (AHCA) passed the House of Representatives in May 2017 by a vote of 217 to 213. Democratic Representatives voted unanimously against it, while 20 Republicans joined them in opposition. A month after the House vote, the Kaiser Health Tracking Poll reported that favorable opinion of Obamacare had risen to over 50 percent for the first time since 2010. Only 30 percent supported the AHCA.[14] As the House repeal vote was being counted, Democrats serenaded Republicans by singing, "Na na na na, na na na na, hey hey, good-bye." The Senate repeal bill was drawing 17 percent support and 55 percent opposition at the end of June 2017 when Republican leaders were forced to delay the vote.[15]

Republicans found it difficult to figure out how to require health insurers to cover people with preexisting conditions without a federal mandate to bring insurers more customers. They tried to do it with huge subsidies for lower-income participants, but conservatives objected that the subsidies would create a new government entitlement.

"We are going to be living with Obamacare for the foreseeable future," House Speaker Paul Ryan lamented after the Republican alternative initially failed. That is something of a miracle. Look at how many near-death experiences the law has been through:

- the death of Senator Kennedy in 2009, which deprived Democrats of the supermajority they needed to end a Senate filibuster;
- the 2010 midterm election in which Republicans won control of the House of Representatives by promising to repeal Obamacare;
- the 2012 Supreme Court ruling that upheld the Affordable Care Act by a vote of 5 to 4;
- the government shutdown in October 2013, when Republicans temporarily cut off funding for the federal government rather than pass a budget that included money for Obamacare;
- a bill to repeal the Affordable Care Act that was passed by Congress in 2016 and vetoed by President Obama;
- the refusal of nearly twenty states to expand Medicaid coverage for the poor, including Texas and Florida, the nation's second and third largest states;
- the 2016 election, which finally produced a Republican Congress and a Republican president who got elected on a pledge to end Obamacare "on day one"; and
- the struggles of the Republican majority in Congress to agree on a replacement bill in 2017.

As of November 2017, Obamacare was still the law of the land, though still under constant threat. Once a benefit is granted to the American people, it becomes very difficult to take it away even if it was not popular initially.

Passing laws without mobilizing solid support from public opinion is often a temptation for presidents, particularly when their party controls Congress. But it is always a risky thing to do in a populist political culture like that of the United States. President Trump said in February 2017, "Nobody knew health care could be so complicated." Oh yes they did.

SIX

The Intensity Factor

The slogans Republican presidential candidates ran on in 2016 were revealing: "Make America Great Again" (Donald Trump), "Believe Again" (Louisiana governor Bobby Jindal), "Reigniting the Promise of America" (Ted Cruz), "Restore the American Dream" (Rick Santorum), "Jeb Can Fix It!" (Jeb Bush) "Heal. Inspire. Revive" (Ben Carson).

They were all about restoring and reviving something. That would be the Old America, when the country was whiter, men were in charge, government was smaller, and religion was more influential. Also, Republicans would quickly add, the United States was more successful, more self-assured, and a more powerful player on the world stage.

Democrats rally to the theme of diversity and inclusion. Sometimes they go overboard, like the San Francisco middle school teacher who refused to announce the results of a student council election because the winners were not diverse enough. "Diversity trumps democracy!" her critics howled until she relented.[1]

Republicans hate political correctness. When challenged during a debate on his opposition to same-sex marriage, Carson said that you "shouldn't automatically assume that, because you believe that marriage is between one man and one woman, you are a homophobe." The left tries to "frighten people and get people to shut up," he added. "That's what the PC culture is all about, and it's destroying this nation."

During the Obama administration, the Republican Party became a resistance movement. Republicans resisted the rise of the New America and its attempt to impose political correctness on our culture. You saw the signs of resistance everywhere, like new voter identification requirements passed in Republican-controlled states. The law in Kansas requires people to provide written proof of citizenship when they register to vote.

Donald Trump's cause was resistance to illegal immigration. He warned that, if he didn't get elected, the Ford Motor Company "will build a new plant in Mexico, and illegals are going to drive those cars over the border." He added, "They'll probably end up stealing the cars."

New Jersey governor Chris Christie, a former prosecutor, called for resistance to the Black Lives Matter movement, which he blamed for rising crime rates. "Police officers are afraid to get out of their cars," Christie said during a primary debate. "They're afraid to enforce the law . . . I am deadly serious about changing this culture."

Marco Rubio's family came to America from Cuba as immigrants in 1956, sixty years before the 2016 election. "I think there's a sense in this country today that somehow our best days are behind us," he said.

"That doesn't have to be true. Our greatest days lie ahead." Inclusion, he said, should be based on values, not political correctness: "whether or not you're coming here to become an American—not just live in America, but be an American."

During the New Hampshire primary debate, Christie ridiculed Rubio for sounding scripted when the Florida senator kept repeating the same charge: "President Obama is undertaking a systematic effort to change this country." That happened to be the essential complaint of the conservative resistance movement: that President Obama brought a different America to power, and "we want the Old America back."

After researching census data on places where Trump did well in the early 2016 Republican primaries, Neil Irwin and Josh Katz wrote in the *New York Times* that "Trump counties are places where white identity politics mixes with long-simmering economic frustration." Trump support was correlated with high numbers of native-born Americans, whites with low education, and people who identify their ancestry as "American." It also correlated with jobs in declining industries such as mining and manufacturing, and with the number of working-age Americans who had dropped out of the labor force. Part of the conflict is the old economy versus the new economy. Opposition to foreign trade was a potent issue for Trump because it signified a new, more global economy.

Social issues such as civil rights, same-sex marriage, abortion rights, and immigration are matters of basic identity for many Americans. They define the battle lines. The Supreme Court has the final say on many of those deeply divisive issues. Court nominations provoke the most pitched partisan battles. That is particularly true when the balance between liberal and conservative justices is at stake, as it was after the death of Justice Antonin Scalia in 2016.

Many of the most heated conflicts in American politics occur over social issues: gun control, illegal immigration, abortion, same-sex marriage, and affirmative action. On some of those issues, conservatives have tended to prevail (resisting firearm regulation), while on others, liberals have won (same-sex marriage). Still others seem to give rise to perpetual deadlock (immigration, affirmative action). How does one side win in a deeply divided country?

In 2015 the Gallup poll reported a striking finding: for the first time since 1991, when Americans were asked to describe their views on social issues, the number calling themselves liberals was tied at 31 percent with the number calling themselves conservatives. In 2009, conservatives outnumbered liberals 42 percent to 25 percent.[2] The percentage liberal has been increasing and the percentage conservative declining since 2009, when Obama took office.

Still, the outcomes of controversies often have less to do with the numbers and more to do with the intensity of opinion and the language used to define the issues. This chapter deals with the intensity factor and chapter 7 with language.

Why Intensity Matters

Polling has a dirty little secret: polls don't measure intensity of opinion very well. Typically, polls can tell you how many people are on each side of an issue but not whether the issue is likely to drive their vote. And that's what really matters to politicians.

Let's say a poll shows a politician that his constituents divide 75 percent to 25 percent in favor of gun control. The politician knows what will happen if he votes for a gun control law. Maybe 10 percent within the 75 percent majority care enough about the issue to vote for him for that reason alone. But he may lose 20 percent out of the 25 percent on the other side. Gun owners may be a minority, but many see gun control as a threat to their Second Amendment rights. It drives their votes. They make sure politicians know it.

Single-issue voting helps explain why intensely committed minorities can hold sway over casually committed majorities. What does it take to activate the majority? Usually a threat, such as a horrifying incident of gun violence or an impending curb on abortion rights. On many social issues, the right is more intensely committed. That's why conservatives have often won battles over gun rights, abortion, and immigration. They are more watchful, better funded, and better organized. They let politicians know that a posse of voters will come after them. "Why are gun owners so politically powerful?" an abortion rights activist once said to me in an interview. "There are more uterus owners than gun owners. And when uterus owners begin to vote this issue, we will win."

The left typically gets passionate over antiwar issues. That's when the passion gap tilts in their favor and Democrats win (2006). But when there is no Vietnam or Iraq controversy, the right is typically angrier and more intense. That's what sustains the talk radio industry.

Single-issue politics is a sort of blackmail: "We don't care what your position is on anything else. If you are with us on our issue, we'll support you. If you are against us, we'll come after you." That is what the anti–Vietnam War movement used to say: "We care only about one thing. Where do you stand on the war?"

On highly divisive issues, the instinct of politicians is to avoid taking any position. The safest thing to do is to say nothing and hope the issue will be decided by the federal courts, where judges are not answerable to the voters. That works, until the politician begins to look irresponsible and risks losing votes for refusing to take a position.

That may have been what convinced Obama to come out in favor of same-sex marriage in May 2012, after Vice President Joe Biden stated his support. Obama's self-described "evolution" on the issue was beginning to look ridiculous. At his campaign appearances, gay-rights activists had started wearing buttons that read, "Evolve Already!" It seemed a reasonable risk for Obama because, by 2012, both sides had roughly equal numbers and similar intensity.

The Gun Issue

Shortly after taking office in 1993, President Clinton said, "I don't believe that everybody in America needs to be able to buy a semiautomatic or an automatic weapon, built only for the purpose of killing people, in order to protect the right of Americans to hunt and practice marksmanship and to be secure." After the 1992 election, Democrats held majorities in both the House and Senate. Having elected the first Democratic president in twelve years, Democrats took decisive action on gun control.

The pressure had been building even before the 1992 election. In May 1991 the House of Representatives voted 238 to 186 to pass the Brady Handgun Violence Prevention Act. That was almost a precise reversal of the vote in 1988 when the House turned down the measure, 228 to 182. What had changed?

Crime, for one thing. Just before the 1991 vote, the US Justice Department reported that violent crimes were up by 10 percent in 1990. Oregon Democratic representative Les AuCoin, casting his first antigun vote after seventeen years in the House, explained: "It is the rising tide of violence in our streets, communities, neighborhoods, schools. You have to be brain dead or an ideological robot not to say in the face of that phenomenon, 'Wait a minute, times are changing.'"

James S. Brady, the presidential press secretary who was shot and permanently disabled in the 1981 assassination attempt on President Reagan, provided an emotional symbol for proponents of the measure to rally around. Reagan, too. He reversed his longstanding opposition to gun control and came out in favor of the Brady bill in 1991. "Ronald Reagan certainly helped," Sarah Brady acknowledged. She was the wife of James Brady. Mrs. Brady became a crusader for gun control, chairing the Brady Campaign to Prevent Gun Violence from 2000 until her death in 2015.

Members of Congress don't like being threatened by single-issue groups. They may respond to the threats, but they resent them. Occasionally, Congress expresses its resentment by defying a single-issue group. It has to be on an easy vote where there is strong public sentiment on the other side. That's what got the Brady Bill passed in 1993, when there was a rising tide of public anger over gun violence. The Brady Bill and the assault weapons ban in 1994 were the last significant gun control measures to make it through Congress. And then what happened? Democrats lost control of Congress for the next twelve years. After the 1994 midterm, Clinton argued that the gun lobby played a big role in his party's defeat. Democrats have been gun-shy ever since. Al Gore rarely talked about gun control during the 2000 presidential campaign. In the final debate with George W. Bush, he said, "None of my proposals would have any effect on hunters or sportsmen or people who use rifles."

Candidate John Kerry went hunting during the 2004 campaign,

claiming, "I will protect the Second Amendment. I always have, and I always will." The National Rifle Association ran an ad against him: "John Kerry, you are not fooling America's gun owners. They know you voted against their gun rights for twenty years. So now you're running away from your record, just like Al Gore did."

The progress made by gun control advocates in the 1990s created a backlash. Opponents of new gun laws felt threatened, and they rallied. The NRA gained seven hundred thousand new members in the year before the 2000 election and had a record four million members by Election Day that year.

Most Americans have always opposed a ban on handguns. Most Americans have also opposed a ban on abortions. Americans don't like to ban anything. Americans believe they have a right to buy a gun or have an abortion. Those rights are protected by the Constitution. But they are not absolute rights. There is a broad public consensus that gun rights and abortion rights can be limited, regulated, and restricted by law like any other right—free speech, for example. The battle is always over how far the government may go in limiting those rights.

On June 26, 2008, the US Supreme Court handed down a landmark gun rights ruling in the case of *District of Columbia v. Heller.* The court ruled for the first time that gun ownership is an individual right guaranteed by the Second Amendment. That right does not have to be connected to service in a militia. Writing for the majority, however, Justice Antonin Scalia said it is "not a right to keep and carry any weapon whatsoever in any manner whatsoever and for whatever purpose."

Shortly after President Obama was reelected in 2012, the horrifying massacre of schoolchildren occurred at the Sandy Hook Elementary School in Newtown, Connecticut. Once again, the outcry for tougher gun laws reached a fever pitch. We began hearing terms like "tipping point" and "game change." Democrats who had been strong supporters of gun rights, such as Senator Joe Manchin of West Virginia, Senator Bob Casey of Pennsylvania, and Senate Majority Leader Harry Reid of Nevada, called for "a new conversation" about guns. New York mayor Michael Bloomberg warned that if Washington failed to pass new gun control legislation, it would be "a stain upon our nation."

Gun rights advocates seemed to be in hiding. A few days after the shooting, NBC News invited thirty-one senators with "A" ratings from the NRA to appear on *Meet the Press*. Not one accepted. Yet despite public outrage, gun control legislation was difficult to pass. Once again, the problem was not public opinion. The public was supportive of measures such as bans on semiautomatic handguns (favored by 52 percent in the *Washington Post*–ABC News poll taken just after the Connecticut massacre) and on high-capacity ammunition clips (favored by 59 percent).

As in the past, intensity had shifted following a sensational incidence of gun violence. Gun control supporters started issuing threats: you'd better support new gun control measures, or else you'll pay a price. But that kind of anger is hard to sustain. Politicians worried: If I support new gun controls, it may be popular right now, but will I pay a price two years from now when only gun owners vote the issue?

"These events are happening more frequently," Connecticut Independent senator Joseph Lieberman said. "I worry that if we don't take a thoughtful look at them, we're going to lose the pain, the hurt, and the anger that we have now."

Intensity is not the only problem. In 2013 a new problem emerged: insularity. More and more legislators represented safely partisan districts. According to statistician Nate Silver, the percentage of safe districts doubled from twenty-eight in 1992 to fifty-six in 2012.[3]

Republicans from safe districts didn't face serious competition from a Democrat. The threat they faced was from a Republican primary challenger.

In 2014, according to the National Opinion Research Center (NORC) at the University of Chicago, Republicans were twice as likely as Democrats to have a gun in the household (50 percent for Republicans; 25 for Democrats).[4] That difference has been widening since the 1970s. Gun ownership declined among Democrats as the party lost many of its rural and conservative supporters. The gun culture has roots in the frontier mentality: we're out here on our own, and we rely on guns to protect ourselves and our families.

Especially if the government fails to protect its citizens. A Republican congressman from Texas told the *Financial Times* that he wished the principal of Sandy Hook Elementary had been armed. "I wish to God she'd had an M4 in her office, locked up, so when she heard gunfire, she pulls it out . . . and takes his head off before he can kill those precious kids."

Foreigners can never quite understand why Americans are so attached to their guns. Many gun rights supporters see guns as the ultimate defense against tyrannical authority. The question came up when I appeared on an Australian television show called *Planet America*, a title that captures the alien nature of the United States to non-Americans. I explained that guns represent individual freedom—something Americans value more than any other people in the world. If you are forced to give up your gun, you become less free.

I have been to gun shows and talked to gun owners. Often they defend gun ownership as the ultimate guarantee of individual rights. Some have told me, "If Jews in Europe had had guns, there would have been no Holocaust." And "If blacks in the South had had guns, there would have been no slavery." That, I explained to my Australian hosts, is a uniquely American mentality.

Following the shooting at an Oregon community college that took nine lives as well as the life of the shooter in October 2015, Obama urged Americans who want to see stronger gun laws to become single-issue voters. "Here's what you need to do," he said. "You have to make sure that anybody that you are voting for is on the right side of this issue." And if they oppose new gun laws? "Even if they're great on other stuff, you've got to vote against them." Gun rights activists do that. For supporters of gun control, however, guns are not usually the sole voting issue.

In fact, Obama quickly undermined his appeal when he compared gun laws to the conservative effort to shut down the federal government unless Planned Parenthood was defunded. "You can't have an issue like that potentially wreck the entire US economy, any more than I should hold the entire US budget hostage to my desire to do something about gun violence," he said. "That would be irresponsible of me." Gun rights activists don't care about being "irresponsible." They care about winning.

Following the Aurora, Colorado, shooting in 2012, in which twelve people in a movie audience were killed and seventy others injured, Sarah Palin said, "Restricting more of America's freedoms when it comes to self-defense isn't the answer. Not when you consider what the reality is. Bad guys don't follow laws." A radio commentator in Washington, DC, denounced the shootings as outrageous and unconscionable but called them "the price we pay for freedom" in the United States.

Immigration

In the 1920s, Republicans made a catastrophic error by writing off the immigrant vote. Beginning in 1928 with the Democrats' nomination of Al Smith, the first Roman Catholic candidate for president, immigrants and their descendants became the core of the New Deal Democratic majority that dominated American politics for nearly fifty years. A century later, Republicans may be making the same mistake again.

The controversy started before Donald Trump. During the 2012 Republican primaries, Mitt Romney said he would veto the proposed DREAM Act (Development, Relief, and Education for Alien Minors) that would allow illegal immigrants brought to the United States as children to become citizens. Romney criticized the Texas law that permitted some undocumented students to pay lower in-state college tuition. He talked about making life so difficult for illegal immigrants that they would "self-deport." He said that Arizona's tough immigration law could be a model for the nation.

The rapid growth in the nation's Latino population can mean two different things politically. In the long run, it is likely to mean more Democratic voters, as more Latinos become citizens, register, and vote. In the short run, it has meant a backlash against illegal immigrants. Which reaction predominates—backlash or empowerment—depends on what part of the country you consider.

Two groups of states have had higher-than-average Latino population growth. One includes states in the interior West, such as Arizona, Nevada, and Colorado. Those states have long had large Latino populations (between 21 percent and 30 percent). All three voted Republican in 2004. Latino voting power helped tilt two of them into the Democratic column in the next three elections. The third, Arizona, voted Republican in 2008, 2012, and 2016 but the margin narrowed. "Immigrants have been in those states for a long time," Brookings Institution demographer William Frey said. "The illegal percentage of those immigrants is somewhat smaller, and people are more accustomed to having immigrants work with them, see them on the streets, see them in the stores."

Other states also experienced higher than average Latino population growth. In Georgia, the Latino population nearly doubled in the first decade of the twenty-first century. The state started out with a very small Latino population (5 percent in 2000). It was up to 9 percent in 2010—rapid growth, but still far below the share in western states.

Frey estimated that states where the influx of Latinos was a recent phenomenon included a higher proportion of illegal immigrants. "Many of them are probably the least likely to be able to assimilate quickly into American life," he said. Those states were "seeing people who are disproportionately illegal, disproportionately less fluent in English, and more likely to not be very well educated."

In those states, Latino empowerment is still a long way off. Some midwestern states such as Ohio and Iowa are closely balanced between Democratic and Republican voters, so even a small Latino vote could tip them into the Democratic column. But those are also states where anti–illegal immigration backlash is strong. "In those states, I think that new immigration . . . will be a tough sell for that population and may not go down very well," Frey said. Indeed, Ohio and Iowa both voted for Donald Trump.

Polls since 2006 have shown consistently that most Americans accept a path to legalization and eventual citizenship for illegal immigrants once a series of requirements has been met. In an October 2015 CBS News–*New York Times* poll, 58 percent of Americans said illegal immigrants should be allowed to stay in the United States and apply for citizenship. Only 26 percent said illegal immigrants should be required to leave. In March 2016, after Donald Trump had become the Republican front-runner, the percentage who supported deporting all illegal immigrants had grown to 36 percent, according to an ABC News–*Washington Post* poll; 61 percent continued to oppose mass deportation.[5]

Does that mean the public supports amnesty? "It is not amnesty," said the late Pennsylvania senator Arlen Specter, the then-Republican chairman of the Senate Judiciary Committee, "because the undocumented aliens will have to pay a fine, they will have to pay back taxes, they will undergo a thorough background investigation, they will have to learn English, they will have to work for six years, and they will have to earn the status of staying in the country and moving toward citizenship."

The public's view of illegal immigration seems to be, if they've been here for a while and can demonstrate that they are hardworking and law abiding, let them stay. On that issue, President George W. Bush parted company with his conservative base. "I believe that illegal immigrants who have roots in our country and want to stay should have to pay a meaningful penalty for breaking the law, pay their taxes, learn English, and work in a job for a number of years. People who meet these conditions should be able to apply for citizenship," he said in 2006.

The conservatives' response: "Nuts." As Representative Cliff Stearns of Florida replied, "A path to citizenship like this is an egregious slap in the face to all those immigrants who sacrificed and respected our laws and entered legally."

Many Democrats supported President Bush on immigration. But they saw him making no progress in convincing the Republican base.

As Senate Democratic leader Harry Reid put it in 2006, "I hope the president will acknowledge how wrong the House Republican approach is to this. They are still talking the same way, Mr. President. They haven't backed down."

In a 2012 Republican debate, Romney said, "The answer is self-deportation, which is [that] people decide that they can do better by going home because they can't find work here because they don't have legal documentation." He added, "We're not going to round people up."

But rounding up people is exactly what some conservatives want to do. Arizona senator John McCain told a town hall in Iowa in 2007, "If you think that you can round up twelve million people and put them in jail, that's fine. I'd be curious where you'd build all those institutions to hold them."

"Arizona!" a voice from the audience called out.

"Arizona," McCain replied. "Okay, thanks. I am not amused."

Members of Congress face strong pressure on the immigration issue—from workers who fear job losses, from Latino voters whom both parties are trying to court, from citizen activists outraged by the idea of amnesty, from business and farm groups who want more low-wage workers, and from labor, civil rights, and religious groups that defend immigrant rights. Nevertheless, a bipartisan Senate compromise on immigration reform supported by President Bush collapsed in 2007 when Republicans voted against it, 38 to 7. The senators were getting an earful from their constituents. Arizona Republican senator Jon Kyl said, "I have learned some new words from some of my constituents." The angry response came as a shock to many Republicans. Conservative radio talk show host Bill Bennett observed, "We've talked to a number of Republican senators, and they confessed to being surprised by the reaction."

What made the difference was intensity. Opponents of immigration reform feel much more strongly about the issue than supporters do. Like gun owners, they vote the issue. In a CNN poll, nearly 80 percent of Americans said they supported a path to citizenship for illegal immigrants who have been in the United States for a number of years, have a job, and pay back taxes. But those who opposed that policy were more intensely motivated: 47 percent of those who opposed a path to citizenship called the issue extremely important, while only 28 percent of supporters felt strongly about it.

As noted, the gun issue becomes two-sided in the immediate aftermath of a sensational incident of gun violence. Do we ever see intensity rise among advocates of immigration reform? We did in 2006, when hundreds of thousands of Latino protesters appeared on the streets all over the country. The protests were driven not by politicians and political activists but by grassroots forces—union and church leaders, Spanish-language radio hosts, plus a new political force: Latino students text-messaging one another to spread the news about school walkouts. Latinos, immigrants, and their sympathizers took to the streets to protest what they regarded as measures that would scapegoat immigrants and minorities.

Supporters of tough anti–illegal immigration measures warned that the protests would backfire. "When John Q. Citizen looked out on the streets and saw hundreds of thousands of people waving Mexican flags and demanding amnesty, I don't think that played well in Peoria," said Representative Tom Tancredo, a Colorado Republican. That may have been true. But the street protests also gave political voice to a coalition that wants the issue dealt with in a more humane and realistic way. The pro-immigrant coalition included businesses and labor unions that depend on immigrant workers, student protesters—and President Bush.

Plus the Catholic Church and charities that could be criminalized for their efforts to aid illegal immigrants.

Opponents were relentless. The House of Representatives had already passed a bill that would make illegal immigrants and those who helped them subject to prosecution as felons. "This bill would literally criminalize the good Samaritan and probably even Jesus himself," Senator Hillary Clinton said. At the same time, Representative Jim Sensenbrenner, Republican of Wisconsin, warned, "I think with the American people and House Republicans, a pathway to citizenship for illegal aliens, aka 'amnesty,' is a nonstarter." And so it was. President Bush said in 2006, "There is a rational middle ground between granting an automatic path to citizenship for every illegal immigrant and a program of mass deportation." So far, no one has found it.

In 2016 the issue paid off for Donald Trump in states where it mattered. Latinos made up 6 percent of the voters in Pennsylvania, according to the network exit poll. Noncollege white voters—Trump's core—were 40 percent. He carried Pennsylvania by about 44,000 votes. Latinos were 31 percent of the vote in California, and noncollege whites, 19 percent. Hillary Clinton beat Donald Trump in California by 4.3 million votes.

In 2012 Mitt Romney told a private meeting of top Republican donors in Florida that if Republicans don't start doing better with Latinos, it "spells doom for us." Want to see what "doom" looks like for Republicans? Look at California. In 1994 Republican governor Pete Wilson embraced Proposition 187, a punitive law that cut off public services for illegal immigrants. Wilson's television ads showed grainy black-and-white footage of Mexican immigrants darting across the border as an announcer intoned, "They keep coming: two million illegal immigrants." Proposition 187 passed with nearly 60 percent of the vote.

It helped get Wilson reelected. Since 1994, California Republicans have paid dearly for that short-lived victory. (Proposition 187 was ultimately struck down by the federal courts.) It brought a huge wave of Latino citizenship applications and voter registration. By 2016, Latinos were nearly one-third of California voters, and 71 percent of them voted for Hillary Clinton.

After voting Republican in six straight presidential elections (1968 to 1988), California has voted consistently Democratic for president since 1992. The state has not elected a Republican US senator and only one Republican governor since 1994 (Arnold Schwarzenegger, a very atypical Republican). Even in 2014, which saw a national landslide for Republicans, Democrats swept all statewide constitutional offices in California as well as thirty-nine out of fifty-three House seats and maintained control of the state legislature.

Michael Madrid, former political director of the California Republican Party, put it this way: "Republicans did with the Latino community in about two years what the Democratic Party couldn't do in thirty years, and that is we mobilized the Latino electorate. The problem is, we mobilized them against us."

The same thing may be happening now on a national scale. Short term, the issue helped Trump get elected. Long term, the impact could reverse. Stuart Spencer, a veteran California political consultant, presaged Mitt Romney's warning of doom when he alerted Republicans in 1997 that the party risks "political suicide and dooms itself to permanent minority status in California" if it does not reach out to Latino voters.[6] The same prediction can be made for the country as a whole.

SEVEN

The Power of Definition

One of the best strategies for winning is to define an issue as a private matter and none of the government's business. It often works because the belief in limited government is so deeply embedded in American political culture. The limited-government position can benefit the left as well as the right. That is what happened in two conflicts from the early 2000s: the Elian Gonzalez controversy in 2000 and the Terri Schiavo controversy in 2005.

As we saw in chapter 1, the Schiavo controversy stemmed from efforts by conservatives in Congress to keep Schiavo, who had been in a persistent vegetative state for fifteen years, on life support. Her husband, who wished to remarry, wanted to allow her to die after her feeding tube was removed. Her parents objected vehemently and found support among religious right activists and leading Republicans, including President George W. Bush and Florida governor Jeb Bush.

Public opinion about the Schiavo case was one-sided. In a CBS News poll, two-thirds of Americans said her feeding tube should not be reinserted. The consensus was revealed on a CBS News poll question: Should Congress and the president be involved in deciding what happens to Terri Schiavo? Only 13 percent said yes. An overwhelming 82 percent said no, including large majorities of conservatives, Republicans, and churchgoers. Two-thirds of white evangelicals said no. As we saw, the public regarded the issue as a case where politicians were trying to exploit an intensely personal family matter for political advantage. Politicians should stay out of it.

After a Florida state court ordered her feeding tube removed, House Republicans voted overwhelmingly to transfer jurisdiction in the case to the federal courts. Many Republican Representatives were concerned about facing a primary opponent who could rally religious conservatives. House Democrats, who were split, may have been worried about facing an opponent who could charge, "You voted to kill Terri Schiavo."

Federal courts, and ultimately the Supreme Court, refused to intervene. Schiavo's feeding tube was removed, and she was allowed to die. Anger over what voters saw as congressional interference in a private matter likely contributed to the ouster of the Republican majority in Congress in the midterm election the next year.

In the Elian Gonzalez case, also in Florida, many conservatives and Cuban Americans were outraged at the idea that a child could be sent back to Cuba to live under Communism after his mother lost her life trying to deliver him to freedom. They angrily opposed the government's position, expressed by Attorney General Janet Reno, that "the law is very clear: a child who has lost his mother belongs with his sole surviving parent."

The public agreed with Reno, according to the polls. But Cuban Americans wanted Elian to remain in the United States, and they received moral support from conservatives. Texas governor George W. Bush issued a statement urging Reno to reconsider. Courts repeatedly upheld the government's decision to reunite the boy with his father. When his Miami relatives refused to surrender the child, federal agents seized Elian in a raid that drew shock and criticism.

Two-thirds of Americans told Gallup they opposed congressional intervention in the Gonzalez case—about the same number who said they opposed congressional intervention in the Schiavo case. The principle appears to be the same: politicians should stay out of private family matters. If intervention is necessary, family disputes should be handled by the courts.

A similar principle applied in the yearlong controversy over President Bill Clinton's impeachment. As noted in chapter 4, a majority was steadfastly opposed to impeachment and conviction. While two-thirds believed Clinton was guilty of lying under oath, two-thirds did not want him removed from office. The more Republicans publicized Clinton's misdeeds, the more the public was convinced that it was just about sex, a private matter.

In all three cases—Elian Gonzalez, Terri Schiavo, and Bill Clinton—liberals defined the issue as government overreach. It's normally a tactic that benefits conservatives. On social issues, however, conservatives often find themselves on the defensive, favoring government interference in personal matters.

Defining the issue to their advantage did work for conservatives in one highly charged case: the confirmation hearings for the nomination of Clarence Thomas to the Supreme Court in 1991. The hearings were a particularly odd event, in part because of the role that public opinion played in determining the outcome. The Republican strategy was to redefine the hearings as a trial. In a trial, the burden of proof is on the accuser. Anita Hill would have to prove that Thomas had harassed her. The issue would become her credibility rather than his qualifications.

No one could personally corroborate Anita Hill's story that she had been sexually harassed by Thomas. And no one could personally corroborate Thomas's story that he had never done so. Witnesses who claimed that Thomas harassed other women or that Hill fantasized about her relationships with men were found to have little credibility. Only two things were established: that it was "out of character" for Hill to lie and that it was "out of character" for Thomas to harass women.

Hill's problem was explaining her behavior: why she continued an apparently cordial relationship with Thomas. Her supporters argued that many people, especially men, "just don't understand" what it is like for a woman who is sexually harassed. "My response was not atypical," Hill contended.

By the end of the hearings, Americans said they found Thomas more credible than Hill by a two-to-one margin.[1] (Among women, the margin was closer but still in Thomas's favor.) The reason had less to do with Hill's motivation than with her behavior. Why had she maintained a relationship with her alleged harasser? Why, as a Yale Law School graduate and an official at the Equal Employment Opportunity Commission, had she failed to report an act of harassment? And why did she not warn her coworkers about Thomas's behavior?

What started out as a confirmation hearing turned into a trial. I tried to explain to the CNN viewing audience that a confirmation hearing is not a trial, to no apparent effect. During the Senate debate, most speakers focused on one issue: who was telling the truth, Thomas or Hill? Only a few senators addressed the real issue of confirmation: Thomas's constitutional philosophy, his judicial experience, and his legal qualifications.

Refusing to confirm Thomas became tantamount to declaring him guilty of an unproven charge. That seemed unfair. Turning the confirmation hearings into a trial was a perfect strategy for deflecting attention away from the issue of whether Thomas was worthy of elevation to the nation's highest court.

What clinched Thomas's victory was his decision to play the racial card. Thomas called the hearings "a high-tech lynching for uppity blacks" and accused his opponents of playing into "the most bigoted, racist stereotypes that any black man will face." African American support for Thomas shot up, from 54 percent favoring his confirmation before the hearings, to 71 percent afterward, according to Gallup–CNN polls.[2]

Southern Democratic senators were the key swing voters, as they had been four years earlier when Robert Bork was up for confirmation to the Supreme Court. Bork advocated an originalist view of the Constitution, as opposed to the view that the Constitution is a living document that changes with the times. He had criticized civil rights and abortion rights decisions. As a result, his nomination drew fervent opposition from civil rights and women's rights groups. Several southern Democratic senators got in touch with me during the Bork proceedings because they wanted to know how their African American constituents felt about his nomination. The most effective argument against Bork— put forth by Senator Edward Kennedy in a floor speech—was that the Appeals Court judge and legal scholar wanted to upset the status quo on civil rights. I informed the senators that the polls showed very little support for Bork among black voters. If they voted to confirm him, they would not only anger their black supporters but also risk reopening racial wounds that had just begun to heal.

In October 1987 Bork was rejected by a Senate vote of 58 to 42. Fifteen southern Democratic senators voted against his confirmation.

In 1991 when Thomas was up for confirmation, I again received calls from southern Democratic senators. This time I had to inform them that the polls showed strong support for Thomas among black voters (including black women).[3] Thomas was confirmed in October 1991 by a vote of 52 to 48. Eight of the eleven Democrats who voted to confirm Thomas were southerners. When Thomas played the race card and won the sympathy of African American voters, many southern Democratic senators responded. The fates of Robert Bork and Clarence Thomas were determined, more than anything else, by the response of African American voters to their nominations.

Abortion

Some liberals would like to ban guns. Some conservatives want to ban abortions. The American people want to be left alone, with just enough government restrictions to protect the public welfare. The debates on these issues tend to polarize around extreme positions. Ban handguns or allow them to be sold without restriction. Ban abortions or allow women to have them for any reason. The American public, however, comes out in between: secure the right but restrict it. If forced to choose, people will tend to favor the position with less government. It is better to have an excess of freedom than an excess of government.

It took a period of time for the Republican Party to come out squarely against abortion rights. In 1976, three years after the Supreme Court's *Roe v. Wade* decision that gave constitutional protection to abortion rights, the Republican Party platform favored "a continuance of the public dialogue on abortion," while supporting efforts to enact "a constitutional amendment to restore protection of the right to life for unborn children." The 1980 platform was less ambivalent. It affirmed Republican Party support for a right-to-life amendment to the Constitution.

With that, Ronald Reagan opened the party ranks to Christian conservatives, many of whom had supported Jimmy Carter in 1976. Subsequent Republican platforms stated unequivocally that "the unborn child has a fundamental individual right to life which cannot be infringed." Religious right voters abandoned Carter for Reagan in 1980 and have since become part of the GOP base.

Ronald Reagan's approach to abortion was more nuanced. Reagan always held fast to his conservative views, but he never denounced Republicans who disagreed with him. His "Eleventh Commandment" was "Thou shalt not speak ill of a fellow Republican."

The text of the 1980 platform plank on abortion said, "While we recognize differing views on this question among Americans in general—and in our own party—we affirm our support of a constitutional amendment to restore protection of the right to life for unborn children." That was the platform on which Reagan first got elected. It defined the Reagan formula: consistency and tolerance.

The abortion issue became explosive in July 1989 as a result of the Supreme Court's decision in *Webster v. Reproductive Health Services*. Antiabortion forces were invigorated by the decision. Prochoice activists felt threatened. Both sides mobilized. What the court did in the *Webster* case was to "modify and narrow" the *Roe* decision that defined abortion as a constitutionally protected right.

Webster changed the standards under which abortion restrictions would be scrutinized and invited states to pass new laws regulating and limiting abortions. Abortion rights, the court argued, were not "beyond the reach of the democratic process." It refused either to uphold or revoke *Roe* for the time being. Instead of defining a new status quo, it invited further legal challenges. Harry Blackmun, the Eisenhower appointee who was the principal author of the *Roe* decision, wrote in his *Webster* dissent, "A plurality of this court implicitly invites every state legislature to enact more and more restrictive abortion regulations in order to provoke more and more test cases."

Actually, the invitation was not implicit: "The goal of constitutional adjudication is surely not to remove inexorably 'politically divisive' issues from the ambit of the legislative process . . . The goal of constitutional adjudication is to hold true the balance between that which the Constitution puts beyond the reach of the democratic process and that which it does not. We think we have done that today." In other words, abortion rights are subject to regulation by government. The court said to politicians, "We're not going to decide the abortion issue—at least not right now. You guys decide. We'll let you know if you go too far."

Most politicians hate the abortion issue. No matter which side they take, they are bound to make some voters angry. They prefer to let the issue be settled by the courts. Then, in the 1989 *Webster* decision, the Supreme Court turned the issue back to the politicians. A prochoice activist said, "The days when politicians can remain silent on choice end right now." A right-to-life leader said of prochoice advocates, "They're not going to be able to hide."

The Power of Definition

The *Webster* case threw antiabortion forces on the defensive even though they prevailed in the decision. *Webster* turned out to be a costly victory. It raised public consciousness of a threat to abortion rights. Representative Richard H. Baker, a Louisiana Republican who switched to the prochoice side said, "There's been no time that public awareness of this matter has been as high as it is now since I've been in public office." An antiabortion activist observed, "The pro-life movement has been organized and active for twenty years, and some of us are tired. The prochoice movement is fresh, so they're operating with a much greater energy reserve. They've really rallied in light of *Webster*."

The prochoice rally did not last long. By 1990, the threat to abortion rights no longer seemed imminent. Few states had moved to criminalize abortions. The threat seemed to diminish, and so did the prochoice impact at the polls. In the 1990 midterm, abortion seemed to have a mixed impact. Before the election, the *Wall Street Journal* listed thirty campaigns where abortion was a key issue. The results were a close split. Abortion rights supporters won fourteen races; opponents, sixteen. Pro-life as well as prochoice governors got elected from both parties (prochoice Republicans in California and Illinois, pro-life Republicans in Ohio and Michigan; prochoice Democrats in New York and Texas; pro-life Democrats in Pennsylvania and Kansas; a prochoice Independent in Connecticut, and a pro-life Independent in Alaska).

The fear factor that *Webster* produced dissipated. Politicians came to realize that it was risky to come out in favor of abortion rights even if most of their constituents were prochoice. They would lose more votes from the antiabortion minority, most of whom would vote against them because of their position, than they would gain from the prochoice majority, few of whom voted simply on that issue. The intensity factor now favored conservatives.

143

Three years after the *Webster* decision, the Supreme Court drew a line between acceptable and unacceptable restrictions. The 1992 case was *Planned Parenthood of Southeastern Pennsylvania v. Casey*. The question before the court was whether to uphold Pennsylvania's Abortion Control Act of 1982. Abortion rights supporters argued that upholding the Pennsylvania law would reverse the *Roe* decision. In fact, the Pennsylvania law did not prohibit abortions. It tried to "control" abortions through a series of restrictions. The American public did not see those restrictions as unreasonable or burdensome.

In the Pennsylvania case, the Supreme Court reaffirmed a woman's constitutional right to abortion as it accepted various restrictions (counseling, a twenty-four-hour waiting period, and parental consent for minors, but not notification of the husband). The Pennsylvania decision was approved of strongly by the public.

Opinions have remained fairly stable for the last twenty-five years. Almost every year, beginning in 1972, the National Opinion Research Center has been asking people whether a pregnant woman should be able to have a legal abortion under various circumstances.[4] Strong majorities (80 to 90 percent) have consistently supported legal abortions if the woman's health is endangered, if she has been raped, or if there is a strong chance that the baby will have a serious birth defect.

The public has narrowly opposed legal abortions (50 to 60 percent) if the family is poor or doesn't want any more children, if the woman doesn't want to get married, or if she wants the abortion "for any reason." Those are all discretionary circumstances. What people have said in these polls is that they do not approve of abortion as a form of birth control. Abortion should be allowed only when there is a more compelling moral argument on the other side. To most people, rape, a threat to the life or health of the mother, or a serious deformity in the child are compelling moral arguments that justify abortion.

To prochoice activists, abortion is a basic human right that cannot be compromised. To pro-life activists, abortion is a sin and a crime and cannot be acceptable under any circumstances. They see abortion as murder, arguing, "No one is allowed to say, 'I personally don't believe in murder, but if you want to go out and kill someone, it is your right.' The law should not interfere." The debate seems to have no middle ground—except in public opinion. For decades, polls have been asking people whether they believe abortion should be legal under any circumstances, illegal in all circumstances, or legal only under certain circumstances.[5] About a quarter say abortion should be legal under any circumstances. About 20 percent say it should always be illegal. The prevailing view (between 51 percent and 58 percent since 2001) has been that abortion should be legal "under only certain circumstances." That's the middle position: abortion should be allowed when it is necessary.

Support for abortion rights under most of the circumstances tested in the NORC polls has been declining slowly since 1972. The basic distinction between discretionary and nondiscretionary circumstances still holds, but over time, more Americans have become uneasy about abortion.

Antiabortion forces have narrowed their focus: away from the basic right and toward specific circumstances where that right can be restricted. In 2007, by a 5-to-4 vote, the Supreme Court upheld the federal Partial-Birth Abortion Ban Act of 2003. That act banned a specific abortion procedure typically performed in the second trimester of pregnancy. When the act was signed into law in 2003, polls showed that a solid majority of Americans supported the ban. A Gallup poll asked about "a specific abortion procedure known as 'late-term' or 'partial birth' abortion, which is sometimes performed on women during the last few months of pregnancy." By 68 percent to 25 percent, the public thought the procedure should be illegal.[6]

Abortion rights supporters framed the issue as an attack on women's rights. "This judgment today is a major strike against a woman's right to choose," Senator Dianne Feinstein said. "The court in this case has, by a narrow five-to-four margin, essentially enacted the first federal abortion ban in this country and has struck down a primary part of *Roe v. Wade*, protection of the health of the mother." Senator Barack Obama expressed concern that the ruling will "embolden state legislatures to enact further measures to restrict a woman's right to choose."

Democrats expressed concern over the broader implications of the ruling: namely, that for the first time, the court had criminalized a specific medical procedure. The court gave lawmakers the go-ahead to counterbalance protection of women's rights with what Justice Anthony M. Kennedy, writing for the majority, called "ethical and moral concerns"—"that the government has a legitimate and substantial interest in preserving and promoting fetal life." The decision created the legal underpinning that allowed states to pass more restrictions on abortion.

As noted, the prevailing view has always been that abortion should be legal "only under certain circumstances." For years, abortion opponents worked to narrow those circumstances. They counted the 2007 decision on the Partial Birth Abortion Ban Act as a major breakthrough. As an abortion rights activist explained to me, "Democrats win on the issue of abortion when it's a larger issue—when it's a right. Republicans win when they keep it narrow. They win with language describing specific procedures."

When the Supreme Court outlawed segregated schools in 1954, the immediate response was explosive. Over time, however, a new consensus on civil rights emerged. Twenty years after the decision, public support for legal segregation had just about vanished. After the court mandated new norms of behavior concerning race, society's attitudes slowly adjusted to the new reality.

That is where the analogy between civil rights and abortion rights breaks down. In the 1973 *Roe* decision, the Supreme Court mandated new norms of behavior concerning abortion. Attitudes did not follow, however. Forty-four years after Roe, no consensus on abortion has emerged. Instead, the issue has become more sharply polarized over time.

We should not expect any quick or easy resolution to the abortion issue. The Supreme Court tried to settle the issue in 1973 and again in 1992 and failed. What makes anybody believe politicians can do a better job? Think of it this way: if the Supreme Court had turned the issue of civil rights over to politicians, we might still be debating school desegregation in state legislatures around the country.

Two Meanings of Affirmative Action

Affirmative action is another issue that is sensitive to definition. Americans distinguish between two versions of affirmative action. Outreach involves measures to help disadvantaged groups catch up to the prevailing standards of competition. Preferential treatment involves suspending those standards and admitting or hiring members of disadvantaged groups who do not meet the standards.

It is fine, the public says, to compensate for past discrimination by means of special training programs, head start efforts, targeted financial aid, talent search programs, community development funds, and the like. Help disadvantaged groups compete, whites say. But do not predetermine the results: no quotas, no preference for one race over another, no dual standards.

A CNN poll taken in 1997 asked half the respondents whether they favored "affirmative action programs for women and minorities." A majority did. The others were asked whether they favored "programs that would give preferential treatment . . . to women and minorities." A majority did not.[7]

Nearly every year between 1987 and 2012, the Pew Research Center survey offered this statement: "We should make every possible effort to improve the position of blacks and other minorities, even if it means giving them preferential treatment." The public has always disagreed by margins of two-to-one or three-to-one. Among whites in 2009, 76 percent disagreed and 22 percent agreed. A majority of Democrats disagreed. At the same time, Pew found that growing numbers of Americans favored "affirmative action programs to help blacks, women, and other minorities get better jobs and education." In 2007, 70 percent of Americans supported such outreach programs.[8]

A Gallup poll press release in July 2013 was headlined, "In U.S., Most Reject Considering Race in College Admissions."[9] The question asked whether college applicants should be admitted solely on the basis of merit, "even if that results in few minority students being admitted," or should applicants' racial and ethnic backgrounds be considered to help promote diversity "even if that means admitting some minority students who otherwise would not be admitted." Answer: stick to merit, 67 percent to 28 percent.

Now here's the headline of a Pew Research Center press release from April 2014: "Public Strongly Backs Affirmative Action Programs on Campus."[10] The Pew question asked, "Do you think affirmative action programs designed to increase the number of black and minority students on college campuses are a good thing or a bad thing?" By better than two to one (63 percent to 30 percent), the Pew respondents said affirmative action is a good thing.

The issue is what people think affirmative action means. Does it mean outreach programs to ensure that qualified minorities get access to schools and jobs? Or does it mean preferential treatment allowing minorities to get access to schools and jobs when they are less qualified? In the 1997 CNN poll, the public was split over the definition. What you thought affirmative action meant determined how you felt about it. Those who favored affirmative action believed, by better than two to one, that it meant outreach to women and minorities. But almost 85 percent of those who opposed affirmative action believed it meant preferential treatment. Most Americans continue to support affirmative action because they believe it means outreach. Critics have the challenge of convincing people it doesn't mean what they think it means.

In April 2014 the Supreme Court upheld Proposal 2, a state constitutional amendment passed by Michigan voters in 2006 that banned "discrimination or preferential treatment" in admissions to state universities. The decision was widely reported as a ban on affirmative action in college admissions. But the Supreme Court refused to rule whether affirmative action is constitutional or not. Instead, it turned the issue over to public opinion. As Justice Kennedy wrote in the controlling opinion, "This case is not about how the debate about racial preferences should be resolved. It's about who may resolve it." In other words, don't ask the court. Ask the people.

What Michigan voters—more precisely, 58 percent of them—said when they passed Proposal 2 in 2006 was that state institutions "shall not discriminate against, or grant preferential treatment to, any individual or group on the basis of race, sex, color, ethnicity, or national origin" in education, public employment, or government contracting. The court ruled that banning preferential treatment is constitutional—if that's what the people want. Kennedy dismissed the claim that "a difficult question of public policy must be taken from the reach of the voters." Taking the case to court, he argued, was a little insulting. He wrote, "It is demeaning to the democratic process to presume that the voters are not capable of deciding an issue of this sensitivity on decent and rational grounds."

What if voters and their elected representatives raise no objection to affirmative action? That's okay, too. In previous cases, the court had allowed the use of race-conscious admissions standards as long as they passed "strict scrutiny"—meaning, only if the institution could demonstrate that alternative approaches to diversity were not working. In his concurring opinion, liberal justice Stephen Breyer argued that the Constitution permits but does not require states to use race-conscious standards. The people have the right to decide not to. Which is what the voters of Michigan did.

The public has handed down its decision on affirmative action: outreach is fine, preferential treatment is not. Liberal justice Sonia Sotomayor seemed to have that distinction in mind when she wrote in her fiery dissenting opinion that she was not going to use the term "affirmative action" because she felt it implied "preferential treatment." Instead, she defended what she called "race-sensitive admissions policies."

Former San Francisco mayor Willie Brown, an ardent defender of affirmative action, once offered this argument: "It's not unlike a poker game where people have been cheating. People have been cheating for years, and they've acquired all the chips. Then all of a sudden, when you catch them cheating, you say, 'No more cheating.' You don't leave them with all the chips. You take the chips away and redistribute the chips." The problem is, when you accuse people of cheating and tell them the government is going to take away their chips, they get angry. They don't think they've been cheating. They believe they played by the rules.

The Pew Research Center has found that, over time, partisanship has become more closely aligned with racial issues such as affirmative action. On the statement, "We should make every effort to improve the position of minorities, even if it means preferential treatment," the gap between blacks and whites remains wide, just as it was twenty-five years ago. But since 1987, Pew reports, the gap between the two parties on this issue has about doubled, from 18 points to 40 points.[11] Democrats, particularly white Democrats, have become significantly more supportive of affirmative action over time, while Republicans remain opposed.

Same-Sex Marriage

The most astonishing transformation of public opinion in our time has been on the issue of same-sex marriage. Support for same-sex marriage was politically poisonous in 2004. By 2016, opposition to same-sex marriage had become a political liability. How did that happen? The answer appears to be personal experience. Once the issue was defined as discrimination against "people you know," the tide of public opposition reversed.

A public backlash against same-sex marriage first materialized after a court in Hawaii ruled in favor of equal marriage rights in 1993.

In 1996 Congress passed, and President Clinton signed into law, the Defense of Marriage Act, which denied same-sex couples the same federal rights as heterosexual couples.

After a court decision made same-sex marriage legal in Massachusetts in 2003, conservative activists and legislators placed antigay marriage measures on the ballot in eleven states in the 2004 election. All the initiatives passed, with an average of about 70 percent support. By mid-2012, measures banning same-sex marriages had been put to a vote in thirty-two states and passed every time.

The target of the populist backlash was federal and state judges who found no compelling constitutional case for discrimination against same-sex couples. In 2010, angry Iowa voters rose up against their state supreme court for giving legal standing to same-sex marriages. Three supreme court justices were up for reconfirmation on the Iowa ballot. They were all fired.

Then something remarkable happened. Public opinion shifted with breathtaking speed. The Pew Research Center shows 2011 as the turning point when public support for same-sex marriage caught up with opposition. Since 2011, every national poll has shown a majority of Americans in favor of allowing same-sex couples to marry legally. By 2015, the margin had become decisive: 57 percent in favor, 39 percent opposed.[12]

How did it happen? The key factor seems to have been personal experiences. In a 2010 CBS News poll, 77 percent of Americans said they knew someone openly gay, up from 42 percent in 1992. In 2013 CNN polling, 57 percent said they have an openly gay family member or close friend, up from 32 percent in 1994. Call it the Dick Cheney effect. Cheney's daughter Mary is openly gay, and the former vice president split with President Bush on the issue of same-sex marriage. Cheney favored leaving the issue up to the states, saying, "Freedom means freedom for everyone." Polls show that people who know someone who is openly gay are far more supportive of equal marriage rights. In an intensely polarized environment, personal experience is a powerful way to change public opinion.

Politicians such as Barack Obama and Bill and Hillary Clinton did not lead public opinion on same-sex marriage. They were forced to catch up with it. A French politician once said, "My people are marching. I am their leader. I must follow them."

In 2015 the Supreme Court handed down a historic decision declaring that marriage equality was a constitutionally protected right. It was a signal victory for the New America, for diversity and inclusion. The Old America capitulated but not without protest. In his dissent, Justice Antonin Scalia expressed contempt for the idea that the Constitution gives people rights to "define and express their identity." Before joining such a decision, he wrote, "I would hide my head in a bag."

The decision met with resistance, of course. That is always the case with controversial Supreme Court decisions, from racial desegregation in 1954 to abortion in 1973. The Republican Party became a resistance movement determined to disempower the New America. Conservatives rallied to the cause of "religious freedom," arguing that Americans should not be forced to violate their religious convictions by accepting same-sex marriage.

Several states passed laws allowing public officials to refuse to authorize same-sex marriages if it offends their religious convictions. Some passed laws allowing businesses to refuse services to gay couples on the same grounds. The big surprise was the business backlash to "religious freedom" laws, notably in Indiana, Georgia, and Arkansas, where the laws ended up being amended or vetoed.

The Old America is rallying to the cause of religious rights. Religion usually puts Democrats on the defensive because they don't want to be seen as the godless party. But Democrats have learned they can fight back by rallying behind the potent cause of diversity and inclusion. Republicans were shocked to discover that gay issues have become as big a political minefield as race. "Any political candidate who is perceived as antigay at the presidential level will never connect with people under thirty years old," a Republican pollster warned before the 2016 election.

There's an old Arab proverb: "Dogs bark, but the caravan moves on." The dogs of resistance are barking. But the caravan is moving on.

EIGHT

The Burden of Indispensability

The Fantasy Decade

Americans have always had conflicting impulses of engagement and withdrawal in world affairs. Withdrawal was the rule between the War of 1812 and World War I. The exceptions were the Mexican-American War (1846–48) over the annexation of Texas and a flirtation with imperialism during the Spanish-American War (1898), which gave the United States control of Puerto Rico, Guam, the Philippines, and, briefly, Cuba. America did not enter World War I until the last year and a half of a war that lasted more than four years, and only after Germany started sinking US ships on the high seas.

After World War I, America rejected the League of Nations and withdrew into isolationism for two decades. In his successful 1920 campaign for president, Warren G. Harding promised a "return to normalcy," which amounted to isolationism. It took Pearl Harbor to blast the United States out of its complacency. The attack occurred more than two years after World War II began, after Hitler had conquered almost all of Europe and Britain stood alone. President Franklin D. Roosevelt used the Lend-Lease Act of 1941 to provide military aid to the Allies without direct US engagement.

Many people expected America to turn inward again after the Second World War. But it did not. A new threat, Communism, had emerged. Farsighted leaders like Harry Truman made a firm commitment to take on the new threat, beginning with the announcement of the Truman Doctrine to a joint session of Congress in 1947. America would "contain" the spread of Communism.

For more than four decades, the Communist threat persisted, and the United States remained engaged. "Ich bin ein Berliner," President John F. Kennedy proclaimed in June 1963. "Mr. Gorbachev, tear down this wall!" President Ronald Reagan declared in June 1987.

Finally, in 1991, nearly forty-five years after the Cold War started, the United States enjoyed two great triumphs. One came in the Persian Gulf War to end the Iraqi occupation of Kuwait, when President George H. W. Bush announced, "By God, we've kicked the Vietnam syndrome once and for all." The other came when President Bush got to announce on Christmas Day what eight presidents before him could only dream of saying: "The Soviet Union itself is no more." Americans hardly bothered to celebrate. The United States was just emerging from recession. In that same speech, Bush declared, "I am committed to attacking our economic problems at home with the same determination we brought to winning the Cold War."

So began a decade of withdrawal, the Fantasy Decade, from 1991 to 2001, much like the 1920s, when prosperity reigned and the rest of the world seemed far away. Americans became complacent once again. The 1990s eventually became a boom decade like the Roaring Twenties. In both cases, the boom was a bubble. In the 1990s sensational domestic events preoccupied the country, such as the federal raid on the Branch Davidians' compound in Waco, Texas, occupied by followers of sectarian religious leader David Koresh; the Oklahoma City bombing and the Columbine High School shootings, as well as the media fixations on the O. J. Simpson trial; the Whitewater controversy involving the Clintons; Monica Lewinsky; Elian Gonzalez; Representative Gary Condit's relationship with Chandra Levy, a missing intern working in Washington, DC, who was later found murdered; and the tragic deaths of Princess Diana and John F. Kennedy Jr.

President Bill Clinton pleaded for engagement in the world. "Choosing isolation over engagement would not make the world safer," he said in 1998. "It would make it more dangerous." But Americans were wary of risk taking in places such as Somalia, where clan warfare resulted in a humanitarian crisis. US intervention led to the loss of eighteen American soldiers and eighty-four wounded. Americans were also wary of what some called "social work" in Bosnia, where Serbia had undertaken a campaign of "ethnic cleansing" of the Muslim population. The United States had a humanitarian interest in Bosnia but no vital economic or security interests. The World Trade Center in New York City was first bombed in 1993. That terrorist attack, in which a truck bomb was exploded in an underground parking garage killing six and injuring a thousand, was prosecuted successfully as a crime, not as an act of war.

In 2001 former secretary of state Henry Kissinger published a book entitled *Does America Need a Foreign Policy?* [1] The United States got the answer on September 11. Once again, Americans were shocked out of complacency. Once again, the United States was threatened. Once again, Americans became engaged. Once again a president confronted an international threat and pledged, "We will not fail."

The Isolationist Impulse

There are two isolationist traditions in American history: one ideological, the other populist.

Ideological isolationists oppose US involvement in the world in principle. In the 1930s, left-wing isolationists such as Senator Gerald P. Nye of North Dakota, a progressive Republican, maintained that the United States had been drawn into World War I by a conspiracy of arms manufacturers ("merchants of death"). Right-wing isolationists like famed aviator Charles A. Lindbergh believed the United States was wrong to sympathize with Britain and Russia against Nazi Germany.

Before the Cold War, US sympathies tended to be anti-fascist and critical of colonialism. The United States was identified with the international left, and conservatives were the most ardent isolationists. Left-wing isolationism weakened when the United States entered World War II on the anti-fascist side. Right-wing isolationism declined after World War II, when America assumed the role of leader of the free world against Communist expansion. The United States became hostile to third world liberation movements, many of which were inspired by Marxism and supported by international Communism. We were identified with the international right, and many liberals came to believe America was on the wrong side of history.

The Burden of Indispensability

Internationalism today is an establishment value. It is endorsed by the entire political establishment, liberal and conservative, Republican and Democratic. When President George H. W. Bush addressed Congress in September 1990 after Saddam Hussein invaded Kuwait, he offered a stirring call to internationalist principle. Our purpose, Bush said, was to "defend civilized values around the world," among them our willingness to "defend common vital interests," "support the rule of law," and "stand up to aggression."

In the Democratic reply to the president's speech, House Democratic leader Richard A. Gephardt said, "This is a cause worth standing and fighting for . . . We are now in the Persian Gulf not simply for oil, or to save emirs and kings, but to defend the most fundamental values of a more stable and decent world."

What never really died was populist isolationism: the sentiment among many Americans that, however noble our purposes, most of what we do for the rest of the world is wasteful, pointless, and unappreciated. Often, as in Vietnam and Iraq, they are right.

Whenever a policy becomes difficult or costly, populist isolationism emerges. In the 1980s, Americans were happy to win easy and decisive military victories in Granada, Panama, and Kuwait. But the public did not support President Reagan's complicated policies of secondhand intervention in Nicaragua and El Salvador.

In 2013 a *New York Times*–CBS News poll asked, "Do you think the United States should or should not take the leading role among all other countries in the world in trying to solve international conflicts?" The answer was loud and clear: it should not, 58 percent to 35 percent.[2] Did the United States have a responsibility to do something about the bloodbath in Syria after more than eighty thousand people [at the time] had been killed? An even louder no, 61 percent to 28 percent. For decades, poll after poll found that the least popular federal government program wasn't welfare. It was foreign aid.[3]

Indispensability

In his second Inaugural Address in 1997, Bill Clinton said, "America stands alone as the world's indispensable nation." Since World War II, whenever there has been a serious threat to world order or to humanitarian values, one rule has applied: if the United States does not do anything, nothing will happen.

What would have happened if the United States had failed to act after Saddam Hussein invaded Kuwait in 1990? Most likely, nothing. Kuwait would have become part of Iraq. Having acted in Kuwait, the first President Bush left the crisis in Bosnia to the Europeans. Bosnia was in Europe's backyard. America had no vital interests there. What happened? Nothing. The Europeans failed to act, and a new horror entered the world's vocabulary: ethnic cleansing. Finally, the United States felt morally compelled to step in and lead a coalition to end the brutality. When atrocities occurred in Cambodia, Rwanda, Congo, and Darfur, the whole world—including the United States—looked away. So nothing happened. The result was genocide.

If America had not led an invasion of Afghanistan, the Taliban would still be in power, harboring terrorists. It is unlikely that anything would have been done to stop Mu'ammar Qaddafi's murderous reprisals in Libya if the United States had not played a crucial role in disabling Libya's air defenses. It is hard to imagine a peace settlement between Israel and the Palestinians that is not guaranteed by the United States.

When the first President Bush called for US intervention to force

Saddam Hussein out of Kuwait, he spoke of "a new world order strug-
gling to be born . . . A world where the rule of law supplants the rule of
the jungle. A world in which nations recognize the shared responsibility
for freedom and justice. A world where the strong respect the rights of
the weak." Why should America assume the world's burden? Because,
the president said, "there is no substitute for American leadership."

The message was that the United States has international interests
as well as national interests. That has been the consensus of the political
establishment since 1947. The American people have never completely
bought into the idea of international interests, however.

Eventually 9/11 happened, and President George W. Bush assumed
his father's commitment to ensuring world order. It was a lot easier for
the second Bush because America had been attacked. "All nations that
decide for aggression and terror will pay a price," he told the graduat-
ing class at the US Military Academy in 2002.[4]

Bush's West Point speech sounded a lot like President Harry Truman's address to Congress in March 1947 when Truman said, "I believe
that it must be the policy of the United States to support free peoples
who are resisting attempted subjugation by armed minorities or by
outside pressures." President Bush was trying to make the case for a
broader US mission, just as Truman did when he called for America to
assume the burden of leading the free world.

President Clinton had warned in 1999 that "the United States
cannot—indeed, we should not—be the world's policeman." This, from
the president who'd ordered military actions in Kosovo, Bosnia, Haiti,
Somalia, Afghanistan, Sudan, and Iraq. The United States may be indispensable, but it will intervene only if the risk of American casualties is
kept to a minimum. The result is a paradox. Every mainstream political
figure endorses the view that the United States must be a world leader.

And every mainstream political figure warns that America must not become policeman to the world.

Limited War?

President Clinton's misfortune was to hold office during the Fantasy Decade, when Americans did not feel threatened. In 1998, when he launched missile attacks on suspected Al Qaeda training camps in Sudan and Afghanistan, he was accused of "wagging the dog"—using a concocted military threat to divert attention from a domestic scandal.

In 2011 President Obama tested a corollary to the rule that if the United States fails to act, nothing will happen. The corollary says that if America does act, it cannot be a limited commitment. It has to be a total commitment or nothing. The Obama administration tested the idea that where the United States has limited interests, it can make a limited commitment. America had limited interests in Libya. Defense Secretary Robert Gates said as much. According to him, Libya "was not a vital national interest to the United States, but it was an interest." [5]

The United States made a limited commitment. The administration called Libya a "kinetic military action," one that is "time-limited, scope-limited . . . in concert with our international partners." The White House asserted that the goal was not regime change, though President Obama said early on, "It is US policy that Qaddafi needs to go."

After an initial show of force that demolished the Qaddafi regime's air defenses, the United States turned over military control to NATO. The administration insisted that Libya would be a short-term commitment, not a long-term engagement. Obama pledged that no US ground troops would be used. The American foreign-policy establishment responded with outrage. The Obama administration seemed to be ignoring the lessons of Vietnam and Iraq (and Lebanon and Somalia).

The issue was this: Can the United States make a limited commitment, using limited resources, for a limited goal? The foreign-policy establishment said no. It had to be a total commitment or nothing. President Obama was determined to show that the answer could be yes, because the alternatives—doing nothing or leading an all-out invasion of a third Muslim nation—were unacceptable.

In fact, Obama saw Libya as setting a new model for military intervention. "This is precisely how the international community should work, "he said," as more nations bear both the responsibility and the cost of enforcing international law."

Syria was another test for Obama. Could America fulfill its obligation to be "the world's indispensable nation" while avoiding a military quagmire? No invasion, no nation building. But Syria was more complicated and more dangerous than Libya. The rationale for intervention in Syria was legal and humanitarian. Legal because President Bashar al-Assad's use of chemical weapons is a violation of international law. Humanitarian because the Assad regime, like the Qaddafi regime, was murdering its citizens.

There were significant constraints on US action in Syria. No one talked about a major commitment of American ground troops—not even Senator John McCain, who called for US support of the Syrian rebels but added, "It does not mean boots on the ground."

Syria was a tough test. "Once you're in, you can't unwind it," Defense Secretary Chuck Hagel and Joint Chiefs of Staff Chairman Martin Dempsey warned a Senate subcommittee. McCain said, "Everything that noninterventionists said would happen in Syria if we intervened has happened." Everything but one thing: Americans were not getting killed.

No Political Wars

Americans hate political wars: wars that are fought for any purpose less than total military victory. That was the problem in Vietnam, where the United States was fighting to win people's "hearts and minds." Americans ended up fighting and dying to save another country's government from a Communist insurrection. In effect, we had involved ourselves in their civil war. The same in Iraq, where Americans were fighting and dying to save a government that was under threat from a sectarian insurrection.

That was also the problem in Somalia, which was supposed to be a humanitarian mission. But the famine in Somalia wasn't caused by a natural disaster. It was caused by politics. All it took to get the United States out was the shocking photo of the mutilated body of a dead American soldier being dragged through the streets of Mogadishu by an angry mob. The result was public outrage over the mission. In the name of saving people from disaster, we were involving ourselves in another country's clan warfare.

Americans believe wars should have a clear military objective— namely, to win. Americans do not have patience for getting involved in other countries' politics. The 1991 Persian Gulf War is the model: win and get out. The war in Vietnam is the antimodel. It was not until 1995 that Robert S. McNamara—as defense secretary, the chief architect of the Vietnam War—acknowledged in his book, *In Retrospect: The Tragedy and Lessons of Vietnam*, that the war was "wrong, terribly wrong."[6] The American people had figured that out twenty-seven years earlier.

"War is nothing but politics by other means," the Prussian general Karl von Clausewitz wrote in his famous treatise *On War* in 1833. To which Americans say, "Bullhockey!" They resoundingly and defiantly reject the notion that war is politics. That was the lesson of Vietnam. And the 1991 Gulf War as well.

The Gulf War proved to Americans that, if we just let the military fight the war, they can get the job done. Immediately after the war, Lieutenant General Thomas W. Kelly, director of operations for the Joint Chiefs of Staff, expressed his appreciation to President George H. W. Bush and the National Security Council for not trying to micromanage the war.

The White House was eager to pull US troops out as quickly as possible, even if their military mission was dangerously incomplete. We wanted to preserve the territorial integrity of Iraq, even if the only way to do so was to leave a murderous dictator in power. And we wanted to avoid responsibility for what happened, even if it meant abandoning the Kurds and the Shiites to Saddam Hussein.

Preemptive War

Most wars must be seen as necessary. The United States is attacked, as at Pearl Harbor in 1941. Or threatened, as we were by the discovery of nuclear missiles in Cuba in 1962. Or there is a gross violation of international norms, as was the case when Saddam Hussein invaded Kuwait, a US ally and oil provider, in 1990. The necessity of war with Iraq in 2003 was not obvious to most of the world, nor to many Americans.

Hearing no convincing alternative argument, many people reached the conclusion that it was a war for oil. Didn't Iraq have the second largest proven oil reserves in the world? Weren't President Bush and Vice President Dick Cheney oil men? Didn't the oil industry contribute huge sums to the Republican Party?

When I interviewed Steve Kretzmann, foreign-policy expert at the Institute for Policy Studies in Washington in 2003, he put it this way: "If McDonald's, the world's largest consumer of potatoes, announces in advance that it's going to buy Idaho, and that the purchase has nothing to do with potatoes, what would you think?" The slogan of the antiwar movement, from Austin to Australia, was "No Blood for Oil."

The rest of the world accepted the idea that Iraq was a war for oil because it did not hear any other convincing explanation. The American public dismissed the idea. By two to one in a February 2003 Gallup poll, Americans said oil was not a reason to take military action against Iraq. Had they heard a more convincing explanation? Yes: 9/11. "September the eleventh should say to the American people that we are now a battlefield," President George W. Bush declared.

Saddam Hussein was a sworn enemy of the United States and a personal enemy of George W. Bush's father. The Bush administration claimed to have evidence that Iraq possessed weapons of mass destruction and was implicated in 9/11. President Bush even called Iraq "the central front" in the war on terror. The idea was that the United States, as a matter of its national security, had to disarm Iraq in order to prevent another 9/11.

In the March 2003 Gallup poll, 88 percent of Americans were of the opinion that Saddam Hussein supported terrorist groups that had plans to attack the United States.[7] In fact, 51 percent believed the Iraqi leader was personally involved in 9/11. For many Americans, the Iraq

War was all about 9/11. That's the reason why Americans initially supported something they had never supported or even imagined in the past: a preemptive war.

When President Bush spoke at West Point in 2002, he explicitly rejected the Cold War policies of deterrence and containment for dealing with terrorism. "We must take the battle to the enemy," the president said, "disrupt his plans, and confront the worst threats before they emerge."[8] Before they emerge? Yes, because the alternative was too dangerous. If Iraq was acquiring weapons of mass destruction and had expressed the intention of using them, should the United States just stand by and wait for Saddam Hussein to commit an atrocity? Should we go after terrorists before they commit an atrocity or wait for another September 11? Bush ordered the future army leaders at West Point "to be ready for preemptive action when necessary."

The idea of preemptive action makes many Americans nervous. Bush argued that preemptive war was the only way to keep Americans safe. "In the world we have entered," the president said, "the only path to safety is the path of action. And this nation will act."

Politically, the Iraq War was the polar opposite of the Persian Gulf War. The Gulf War was more controversial at the outset because the United States had not been attacked. But America got out quickly in 1991. No occupation, no controversy. It was fast, decisive, relatively cheap, and clearly about oil.

When the Gulf War resolution came before Congress in January 1991, Democrats were solidly opposed. Democrats in both houses voted against war (45 to 10 in the Senate, 179 to 86 in the House). When the Iraq War resolution came before Congress in October 2002—one year after the 9/11 attacks—Democratic opposition was not as solid. House Democrats still voted against going to war but by a narrower margin

(126 to 82). Senate Democrats voted in favor, 29 to 21. Five Democratic senators with presidential ambitions voted for war: John Kerry, John Edwards, Joe Biden, Christopher Dodd, and Hillary Clinton.

Burned by failing to support the "triumphant" Gulf War in 1991, many Democrats didn't want to make the same mistake again. So they made a different mistake. They supported a war that quickly lost public support.

Getting Out

Public support for the war in Iraq eroded much faster than was the case in either Korea or Vietnam. The view that the United States had made a mistake sending troops to Iraq reached a majority in early 2005, when American combat deaths totaled about 1,500. In Vietnam, that did not happen until after the 1968 Tet offensive, by which time US losses totaled over 20,000.[9] That was when newscaster Walter Cronkite returned from Vietnam and told Americans that the Vietnam War had become a stalemate. The United States could not win. The reverse happened in Iraq. The 2003 victory turned sour as American forces were unable to extricate themselves and casualties mounted. The public wanted the same thing in Iraq as they had wanted in Korea and Vietnam: to win and get out. But the United States did not win in Korea and Vietnam and found it difficult to get out in all three places.

The 2006 midterm election was a referendum on Iraq. The voters expressed no confidence in President Bush's leadership. They turned both houses of Congress over to the Democrats. The new House speaker, Nancy Pelosi, said after the election, "Nowhere was the call for a new direction more clear for the American people than in the war in Iraq."

"It is clear that we need to change our strategy in Iraq," Bush replied in January 2007. That was when he announced "a new way forward." But his plan shocked the country. He announced, "I have committed more than twenty thousand additional American troops to Iraq." The plan for a surge was defiant of public opinion. And the public didn't like it. By better than two to one in a CNN poll (66 percent to 32 percent), Americans opposed sending additional US troops to Iraq.[10]

The surge brought an outpouring of rage from Democrats. The 2006 midterm had been a decisive repudiation of the war. Bush's surge two months later looked like a gesture of contempt for the voters. Democrats were virtually united in their opposition; 88 percent opposed the troop buildup. There was even criticism from Republicans. Senator Chuck Hagel of Nebraska, a decorated Vietnam veteran and a Republican, called Bush's troop buildup "the most dangerous foreign-policy blunder in this country since Vietnam." Hagel, later to become President Obama's secretary of defense, spoke for the 30 percent of Republicans who opposed the surge.

Americans have always had confidence in the capabilities of the US military. They never had confidence in the capabilities of the Iraqi government—a government that wasn't even capable of managing Saddam Hussein's execution. Americans were wary of the notion that our success depended on the Iraqi government's ability to achieve political reconciliation.

In the year following the surge, the public's view of the Iraq War went through yet another twist. With the arrival of more US troops, the violence in Iraq began to subside. The number of Americans who felt "the US military is making progress in improving conditions in Iraq and bringing an end to violence in that country" rose from 47 percent in August 2007, to 52 percent in February 2008, to 54 percent in June 2008, according to CNN polls.[11] But the impression of military progress did not increase public support for the war. The number of Americans who favored the war barely changed: 31 percent in January 2007, when the troop buildup began; 30 percent in June 2008. Two-thirds continued to oppose the Iraq War.[12] Most Americans just wanted it over.

Nevertheless, the surge worked. The military situation in Iraq stabilized temporarily, long enough to give the United States cover to start withdrawing troops. So what happened in the United States? Politically, the Iraq issue began to disappear from the agenda. The war never became popular. Americans continued to regard it as a mistake. But by the time of the 2008 presidential election, Iraq was no longer a major issue. On Election Day 2008, only 10 percent of the voters cited the war in Iraq as the biggest issue facing the country. Nearly two-thirds cited the economy.

The Failure of Nation Building

Afghanistan was front and center on the nation's radar screen for a few months after the 9/11 attacks. US-led military strikes began in October 2001. By December, the Taliban regime was out of power. For the next five years, Iraq dominated the foreign-policy agenda. Afghanistan was the forgotten war.

When Barack Obama took office in 2009, the United States had been fighting in Afghanistan for eight years. But to many Americans, Afghanistan looked like a new war. In 2009, even with 130,000 US troops still in Iraq, Iraq was becoming the forgotten war. Suddenly Afghanistan grabbed public attention, starting with Obama's decision to send 21,000 additional troops. He described Afghanistan as a "war of necessity" rather than a "war of choice" like Iraq. The problem was that the necessity had occurred eight years earlier, immediately after 9/11.

Obama's liberal base abandoned him on Afghanistan. In the CNN poll, opposition to the war grew fastest among Democrats, from 55 percent opposed in April 2009 to 73 percent opposed in September.[13] What changed wasn't the nature of the enemy. The Taliban and Al Qaeda remained perfect enemies for Americans: barbaric, intolerant, and threatening. What changed was the character of the war. What started as a limited counterterrorism campaign turned into a difficult and costly exercise in nation building.

General Stanley McChrystal, the top US commander in Afghanistan in 2009, wrote a classified counterinsurgency strategy that said, "Protecting the people is the mission. The conflict will be won by persuading the population, not by destroying the enemy."[14] That's a political war, the kind Americans hate. Once again, the United States was fighting to build confidence in another country's government. Just as we tried and failed to do in Vietnam and Iraq.

The August 2009 election in Afghanistan was supposed to solidify popular support for the Hamid Karzai government. Instead, it raised issues of fraud and mismanagement and threw a shadow over that government's legitimacy. Americans were fighting and dying for a government that stole elections.

Afghanistan doomed the Bush Doctrine. The Bush Doctrine was promulgated by the president in his second inaugural address on January 20, 2005: "The survival of liberty in our land increasingly depends on the success of liberty in other lands." That is an arguable proposition. Would the United States really be more secure if countries such as Saudi Arabia became democracies? When Egypt and Gaza and Turkey held elections, Islamist parties won. Nor is it clear that US policy makers understand enough about other countries' politics and cultures to turn them into functioning democracies.

The United States did succeed in building functioning democracies in Germany and Japan following World War II. Two exceptional conditions made those ventures a success. First, Germany and Japan had powerful preexisting national identities, even if those identities were exaggerated and distorted under fascism. Second, both countries faced total defeat and unconditional surrender after World War II. America had both the authority and the legitimacy to rebuild their national institutions. Those conditions did not hold in Iraq and Afghanistan, where national identities were weaker and the US objective was more limited ("regime change"). In Iraq and Afghanistan, unlike Germany and Japan, the United States was seen as the invader.

Back in 2000, in a campaign debate with Al Gore, George W. Bush warned, "If we don't stop extending our troops all around the world in nation-building missions, then we're going to have a serious problem coming down the road." As we did.

A New Cold War?

For a year after the 9/11 attacks, the American public was united. President Bush's job approval rating hit 90 percent in the September 2001 Gallup poll—the highest rating ever recorded for any president (just above his father's 89 percent at the end of the 1991 Gulf War). His job rating remained above 50 percent for more than two years; among Democrats, for one year.[15] During that period, the country experienced what looked like an era of good feeling; an era of national solidarity in the face of a dire threat.

The closest analogy to the war on terror was supposed to be the Cold War: an open-ended conflict with no definitive outcome in the foreseeable future. The enemy was an "ism": first Communism, later terrorism. It was a global confrontation. The United States divided the world into our side and their side. "Either you are with us, or you are with the terrorists," Bush said on September 20, 2001.

During the Cold War, Americans were obsessed with the nuclear threat. After 9/11, we were obsessed with the threat of terrorism. US citizens pursued airport security with the same zeal we once built fallout shelters and practiced "duck and cover" exercises. Perhaps the closest parallel to the fear Americans felt after 9/11 was the 1962 Cuban Missile Crisis that brought the world to the brink of nuclear war.

The Cold War taught the country some important lessons that were applied to "America's New War." In the early years of the Cold War, Americans were preoccupied by "the enemy within." After 9/11, President Bush insisted that the Islamic religion, and Muslim Americans in particular, were not the enemy. "This is civilization's fight," he said, being careful to include Muslims: "We respect your faith . . . The terrorists are traitors to their own faith, trying, in effect, to hijack Islam itself."

The early years of the Cold War were marked by the unsubtle and inflexible diplomacy of Secretary of State John Foster Dulles: "brinkmanship" and "massive retaliation." President George W. Bush seemed to understand that the war on terror would be fought in a world of complex competition, shifting allegiances, and sometimes devious diplomacy. For example, the United States quickly lifted its antinuclear sanctions on Pakistan. The administration contemplated an opening to Iran if it would help us.

The Cold War lasted forty-five years. It was costly, difficult, and often controversial. When the conflict began, there was considerable doubt that the American people would have the stomach for a massive, open-ended, global commitment. But through it all, Americans sacrificed and endured. In the end, Communism collapsed, owing in no small measure to the relentlessness of US opposition.

The analogy with the war on terror does not hold. The war on terror lasted barely twelve years. President Barack Obama declared an end to it on May 23, 2013: "We have now been at war for over a decade." From now on, "we must define our effort not as a boundless 'global war on terror' but rather as a series of persistent, targeted efforts to dismantle specific networks of violent extremists that threaten America." [16] Obama was describing more a police action than a war.

The war in Iraq undermined public confidence in the war on terror. In 2005 the White House used the "war on terror" to try to boost sagging support for the war in Iraq. As Bush's White House spokesman said in June 2005, "We are fighting the terrorists in Iraq so we don't have to fight them here at home."

Public satisfaction with the way things were going in the war on terror was the lowest since 9/11, according to Gallup. It was not because Americans felt more threatened. They didn't. The number who said further acts of terrorism against the United States were likely in the near future had gone down, from more than 50 percent a year earlier to just over a third in 2005. [17] Discontent with the war in Iraq eclipsed terrorism. In a June 2005 *New York Times*–CBS News poll, more than three times as many Americans mentioned Iraq as mentioned terrorism as the most important problem facing the country. [18] When President Obama declared an end to the global war on terror, he acknowledged that the threat of terrorism had not disappeared. It had "shifted and evolved" to a smaller scale, as was the case before 9/11.

America had experienced terrorist attacks before 9/11: on a US Marine barracks in Lebanon in 1983, on the Khobar Towers military residence in Saudi Arabia in 1996, on US embassies in Kenya and Tanzania on the same day in 1998, and on the destroyer USS *Cole* off the coast of Yemen in 2000. The World Trade Center in New York was first bombed in 1993 and, as noted earlier, it was treated not as an act of war but as a crime. The perpetrators were apprehended and brought to justice.

During the 2004 campaign, Republicans skewered John Kerry's "law enforcement" approach to counterterrorism. In a *New York Times Magazine* interview, Kerry compared terrorism to prostitution and illegal gambling. He pledged to reduce it to the point where "it's something that you continue to fight, but it's not threatening the fabric of your life." The Bush campaign quickly released a television ad asking, "How can Kerry protect us when he doesn't understand the threat?" [19]

Did President Obama propose returning to the law enforcement approach used after the 1993 World Trade Center bombing? Not exactly. What he proposed could be called "law enforcement plus." "Despite our strong preference for the detention and prosecution of terrorists," Obama said, "sometimes this approach is foreclosed." Terrorists hide out in remote and inaccessible locations. They are protected by local populations. Other governments cannot or will not cooperate with the United States. What do we do then? The president's answer was drones.

He defended the use of drones ("targeted lethal action") as an alternative to military intervention.[20] He called drones "the course of action least likely to result in the loss of innocent human life." Drones, Obama argued, must be measured "against the history of putting American troops in distant lands among hostile populations."

Obama's New America coalition was forged out of antiwar

activism. He first rose to prominence as an opponent of the war in Iraq. His approach to counterterrorism was commensurate with his antiwar roots. "Unless we discipline our thinking, our definitions, our actions," he said, "we may be drawn into more wars we don't need to fight."

Americans supported the use of drones (65 to 75 percent in various polls), so long as they were not used inside the United States.[21] The president admitted that drone strikes raise troubling legal questions. But he insisted that the strikes continue, albeit with stronger safeguards and more transparency. They were his alternative to Bush's policy of preemptive war.

The Islamic State Challenge

In 2014 President Obama dismissed the Islamic State of Iraq and Syria (or ISIS) as "jihadists who are engaged in various local power struggles and disputes, often sectarian." Then they grabbed huge swaths of territory in Syria and Iraq, terrorized the local populations, and committed grisly murders of Americans. The public sees ISIS as bloodthirsty fanatics who must be eliminated by force. Despite the public's revulsion against ISIS brutality, Americans ruled out the use of US ground troops. And the president promised not to dispatch any. Americans are okay with air strikes, intelligence support, and military aid to local militias.[22] We want to fight this war by technology and by proxy. With no US casualties.

Who are our allies in this fight? And can we trust them to fight ISIS and not one another? That is exactly the political thicket Americans will not tolerate. They want to win a clear-cut military victory, destroy ISIS, and go home. During the 2016 Republican presidential campaign,

Texas senator Ted Cruz vowed to "carpet bomb ISIS into oblivion." Donald Trump said he would "knock the shit out of 'em" and then "take the oil." As we learned in Vietnam and Iraq, the public doesn't trust unreliable foreign allies or wish to get involved in other countries' civil wars.

Benjamin Rhodes, President Obama's deputy national security adviser, captured the sentiment of the nation's establishment perfectly in 2013 when he made this point to the *New York Times* during the debate over Syria: "One thing for Congress to consider is the message that this debate sends about US leadership around the world: that the US for decades has played the role of undergirding the global security architecture and enforcing international norms. And we do not want to send a message that the United States is getting out of that business in any way."[23]

The problem is that many Americans want to send that very message. A Pew poll taken for the Council on Foreign Relations in December 2013 found that a majority of Americans (52 percent) endorse a radically alternative view to that of the establishment: namely, that the United States "should mind its own business internationally and let other countries get along as best they can on their own." That was the highest level of isolationism measured in nearly fifty years.[24]

A Populist Foreign Policy

Thanks to Donald Trump, we now know what a populist foreign policy looks like: in Trump's words, "I'm not isolationist, but I am America First." When an interviewer first mentioned the slogan "America First," Trump said, "I like the expression," giving the impression that he had never heard the term before. The America First Committee, founded in 1940, opposed any US involvement in World War II and included isolationists and Nazi sympathizers.

"'America First' will be the major and overriding theme of my administration," the presidential candidate said when he delivered a speech defining his foreign policy in April 2016. "I will view as president the world through the clear lens of American interests." If our NATO allies won't pay their fair share of the cost of defending them, "the US must be prepared to let those countries defend themselves." He said America must be "willing to leave the table" if we can't get the deal we want. And "our military dominance must be unquestioned—and I mean unquestioned—by anybody and everybody."

Trump horrified the editors of the *Washington Post* when he said he wanted to renegotiate NATO. ("We certainly can't afford to do this anymore.") When asked whether the United States gains anything by having military bases in South Korea and Japan, he replied, "Personally, I don't think so." He said South Korea is "a wealthy country" that he had "great relationships with." ("I have buildings in South Korea.") His complaint? "We are not reimbursed fairly for what we do." Hillary Clinton accused Trump of "turning our alliances into a protection racket." You pay us, and we'll protect you.

Trump's approach to ISIS exhibited markers of isolationism. "I would knock the hell out of ISIS in some form," he told the *Post*'s editors. "I would rather not do it with our troops, you understand that. Very important." His plan was to use unrestrained air power and get Muslim countries to provide the ground troops. He said he would find it "very, very hard" to send thousands of US ground troops to the Middle East, even if the generals at the Pentagon recommended it. How would Trump persuade other countries to commit troops? He threatened to halt oil purchases and end the US alliance with Saudi Arabia unless it committed ground troops. "Without us, Saudi Arabia wouldn't exist for very long," he told the *New York Times*. That's called bribery.

Trump called it negotiation. He said the key to negotiation is unpredictability: "We have to be unpredictable. We're totally predictable. And predictable is bad." That's how he justified shifting positions on issues like the war in Iraq.

But military alliances are based on predictability. If a NATO ally is attacked, the attacker has to know that the United States will retaliate. "We need steady hands," Hillary Clinton told the American Israel Public Affairs Committee (AIPAC) in 2016, "not a president who says he's neutral on Monday, pro-Israel on Tuesday, and who-knows-what on Wednesday because everything is negotiable."

Suppose Russia were to attack Estonia, a member of NATO. Would the United States send troops to defend little Estonia, population 1.3 million, as the NATO treaty obliges us to do? Trump asked, "Why are we always the one that's leading, potentially, the Third World War with Russia?" The whole point of NATO is that Russia can't be certain we won't come to Estonia's aid. The issue did not come up when the Russians intervened in Ukraine in 2014 because Ukraine is not a member of NATO.

Trump was repudiating the framework of US foreign policy since 1947. The establishment of both political parties continues to defend that commitment. Hillary Clinton told AIPAC, "We need America to remain a respected global leader, committed to defending and advancing the international order."

But the Cold War is over, and Trump sees no necessity for the United States to continue to bear that burden. "NATO was set up when we were a richer country," he said. "We are a poor country now." What about America's international interests and its commitment to defend world order and humanitarian values? As noted earlier, Obama's deputy national security adviser warned during the debate over Syria, "We do not want to send a message that the United States is getting out of that business in any way." That's the message Trump was sending. Millions of Americans were eager to endorse it.

As president, Trump appeared to abandon his isolationist message when he authorized a missile strike on a Syrian air base in retaliation for the use of chemical weapons. Commentators didn't know what to make of it. Cynics accused President Trump of wagging the dog, to distract from his domestic woes. Trump, who is known to respond more to visual images than to written analysis, told reporters, "That attack on children yesterday had a big impact on me—big impact. That was a horrible, horrible thing. And I've been watching it and seeing it, and it doesn't get any worse than that."

Some of his strongest supporters on the extreme right denounced Trump for abandoning his campaign pledges not to get involved in foreign adventures. "This is definitely not what we voted for," one of them declared in a livestream broadcast. The more conspiracy minded argued that Trump had been duped into changing positions by fake footage or by a staged chemical attack.

Isolationism is not pacifism. It means a refusal to get involved in other countries' problems unless they have a direct impact on US interests. If America is attacked or its interests threatened, we respond with overwhelming and decisive force. We win. Then we get out. Trump told the *Washington Post* editorial board, "I'm a counterpuncher. Meaning, if I get hit, I'm going to hit back harder." That is the ruling principle of his foreign policy: if we get hit, we hit back harder. Senior military officials described the Syria strike as "proportional" and not intended to signal a long-term engagement in the Syrian civil war.

President Trump did not see himself as a flip-flopper with the Syrian strike. He simply redefined the issue to fit his predilections. "Tonight I ordered a targeted military strike on the air base in Syria from where the chemical attack was launched. It is in the vital national security interest of the United States to prevent and deter the spread and use of deadly chemical weapons." When our vital interests are threatened, the United States will respond forcefully. Even isolationists follow that logic.

President Trump appeared to embrace the idea of international interests when he spoke in Warsaw, Poland, on July 6, 2017.[25] But the international interests he endorsed were not global security or international norms. They were more ethnocentric. Trump called for a defense of the values of "our civilization" and "the West" against the threat of "radical Islamic terrorism." Columnist Peter Beinart pointed out that "the West is a racial and religious term" meaning "largely Christian" and "largely white." And therefore in line with the "alt-right" doctrine of white nationalism. An explicit rejection of pluralism and diversity.[26]

Trump's affinity for Russia and its president, Vladimir Putin, troubles a lot of Americans, including many conservatives. Trump has also made positive comments about the repressive governments of Saudi Arabia, Egypt, the Philippines, Poland, India, and Turkey. Viktor Orban, Hungary's right-wing leader who called Muslim refugees a threat to Europe's "Christian roots," has expressed admiration for Trump. What these governments have in common is authoritarian nationalism.

"We must work together," Trump said in Warsaw, "to confront forces, whether they come from inside or out, from the South or the

East, that threaten over time to undermine these values and to erase the bonds of culture, faith, and tradition that make us who we are . . . We celebrate our ancient heroes and embrace our timeless traditions and customs."

In his 2002 West Point speech, President George W. Bush had said, "More and more, civilized nations find ourselves on the same side, united by common dangers of terrorist violence and chaos." Bush was talking about a defense of civilization; a universal value. Trump was talking about a defense of a particular civilization: "the West." As if to prove the superiority of Western civilization, Trump said in Warsaw, "We write symphonies." For Trump, our international interests are an extension of his definition of our national interest: protection from cultural invasion by alien outsiders.

NINE

Successful Challenges

Political strategist Alan Baron used to tell the story of managing the 1964 Democratic campaign in his native Sioux City, Iowa. An unemployed teamster was seeking a state senate seat that had not been held by a Democrat for decades. He asked for $300 to rent a truck, decorate it with pictures of President Lyndon Johnson and Governor Harold Hughes and drive it around town on Election Day to get out the vote.

Resources were tight, and Baron had to turn him down. But the candidate raised the money and rented the truck on his own. On Election Day, the entire Democratic ticket was elected: LBJ, Hughes, the state senate candidate—even a blank space for county attorney, despite no Democrat on the ballot.

"You see," the candidate said to Baron, "the truck worked."

"If only Adlai Stevenson had known about the truck," Baron replied.

To win, you need the right conditions as well as the right candidate and the right campaign message. Some elections are unlosable. There was virtually no way Lyndon Johnson could have lost the 1964 election, even if the Republicans had not made it so easy for him. Many elections can go either way. Is there some kind of law that governs the success of a candidate and strategy? I think there is. I call it the Law of the Missing Imperative. The party out of power in the White House has to discover what voters want that they are not getting from the incumbent and figure out how to market it. Even if the incumbent isn't running for reelection, the president's party and record are still on the ballot.

Presidential campaigns are essentially exercises in market research. The US political system, like its economic system, functions in a supremely opportunistic capitalist culture. If there is a market, there is likely to be a product. When the opposition party finds a product—in other words, a candidate—that meets the needs of the political market, it wins.

There are, of course, plenty of failures in the political market just as in the economic market. Remember New Coke? Corfam leather substitute for shoes? Betamax videotapes? They were all flops, like Barry Goldwater, George McGovern, John Kerry, and Mitt Romney. They might have been good products. But there was not a big enough market for them when they were launched. Timing is everything.

1960: Youth

In 1960, after eight years of President Dwight Eisenhower, voters worried that the country was slowing down. They feared America was losing the edge to the Soviet Union in military power and technology, especially after the Soviets launched the Sputnik space satellite in 1957. Moreover, Eisenhower was the first president whose medical issues—heart disease, gastrointestinal problems—were covered graphically on television. His age and health problems seemed to signify the country's loss of momentum. Americans were looking for a leader who offered youth, dynamism, and vigor.

That was John F. Kennedy, who promised to "get the country moving again." JFK symbolized the coming to power of a new generation of Americans, born in the twentieth century, who had fought and won World War II. Elected at age forty-three, Kennedy remains the youngest president ever elected.[1]

Kennedy fit, or designed his campaign to fit, the mood of the country. The 1960 election saw the closest national popular vote for president in US history (Kennedy won by 112,827 votes, or 0.17 percent). Voters were ambivalent—not so much polarized as torn between continuity and change. The unemployment rate had been declining since the 1958 recession. Eisenhower's job approval rating was a strong 58 percent. The biggest issue was the Cold War and the perception of growing Soviet power, including a nonexistent "missile gap" that triggered alarm from Democrats. Four presidential debates focused almost exclusively on foreign policy. (Ever hear of Quemoy and Matsu?) The market for change was not overwhelming in 1960. But Kennedy managed to eke out a narrow victory by capturing the theme that fit the moment: youth.

1968: Order

In the late 1960s, the United States was shattered by racial violence, the Vietnam War, and campus protests. Turmoil and disorder reached a peak in 1968: the Tet offensive in Vietnam, the assassinations of Dr. Martin Luther King Jr. and Robert F. Kennedy, disruptions on American college campuses, the breakdown of law and order in US cities, rioting and a police rampage at the Democratic National Convention in Chicago. In 1968, voters wanted an experienced professional who could hold the country together. It was one of the rare years in which voters were not looking for an outsider untainted by Washington. They wanted an experienced political insider.

Richard M. Nixon had held almost every top office in government: congressman, senator, vice president. Having lost the presidency narrowly in 1960 and then the race for governor of California in 1962, his political career seemed over. The morning after his devastating defeat for governor, Nixon had announced, "You won't have Nixon to kick around anymore because, gentlemen, this is my last press conference." ABC broadcast a documentary, *The Political Obituary of Richard Nixon.*[2]

In 1968 Nixon was resurrected from the political grave. He had something to sell—order—and a market that wanted to buy it. Joe McGinniss wrote a best-selling book about Nixon's shrewd marketing campaign, *The Selling of the President.*[3] Toward the end of the campaign, Nixon started using the theme "Bring Us Together." One of his aides had seen a young girl carrying a sign that said "Bring Us Together Again" at a whistle-stop in Ohio. In his victory speech, Nixon mentioned the sign and said, "That will be the great objective of this administration at the outset: to bring the American people together."

Nixon was well situated to claim the center in 1968. In the contest for the Republican nomination, he was in the center, between Nelson Rockefeller on his left and Ronald Reagan on his right. The fall campaign found Nixon in the center again, with Hubert Humphrey on his left and George Wallace on his right. Everywhere Humphrey and Wallace went, it looked like a riot might break out. Nixon sold order, and Americans bought it. Once again, the margin was narrow—less than 1 percent—because some of the vote for change was captured by George Wallace, who ran as an Independent and got 13.5 percent of the vote.

1976: Morality

Americans elected Nixon. They got Watergate. In August 1974, the Watergate scandal, involving a break-in at the offices of the Democratic Party and a White House cover-up of the crime, forced President Nixon to resign from office or be impeached. In 1976 one candidate understood what Americans were longing for after Watergate. Jimmy Carter, a one-term governor of Georgia, came out of nowhere and overwhelmed a field of strong Democratic contenders with a simple message: "I will never lie to you." Americans had been shocked by Nixon's behavior in the White House and dismayed by Gerald Ford's decision to pardon him. Carter's deep religious convictions convinced voters that he had strong moral values and would restore integrity to the White House.

Carter's primary campaign was a masterpiece of political strategy. He took on his leading rivals one by one and beat them on their own turf: George Wallace in a southern state (Florida), Morris Udall in a progressive state (Wisconsin), and Scoop Jackson in a union state (Pennsylvania). In the later primaries, his opponents formed a stop-Carter coalition that created some setbacks for the front-runner. (Frank Church won Nebraska and Oregon; Jerry Brown won Maryland and Nevada.) But it was too late to stop Carter.

Liberals were suspicious of Carter, a southern white moderate. But Carter's embrace of civil rights and his strong support from African American voters convinced them to back him. In the end, it was the Watergate scandal that created Carter and his message of morality that sold him to the voters.

1980: Leadership

Jimmy Carter retained his image of integrity throughout his one term in office. But there was something voters were missing: leadership. The president was derided by his critics as wishy-washy. He faced immense challenges: an energy crisis, gasoline shortages, out-of-control inflation, a tax revolt, recession, the Soviet invasion of Afghanistan, a revolution in Iran that led to the Iranian hostage crisis. In those tumultuous times, Carter often seemed hapless and ineffectual, buffeted by forces beyond his control.

Enter Ronald Reagan, who probably could not have gotten elected in any year except 1980. He frightened too many voters. The race was close until the last week of the campaign. Voters worried that Reagan was dangerous; that electing him would be too much of a change. They feared he might start a war or slash government spending for seniors. But in 1980, in the atmosphere of crisis under Carter, Reagan's strength of conviction and strong sense of direction struck a powerful chord.

For conservatives, 1980 is the Year One, the year they finally won their long struggle to gain ascendancy over the Republican Party. Everything before Reagan's election is prehistoric, with the exception of

Barry Goldwater in 1964. Goldwater was a prophet. He pointed the way but did not enter the promised land.

The year 1980 brought into focus the great changes in American politics that began in the 1960s, were temporarily interrupted in the mid-1970s, and would continue through the 1980s, 1990s, and into the new century. By 2016, those changes had wrought a polarized and gridlocked political environment. The battle lines of the confrontation between the New America and the Old America became clearly visible in 1980.

Mindful of Barry Goldwater's catastrophic performance, Ronald Reagan gave a cautious and conciliatory acceptance speech at the 1980 Republican National Convention. "It is essential," he said, "that the integrity of all aspects of Social Security be preserved."

The first stirrings of Old America had become apparent with the Goldwater campaign in 1964. Goldwater's opposition to the Civil Rights Act brought him the support of southern whites. In 1972 Nixon used his Southern Strategy to solidify the Republican hold on the white South. On the left, the emergence of the New America had become evident with the George McGovern campaign in 1972, when the Democratic Party embraced social liberalism and repudiated its Cold War commitment to anti-Communist military intervention.

Goldwater and McGovern lost. Reagan won. He was the whole conservative package. To the Republican Party's traditional economic conservatism and its more recent racial-backlash support, Reagan added an appeal to the religious right, even though Reagan himself was not particularly religious.

The 1980 campaign challenged the conventional wisdom of the supposedly inherent "centrism" of American politics. When a moderate or centrist candidate runs against a candidate perceived as more ideologically extreme, the moderate is supposed to win, just as in 1964 and 1972. That is especially true if, as in those years, the moderate is the incumbent.

The 1980 election was driven by dissatisfaction with President Carter. Reagan won with a bare majority of the vote (50.8 percent). But his margin over Carter was decisive (9 points) because John Anderson received more than 6 percent of the vote. Anderson, a Republican congressman from Illinois, ran as an Independent and appealed to liberal Democrats who didn't like Carter and to moderate Republicans who objected to Reagan.

One other thing doomed Carter's reelection: the country went into recession in January 1980. America has suffered from ten recessions since 1950. All but one of them (1980) began during a Republican administration.[4] Democrats do not tolerate recessions very well. The recession helped fuel Senator Edward Kennedy's ultimately unsuccessful challenge to Carter's renomination in the 1980 Democratic primaries.

The surprisingly decisive Republican margin came about as a result of a late swing. CBS News and the *New York Times* reinterviewed almost all of the 2,264 registered voters whom they had originally interviewed a few days before the election. Thirteen percent reported a change from their preelection preference. This group switched from two to one for Carter to nearly two to one for Reagan in the last few days of the campaign.[5]

I remember the last week of that campaign well. The event that precipitated the late swing was the one and only debate between Reagan and Carter on October 28. (Reagan had previously debated John Anderson when Carter refused to show up because Anderson was included.) It was at the October 28 debate that Reagan reassured voters that he was a safe alternative, mostly with his closing statement: "Are you better off than you were four years ago?"

Before the debate, ABC News announced a viewer call-in poll. At the end of the debate, viewers were invited to call one number if they thought Carter had won the debate and another number to pick Reagan. It was anything but a scientific poll. Not only were respondents self-selected, but they could call as many times as they wished—at a charge of fifty cents per call.

When the results were announced after the debate, an incredible seven hundred thousand calls had been made. Two out of three callers preferred Reagan. I was working with the *Los Angeles Times* poll that year, and we discovered that, as news of the poll result got out, more and more people came to the conclusion that Reagan had won. An unscientific poll made the outcome of the debate a "fact."[6] With that, the floodgates burst. Day by day, we saw Reagan's support building among voters who did not believe Carter deserved to be reelected but had been put off by Reagan's "radical" image. One could argue that the last fifteen minutes of the 1980 debate and the phony poll result changed the course of history for decades thereafter.

The 1980 election also brought new social issues into presidential politics. For the first time, the candidates and parties took strong and divergent positions on women's rights and abortion. The Republican platform went on record in opposition to the Equal Rights Amendment (ERA) for women, which would have prohibited legal discrimination on the basis of sex and came three states shy of the thirty-eight needed for ratification, and in favor of a constitutional amendment to prohibit all abortions. The party went so far as to require that any federal judge appointed by a Republican president be explicitly opposed to abortion.

The Democrats pledged to withhold party support from any candidate who opposed the ERA. On abortion rights, Democrats supported the use of federal funds to subsidize abortions for poor women.

When you look at the 1980 vote, you see the evidence of ideological shift. Reagan's gains over Gerald Ford's 1976 vote were largest among labor union families, manual workers, white southerners, Catholics, seniors, and the non-college-educated—all groups that had been core supporters of the New Deal Democratic coalition. The support that Carter lost from women, the college educated, young voters, Protestants, higher-status groups, independents, and nonsoutherners went disproportionately to John Anderson.[7]

What happened in 1980 might be described as an unraveling of the strained fabric of New Deal Democratic loyalties. It was Carter's weakness, not itself an ideological issue, that caused the threads to unravel. But once the fibers started to come apart, they were pulled in different directions, some to the right by Reagan and some to the left by Anderson. Ideology had more to do with the direction of change than with the momentum behind it.

One thing clearly contributed to the increasing polarization of the two parties: the fact that moderates in both parties had been given a chance and were seen as having failed. Ronald Reagan succeeded four failed presidents in a row, two Democrats and two Republicans: Lyndon Johnson, who lost support in his party and declined to run for reelection; Richard Nixon, who was forced to resign; Gerald Ford, who couldn't get elected; and Jimmy Carter, who got fired. After those bitter experiences, Americans were desperate to see a leader succeed. Voters were ready to try something different in 1980. Even something radically different.

Reagan's deeply conservative views, which might have been a

handicap in another year, made him seem like a man of strong principles and convictions—just what the country needed after four years of "wishy-washy" leadership. He was the un-Carter.

1992: Empathy

Republicans kept the White House for twelve long years after 1980. George H. W. Bush got elected in 1988 essentially as a third term for Reagan. As we will see in chapter 10, Democrats tried to run a nonideological campaign in 1988, but their candidate, Michael Dukakis, was relentlessly attacked as too liberal. After the 1988 defeat, Democrats were forced to recalibrate their message. Were they too far out of the mainstream? Too liberal? Too wedded to big government? That critique would have been tested if Democrats had nominated their dream candidate in 1988: New York governor Mario Cuomo. But Cuomo declined to run. Instead, Democrats turned in the other direction, to Bill Clinton, chairman of the centrist Democratic Leadership Council, who fashioned himself a "New Democrat" and an advocate of the "third way."

By 1992, the first President Bush was in deep trouble. In 1991 he had won the Gulf War and stood astride the world like a colossus. A year later, he was toast. The problem was empathy, his seeming inability to understand what ordinary Americans were going through in the recession. He appeared remote and out of touch, unable to connect with working people.

Part of the problem was that Bush was born to wealth and privilege. It confirmed the most damaging stereotype of the GOP: that Republicans are the party of wealth and privilege. Republicans find it easier to elect candidates who were born to modest circumstances and made their own way in the world: Dwight Eisenhower, Richard Nixon,

Ronald Reagan. Both Presidents Bush got in trouble when the economy went sour on their watches. How could they possibly understand what ordinary people, facing the loss of their jobs, their homes, and their health insurance, were going through? As Texas governor Ann Richards declared famously in 1988, taunting George H. W. Bush for his wealth as well as his inarticulateness, "Poor George. He can't help it. He was born with a silver foot in his mouth."

Republicans faced that problem again in 2012 when the party nominated Mitt Romney. Romney made matters worse by constantly saying things that exposed him as out of touch, such as "Corporations are people." Democrats can get away with highborn candidates such as Franklin D. Roosevelt and John F. Kennedy. They become traitors to their class, and voters admire them for it. For Republicans, however, it's always a risk.

Bill Clinton was certainly not born to wealth and privilege. His ability to connect with voters is legendary. He felt your pain. Later, it became a joke, but empathy was the missing imperative that got him elected in 1992.

Underlying the chaotic twists and turns of the 1992 campaign was one of the most spectacular collapses in public support for any president in American history. George H. W. Bush went from 89 percent approval in March 1991, in the aftermath of victory in Operation Desert Storm, to 33 percent approval in October 1992, a year and a half later. Both he and Jimmy Carter had major foreign-policy achievements, but they counted for little politically because both presidents saw the economy deteriorate on their watch. Carter and Bush were defeated for re-election, and their parties paid a heavy price. The lesson of their defeat was: don't ignore the economy, stupid.

The larger message for all presidents is that foreign policy cannot save you, but it can destroy you. The Vietnam War destroyed Lyndon Johnson in 1968, despite his strong record on the economy and civil rights. A foreign-policy triumph could not save George H. W. Bush in 1992 when the economy tanked.

The 1992 election was a massive vote of no confidence in President Bush. Some Republicans still blame Ross Perot for their loss. But it wasn't that simple. Bush lost about equal numbers of votes to Clinton and Perot. When Perot voters were asked how they would have voted if Ross Perot's name had not been on the ballot, equal numbers said Clinton and Bush.[8]

Perot did attract a lot of former Bush voters. But they were furious at Bush, and most never would have voted to reelect him. Perot's candidacy was actually a bigger threat to Clinton. When Perot was running first in the polls, in May and June 1992, Clinton was coming in third. Perot (temporarily) got out of the race in July 1992 on the day Bill Clinton accepted the Democratic nomination. Perot declared upon withdrawing, "The Democratic Party has revitalized itself." Two-thirds of Perot's supporters immediately went to Clinton. Perot reentered the race in October and participated in all three debates but never recovered his early support. Moreover, when Perot started picking up support after the final presidential debate on October 19, his gains came mostly at Clinton's expense. In the end, Perot did not split the Republican vote. He split the anti-Bush vote, which is to say the vote for change. Perot did not deny Bush his second term. He denied Clinton his majority.

President Bush was challenged in the Republican primaries by an antiestablishment conservative, Patrick Buchanan. When an incumbent is threatened by a serious primary challenger, it always means trouble, even if the incumbent wins the nomination. In 1976 President Ford fended off a tough challenge from Ronald Reagan and was mortally wounded in the process. So was President Carter when he faced a challenge from Edward Kennedy in 1980. Challenges to President Johnson's renomination in 1968 from Senators Eugene McCarthy and Robert Kennedy led Johnson to withdraw. Buchanan's 1992 challenge to President Bush was not nearly as severe. It barely lasted beyond the New Hampshire primary, where Buchanan gave Bush a scare. But it revealed the depth of conservative disaffection with Bush as well as the willingness of angry conservatives to take on a president of their own party who had committed the cardinal sin of agreeing to a tax hike. Buchanan's antiestablishment revolt in some ways presaged the Donald Trump rebellion of 2016.

The most remarkable phenomenon of 1992 was Ross Perot. The diminutive Texas billionaire captured nearly 20 percent of the vote—the highest vote for an independent or third party candidate for president since 1912, when Theodore Roosevelt, a former president running on the Bull Moose ticket, came in second with 27 percent of the vote. The incumbent in 1912, William Howard Taft, came in third. The split in the Republican vote enabled Woodrow Wilson to get elected with 42 percent of the vote.

The Perot faith had one central belief: politics is the enemy of problem solving. That view is a core element of American populism. Why can't we solve the deficit? Because politics gets in the way. Why can't we deal with climate change? Too much politics. The Perot style of antiestablishment populism reemerges in a new guise every time Washington seems incapable of solving the country's problems. We saw it again with the emergence of another businessman and nonpolitician: Donald Trump in 2016.

Perot ran again in 1996 as the nominee of his newly organized Reform Party. But the novelty had worn off. More important, the country felt that things were picking up under President Clinton. The technology-driven boom (or bubble) of the late 1990s was under way. Voter anger and anxiety had diminished. Perot's support dropped from 19 percent in 1992 to 8 percent in 1996.

Historian Richard Hofstadter once wrote, "Third parties are like bees. They sting and then they die." In 1992 Ross Perot stung. In 1996 he died.

2000: Character

Two weeks before the 2000 election between Al Gore and George W. Bush, I was working in the CNN newsroom when a high-level network executive came over to me and asked, "Who's going to win?"

I replied, "I think this will be the first presidential election since 1968 when the night before the election, we won't have any idea who's going to win."

A month later, I saw the executive again. "You were right," he said. "But what you didn't tell me was that two weeks after the election, we still wouldn't know who was going to win."

First we had the 2000 campaign in which issue differences were muted and voters could have gone either way. In most elections, one of two themes prevails: "You've never had it so good," or "It's time for a change." In 2000, voters felt both ways. In overwhelming numbers, they said this was the best economy of their lifetime. Also in overwhelming numbers, they thought the country needed a change of leadership. Hence, the excruciating closeness of the result.

Voters were not deeply engaged in the campaign. Turnout in the primaries was the second lowest to that date.[9] Only 1996, when there was no contest for the Democratic nomination, saw lower turnout. The audiences for the October debates were at near-record lows. There was no great overriding issue roiling the electorate. When there are no big issues driving the vote, small differences take on more importance. That happened in the 1960 election, which also took place at a time of peace and prosperity. The cliché that year was, "Tweedledum and Tweedledee. Not a dime's worth of difference between 'em." Arthur Schlesinger Jr. wrote a book aimed at liberals entitled *Kennedy or Nixon: Does It Make Any Difference?* [10]

If there were no big issues in 2000, how did voters make up their minds? A lot of it was personal. They saw Al Gore as not particularly likable. And George W. Bush as not particularly knowledgeable. It drove Democrats crazy that voters seemed to care more about likability than knowledgeability. My God, didn't people understand they were electing a president of the United States? Well, yes. But there was no big problem out there that needed fixing. No economic crisis. No mounting budget deficit. No (apparent) foreign threat.

If voters thought something needed fixing, they'd hire someone with the know-how to fix it. They elected Richard Nixon twice, and no one ever called Nixon likable. They elected Nixon in 1968 because he seemed to have the knowledge and experience to fix what was wrong. Nixon had lost in 1960 when nothing much was wrong, and voters went for the guy they liked better. Gore played the Nixon role in 2000; the knowledgeable candidate who was hard to like. Bush played Ronald Reagan, the likable candidate whose knowledgeability was in question.

When an election is close, it gives the impression that voters are deeply polarized. But a close vote can mean something else: namely, that voters can't make up their minds. They see things they like and dislike about both candidates. Pollsters know that when a poll question gets a fifty-fifty response, it can mean that people are sharply divided, or, as is often the case, that they have mixed feelings and that many are picking an answer at random. Ask people which they would prefer, ice cream or apple pie, and you would probably get close to a fifty-fifty split. Not because the public is deeply polarized between pie and ice cream, but because most people like both and have trouble making up their minds. They choose at random. That's what happened in the close election of 1960. It seemed to happen again in 2000, when voters were ambivalent about the election, the candidates, and the country.

The strange thing about the 2000 election was that it should not have been close. The country was in its tenth year of economic recovery, an all-time record. President Clinton's job approval rating was over 60 percent. That was higher than Reagan's in 1988, the year the elder George Bush was elected to succeed him. Every forecasting model said Gore should have been an easy winner. But forecasting models tend to ignore personal factors.

In 2000, when George W. Bush spoke about a new image for the Republican Party, he was trying to put aside the image of the GOP from the 1990s. Specifically, Bush had nothing to do with three highly controversial events that defined the Republican Party during the previous decade.

One was the harsh and divisive 1992 Houston convention. Pat Buchanan said in his prime-time convention speech, referring to the riots in Los Angeles following the acquittal of the police officers on trial for the brutal beating of Rodney King, "As [the troops] took back the streets of Los Angeles, block by block, so we must take back our cities, and take back our culture, and take back our country." He showed no trace of Reagan-like optimism or expansiveness. He also said ominously, "It is a cultural war, as critical to the kind of nation we will one day be as was the Cold War itself."

The second signal event was the Gingrich revolution. The 1994 election was a high point for Republicans, when they finally realized their dream of taking control of Congress after forty years in the wilderness. It was the year of the angry white man. Congressional Republicans assumed that a negative, confrontational style would continue to pay off for them. Clinton outsmarted them, however. He stole their agenda and forced Republicans farther and farther to the right. When they shut down the federal government twice in 1995 and 1996, for a total of twenty-seven days, angry white men turned on Congress.

The GOP's harsh, combative style reached a climax in the third defining event of the 1990s: impeachment. Which ended up overthrowing House Speaker Newt Gingrich, not President Bill Clinton.

George W. Bush and Dick Cheney were clean. They had nothing to do with the Houston convention or the Gingrich revolution or impeachment. Bush wanted to reach back to a more positive conservative style: Reagan conservatism, not Gingrich conservatism. The two brands of conservatism were not different on principles. But they differed in style. Bush was trying to revive the Reagan image of the party: tolerant, compassionate, and inclusive, with a little of his father's "kinder, gentler" thrown in. Bush's Republican Party was supposed to be his father's party, the pre–Newt Gingrich GOP.

Bush took one trick right out of the Bill Clinton playbook. As president, Clinton pulled off one of the neatest political tricks in modern times. Every time the Republican Congress passed extreme legislation, Clinton would respond by saying, "I'm for that but not that much." It was a deft political move. Congress would pass a balanced budget. President Clinton would say, "I'm for a balanced budget, too, but I am going to veto this bill because it goes too far. It endangers Medicare,

Medicaid, education, and the environment." Eventually Congress passed a balanced-budget bill more to his liking, and he signed it.

Congress would pass welfare reform legislation. Clinton vetoed welfare reform bills—twice—saying essentially, "I'm for welfare reform, too, but not that much. This bill is too harsh." He demanded that Congress pass a welfare reform bill he could sign. And it did. This enabled him to carry off a remarkable political feat: he stole the Republicans' issues and stood up to them at the same time.

Bush carried off a comparable political feat in the way he dealt with conservatives in his party. His approach was essentially to say, "I endorse your positions, but I embrace your adversaries." Thus, Bush joined with conservatives in opposing same-sex marriage. But he also welcomed gay supporters, becoming the first Republican nominee for president to invite gay and lesbian support for his campaign. Bush firmly opposed abortion rights, but after he took office, he welcomed abortion rights supporters such as former New Jersey governor Christine Todd Whitman into his administration. He opposed affirmative action but did not make opposition to affirmative action a litmus test for his campaign or for his administration. That seemed to be what Bush meant when he called himself a compassionate conservative. He was saying to moderates, I don't agree with you, but I don't hate you or reject you. It was "nice conservatism," as opposed to the "nasty conservatism" of Newt Gingrich, Tom DeLay, and talk radio commentator Rush Limbaugh.

Why was the 2000 election so close? As usual, it was all about sex. The gender gap, to be precise. According to exit polls, the election wasn't even close among men. Men voted for Bush by an 11-point margin. The election wasn't close among women, either, as they voted for Gore by an 11-point margin. The election was a gender showdown, fought to a standoff: Bush, the president of men, versus Gore, the president of women.[11] The gender gap had been a feature of American politics since 1980, but we had never seen anything like this before: competing landslides.

Women, on the average, tend to be more risk averse than men. I was once criticized by feminists for saying that, but there is proof: women make up fewer than 10 percent of state and federal prisoners in the United States.[12] All crimes involve risk taking. Women are less likely to take risks. Especially stupid risks. Women tend to place higher value on the safety net, which is the main reason they supported Gore. Men are more inclined to be risk takers. George W. Bush came out of the worlds of sports and business. Those are stereotypically male worlds, where risk taking is expected and rewarded.

Bush campaigned on the theme of competition and risk taking. In his acceptance speech at the Republican National Convention, Bush promised younger workers, "We will give you the option—your choice—to put a part of your payroll taxes into sound, responsible investments." On education, he said, "When a school district receives federal funds to teach poor children, we expect them to learn. And if they don't, parents should get the money to make a different choice."

Bush used his convention speech to draw a contrast with Al Gore. "Every one of the proposals I've talked about tonight, he has called 'a risky scheme,' over and over again. It is the sum of his message: the politics of the roadblock, the philosophy of the stop sign." He went on to mock Gore. "If my opponent has been there at the moon launch, it would have been a 'risky rocket scheme.' If he had been there when Edison was testing the light bulb, it would have been 'a risky anticandle scheme.'"

Al Gore repeatedly called Bush "risky," "irresponsible," and "reckless." He told New York financial leaders, "I believe George W. Bush's entire economic agenda is built on a foundation of irresponsibility and risk." He characterized Bush's tax cut as a "risky tax scheme for the wealthy" and called Bush's proposal to allow some Social Security money to be invested privately "his secret plan to privatize Social Security."

Gore's paradigm was the safety net. He pledged to secure it. Gore told a Cleveland audience, "First, let's make Social Security financially sound into the second half of this new century, and make Medicare financially sound for at least another thirty years." In Cleveland, Gore pledged to "set aside some money for a rainy day, to be absolutely certain that we never spend money we don't have." Hence, the famous "lockbox," Gore's metaphor for protecting payroll tax revenues from being used for anything except social security and Medicare benefits. Bush was betting that Americans were willing to take risks in 2000 precisely because they felt secure and prosperous, while Gore tried to portray Bush as cocky and reckless. Gore's campaign theme was, in essence, "Safety First."

As president, Bush was as good as his word. His tax cut took a big risk with the nation's economy and public debt. The Iraq War put US lives and treasure at risk, as well as America's standing in the world. Unlike his father, George W. Bush never touted the virtue of "prudence."

The Clinton years equalized the strength of the two parties. What Bill Clinton did was blur party differences on economic policy while creating a deep division over values. Clintonism was a policy of the center—the "third way"—between left and right. A lot of it was lifted from Republicans. And it worked. It brought the country peace, prosperity, declining crime rates, and declining welfare rolls. On Election

Day 2000, two-thirds of Americans thought the country was headed in the right direction.[13]

President Clinton created a consensus on policy but not on values. While voters were not deeply polarized in 2000, the election results were not random. Voters made their choice on the basis of values and lifestyle. "Lifestyle" is a 1960s word, and Bill Clinton was a creature of the sixties. Liberals liked Clinton's values, not his centrist policies. Conservatives hated Clinton's values. They were the values of the sixties.

Gore tried to keep a distance from Clinton. He named Joe Lieberman, a fierce critic of President Clinton's behavior, to the ticket. But Gore was always Clinton's man. Voters who hated Clinton came out strongly against Gore. Consensus on policy. Divided on values. That was America at the turn of the twenty-first century.

What voters were looking for in 2000 became clear at the beginning of the campaign, when John McCain won the New Hampshire primary. McCain was the un-Clinton. McCain's campaign theme captured the missing imperative most clearly: "straight talk." McCain traveled across New Hampshire on a bus he labeled "the Straight Talk Express." Clinton was anything but a straight talker. I recall asking audiences in 2000—many of whom were wildly enthusiastic about Clinton—if they could recall anything memorable that President Clinton had said. There would be a moment of silence, and then the audience would begin to laugh nervously. Eventually someone would raise a hand and reply, "I did not have sexual relations with that woman." I asked if they could recall any other memorable Clintonism. Someone usually said, "I didn't inhale." Anything else? "It depends on what the meaning of 'is' is."

Those are precisely the opposite of straight talk. They explain the initial success of McCain's marketing strategy. It showcased McCain's strength, not only in contrast to Clinton but also in contrast to George W. Bush, who couldn't talk straight, and to Al Gore, who had defended himself from charges of campaign finance violations by claiming that "no controlling legal authority" could say otherwise. If McCain had managed to win the Republican nomination in 2000, my guess is that he would have won the election fairly handily. But McCain's decision to challenge conservative control of the Republican Party doomed him.

In the end, Clinton's personal flaws opened the way for George W. Bush to run as a man of character in 2000. He could do it mostly because of the brand name Bush. Even though he was fired by voters after one term, the first President Bush had a reputation for honor and integrity—qualities that voters did not readily associate with Bill Clinton. In 2000 George W. Bush promised to uphold his family's reputation for good character by pledging, "When I put my hand on the Bible, I will swear to not only uphold the laws of our land. I will swear to uphold the honor and dignity of the office to which I have been elected."

The character message was not enough to convince a majority of Americans to switch parties at a time when the economy was booming and President Clinton's job approval rating was 57 percent. But it was enough to get voters to accept Bush as the new president.

2008: Uniter

Barack Obama had unique qualifications to be what George W. Bush had called himself: "a uniter, not a divider." Obama was both black and white. He was from a new generation. Most important, he was the first nationally prominent African American politician who did not come out of the civil rights movement. The race issue had never been central to his politics, as it had been for Jesse Jackson and Al Sharpton.

Obama was not part of the culture wars of the 1960s that shaped the nation's two baby boomer presidents, Bill Clinton and George W. Bush. Obama could speak the language of faith that makes many Democrats uncomfortable. He promised to reach out to Republicans and govern in a spirit of bipartisanship.

In a normal political year, partisans look for a fighter to carry the party's banner. Democrats had that choice in 2008. Hillary Clinton promoted herself as a fighter. She said in Ohio, "When I say I will fight for you, I will. It's what I've always done." Obama repudiated attack politics. He claimed to offer "a new politics" of consensus building and unity. In Dallas, he described "a choice between a politics that offers more of the same divisions and distractions . . . or a new politics of common sense, of common purpose, of shared sacrifices and shared prosperity." Obama's call for a new politics of consensus struck a nerve, while Clinton's combative message backfired. Obama's message was more in tune with what voters were looking for: someone who could end the bitter partisan warfare that had dominated American politics since 1980.

Clinton tried to portray Obama as weak and naive: "The idea that you're going to escape the Republican attack machine and not have high negatives by the time they're through with you, I think is just missing what's been going on in American politics for the last twenty years." Obama's response: "We're going to need somebody who can break out of the political patterns that we've been in over the last twenty years." The last twenty years included the Clinton wars of the 1990s.

Hillary Clinton tried to run on her experience. "Change is just a word unless you have the experience to make it happen," she said in February 2008. Obama's response? Judgment matters more than experience. Experienced people got us into Iraq. "On what I believe was the single most important foreign-policy decision of this generation, whether or not to go to war in Iraq, I believe I showed the judgment of a commander in chief," Obama said at the Democratic debate in Texas. "And I think Senator Clinton was wrong in her judgments on that."

By 2008, the war in Iraq was no longer central to the presidential campaign. Democrats had vented their anger over Iraq in the 2006 midterm election, and the war seemed to be winding down. But the Iraq issue was crucial in selling Obama to his party. In October 2002 Senator Clinton—along with John Kerry and John Edwards—had voted to authorize the use of force in Iraq. That same month, Obama, then an obscure Illinois state senator, delivered a stirring speech in Chicago opposing the war. "I know that even a successful war against Iraq will require a US occupation of undetermined length, at undetermined cost, with undetermined consequences...I am not opposed to all wars. I am opposed to dumb wars." Fortunately for Obama, a portion of that speech was preserved on video. It substantiated his claim that he had been right about Iraq from the start.

Obama appeared to understand that American government demands consensus. All lasting policy achievements are built on consensus. In his criticism of Clinton's approach to health care reform during the Texas debate, Obama said, "We can have great plans, but if we don't change how the politics is working in Washington, then neither of our plans is going to happen, and we're going to be four years from now debating once again how we're going to bring universal health care to this country."

Ultimately, Republican John McCain came to acknowledge the demand for bipartisan consensus. He promised, "I will, as I often have in the past, work with anyone of either party to get things done for this country." But Obama had the first claim on the issue. He said in a 2007 Democratic debate, when eight contenders were in the race, "We are all very qualified for the job. The question is who can inspire the nation to get beyond the politics that have bogged us down in the past."

Hillary Clinton's base was traditional Democratic partisans: women, seniors, blue-collar voters, Catholics, and Latinos. Obama's base was young voters, affluent professionals and Independents, as well as African Americans who joined the Obama movement after they saw Obama win white votes in Iowa. Neither candidate could make inroads into the other's base. That's why the Democratic primary campaign stretched on so long. It turned into trench warfare, with each side trying to rally higher turnout from its base.

Obama's support among white voters looked very much like that of previous progressive Democrats: Eugene McCarthy in 1968, George McGovern in 1972, Gary Hart in 1984, Michael Dukakis in 1988, Paul Tsongas in 1992, Bill Bradley in 2000, and former Vermont governor Howard Dean in 2004. None of them except Obama got many black votes in the Democratic primaries. The African American vote gave Obama his crucial edge.

What was Obama's problem with white working-class voters? Was it race or class? Race clearly was a factor in Obama's weakness in the Appalachian region. Clinton beat Obama soundly in West Virginia, Kentucky, Arkansas, and Tennessee—states with large numbers of Appalachian whites and relatively few African Americans. But Obama's problem seemed bigger than race. As Stuart Rothenberg, editor of the *Rothenberg Political Report*, explained, "He talks at thirty-five thousand feet. He's much more of a professor giving a lecture than he is a candidate trying to connect with real people."

In Pennsylvania, white noncollege Democrats who said race was an important factor in their vote went for Clinton over Obama by four to one (79 percent to 20 percent). But only one Democrat in eight said race was an important factor. Four in five white working-class Democrats said race was not important. They voted for Clinton, too, by better than two to one (68 percent to 32 percent).[14] Which suggests that Obama's problem with those white voters was only partly racial. A lot of it was cultural.

Obama's educated upper-middle-class perspective suddenly became evident when his remarks at a San Francisco fund-raiser came to light. That's where he talked about blue-collar workers in Pennsylvania's small towns becoming "bitter" about their economic problems and clinging to "guns or religion" as a way to "explain their frustrations." Obama seemed to be saying that anxious workers turn to religion and guns because they are bitter and frustrated with their lives. The implication was that their values and lifestyle are irrational; that they are distractions from their true interests.

Obama's remarks drew a storm of protest from voters who felt they showed a lack of respect for rural and working-class values. A drawing of Obama with his nose in the air quickly made its way around conservative websites. The caption: "Snob. It's an elitist thing. You wouldn't understand." Hillary Clinton seized the opportunity to call Obama's remarks "elitist" and "out of touch." At one point, Clinton said, "People don't need a president who looks down on them."

Few Democrats do well with white working-class voters anymore. Jimmy Carter lost them in 1980. Walter Mondale lost them in 1984. Michael Dukakis lost them in 1988. Al Gore lost them in 2000. And John Kerry lost them in 2004. The average margin? Twenty-two points. The only Democratic presidential candidate who was competitive among white blue-collar voters in recent decades was Bill Clinton, who ended up tied with George H. W. Bush among noncollege white voters in 1992. He led Bob Dole by 1 point in 1996. And Obama? In November 2008 Obama lost noncollege white voters by 18 points and in 2012 by 25 points. In the 2014 midterm, noncollege white voters favored Republican House candidates by a gigantic margin: 64 percent to 34 percent.[15] In 2016 those voters were Donald Trump's core backers.

Obama won the nomination in 2008 by putting together an unusual coalition of "NPR Democrats" and African Americans. He defeated Hillary Clinton. But only barely (0.1 percent of the total popular Democratic vote). Clinton led Obama narrowly in the 2008 Democratic primary vote, but Obama led Clinton by better than two to one in the much smaller Democratic caucus vote.[16]

A primary is an election. A caucus is a meeting. Caucuses require a greater commitment of time and effort. They usually don't have a secret ballot. Caucus participants typically have to stand up in front of their friends and neighbors and God and everybody and declare publicly which candidate they are supporting. That's something most ordinary voters are reluctant to do. As a result, caucuses tend to be dominated by political activists. In 2008, Democratic activists favored Obama.

The 2008 election was driven more by events than by the campaign. Big events have big consequences. The financial crisis of 2008 was a big event. The campaign? Not so much. The debates, for instance, did not have much impact. The financial crash did.

Almost six in ten Americans believed the country was headed for another depression like the one in the 1930s. In early October 2008, 75 percent of voters who thought a depression was very likely were voting for Obama. Somewhat likely? 65 percent for Obama. Not very likely? A close split. Those who believed another depression was not likely at all? 63 percent for McCain.[17]

Obama won the election on the issues. On November 4 a solid 58 percent of the voters said their candidate's positions on the issues was what drove their vote; they went 60 percent for Obama. Just 39 percent said their vote was driven by their candidate's personal and leadership qualities. They went nearly 60 percent for McCain.[18]

Obama's victory was a victory for the New America, which meant, above all, young people. He got an amazing two-thirds of the vote among voters under thirty and just over half the vote among voters thirty to sixty-four years old. The only age group that voted for McCain was seniors. Literally, the Old America.[19]

In order to win the Republican nomination, John McCain had to do something he did not do when he first ran in 2000: accede to the conservative ascendancy over the Republican Party. It was symbolized by his victory in the South Carolina Republican primary. South Carolina, the conservative state that had ended the McCain campaign for the Republican nomination in 2000, crowned him the victor in 2008. McCain's choice of Sarah Palin as his running mate undermined any remaining pretense that he could be a unifying force.

In his victory speech on election night, Obama stated that Americans had "sent a message to the world that we have never been a collection of red states and blue states—we are and always will be the United States of America." It is a terrible irony that Obama failed to deliver on his promise. Elected as a uniter, Obama's policies intensified the country's political polarization. According to the Gallup poll, Democrats and Republicans were more divided over Obama's performance in 2016 than they had been over Clinton's and George W. Bush's when they left office.

Obama was the fourth president in a row who promised to unite the country and failed. The problem wasn't Obama. The problem was the standoff. No president could end it. In 2016, as we will see in chapter 11, the winning candidate didn't even bother to try.[20]

TEN

Failed Challenges

M any challengers have tried and failed to find the missing imperative. Sometimes they failed because of timing—a good message but the wrong year. Sometimes they failed because the candidate did not fit the message. And sometimes they failed because voters were not really missing what the opposition party believed they should be missing, either because the voters did not want it or because they already had it.

1964: Choice

In 1964 Barry Goldwater said he was running for president to offer voters "a choice, not an echo." It turned out to be a choice voters were not interested in.

Probably no Republican could have gotten elected in 1964. The nation was still in shock over the assassination of President Kennedy, and the economy was doing well. There were signs of impending conflict—civil rights protests, a still small-scale war in Vietnam—but the turmoil of "the sixties" had not yet hit. The year 1964 did not see a big market for change, much less for a clear-cut "choice."

Goldwater's candidacy was driven by conservatives who had felt frozen out of national politics since the 1920s. Conservatives had to endure twenty years of Democrats in the White House (FDR and Truman), followed by eight years of moderate Republican government under President Eisenhower. The final straw was the restoration of Democratic rule under Kennedy and LBJ.

Goldwater's issue was anti-Communism. Conservatives objected to the policy of "containing" Communism first articulated by President Truman and sustained by President Eisenhower. Conservatives didn't want to contain Communism. They wanted to roll it back to the point where the Soviet Union could be isolated and then defeated. After the world went to the brink of nuclear war during the Cuban Missile Crisis of 1962, those policies seemed reckless and provocative. To talk about liberating the "captive nations" of Eastern Europe came across as dangerous, though it eventually happened twenty-five years later. The famous "daisy ad," which ran precisely once on network television, depicted the Republican candidate as someone who was likely to blow up the world. The ad, which showed a little girl picking petals off a daisy and counting them, transitions to a countdown ending with a nuclear explosion. "These are the stakes," President Lyndon Johnson's voice-over intones gravely. "To make a world in which all God's children can live, or to go into the dark. We must either love each other, or we must die."

In accepting the vice presidential nomination, Hubert Humphrey electrified the Democratic convention when he said, "Most Democrats and Republicans in the Senate voted for the $11.5 billion tax cut . . . but not Senator Goldwater. Most Democrats and Republicans in the Senate—in fact, four-fifths of the members of his own party—voted for the Civil Rights Act, but not Senator Goldwater." The litany went on: . . . "the establishment of a United States Arms Control and Disarmament Agency . . . an expanded medical education program . . . the National Defense Education Act . . . the United Nations in its peacekeeping functions." As he listed Goldwater's transgressions, the crowd roared in response, "But not Senator Goldwater!"

Goldwater did not help his cause when he told the Republican convention, "I will remind you that extremism in the defense of liberty is no vice. And let me remind you also that moderation in the pursuit of justice is no virtue."

Goldwater certainly offered voters a clear-cut choice in 1964, but it was a choice they found extreme and dangerous in a year when change was not a priority. The assassination of President Kennedy and the accession of President Johnson the previous November was enough change for most Americans. Nevertheless, the Goldwater campaign did set in motion the conservative takeover of the Republican Party. In 1964 Ronald Reagan delivered a nationally televised speech on behalf of the Goldwater campaign. Its title? "A Time for Choosing." That time was not 1964. But it did come about sixteen years later.

1972: Peace

The McGovern movement is often seen as a bookend to the Goldwater movement. Republicans moved right in 1964 when they nominated

Goldwater, who was soundly repudiated by the voters (38 percent of the vote). Democrats moved left in 1972 when they nominated George McGovern, who was soundly repudiated by the voters (38 percent of the vote). Nevertheless, both candidates had an enduring impact on their parties. Republicans were transformed into a conservative party, while liberals became the dominant influence in the Democratic Party.

In 1972, anti–Vietnam War voters remained intensely angry after the establishment candidate, Hubert Humphrey, "stole" the Democratic nomination at the tumultuous 1968 Democratic convention in Chicago. Two antiwar candidates, Eugene McCarthy and Robert F. Kennedy, had won the 1968 Democratic primaries. Humphrey, who did not compete in the primaries, got the nomination because of his support from party bosses such as Chicago mayor Richard J. Daley.

For the next four years, antiwar voters were a movement in search of a leader. After the 1968 convention, McGovern cochaired the commission that rewrote the party's nominating rules. Beginning in 1972, party nominees were to be chosen by ordinary voters participating in party primaries and caucuses. The insiders who had given Humphrey the nomination were shoved aside. Antiwar activists dominated the process in 1972 and propelled McGovern to the Democratic nomination, starting with his surprise victory in the Iowa caucuses and his strong second-place finish (to Senator Edmund Muskie from nearby Maine) in the New Hampshire primary.

The irony of the 1972 election was that American voters had turned decisively against the war in Vietnam. In the end, however, they did not vote for the antiwar candidate. That was partly because of McGovern's association with left-wing causes. The Nixon campaign labeled McGovern the candidate of "acid, amnesty, and abortion." It was also because of the chaotic Democratic convention that saw McGovern deliver his acceptance speech at three o'clock in the morning Eastern time. And because of his disastrous choice of Senator Tom Eagleton as his running mate. When Eagleton's medical record revealed that he had undergone electroshock therapy, McGovern proclaimed himself "one thousand percent" behind his choice—but subsequently dropped him from the ticket in favor of R. Sargent Shriver.

A major reason for McGovern's failure was that voters fed up with the war did not see him as the better choice for peace. As we saw in chapter 1, the country was antiwar but not dovish. When President Nixon was elected in 1968, he was reported to have a "secret peace plan" to end the war. Nixon never actually said that. In off-the-record briefings, Nixon and his aides encouraged antiwar journalists to believe he had a peace plan.[1] Four years later, the war was still going on, and voters were likely to hold Nixon accountable for not ending it. So President Nixon promised "peace with honor" and trotted out Henry Kissinger, his national security adviser, to announce that "peace is at hand." It wasn't. US troops continued active combat for nine more months. US personnel were finally evacuated in April 1975, almost nine months after Nixon had resigned.

The peace theme did not work for McGovern even though voters desperately wanted peace in 1972. The Republican campaign managed to convince them that Nixon was the more reliable choice for peace, especially because Nixon had already reduced the US troop commitment by more than 90 percent.

1984: Fairness

The 1984 election was a vote of confidence in Ronald Reagan, just as the 1980 election had been a vote of no confidence in Jimmy Carter. It also showed more clearly the outlines of the New America coalition that was coming to define the Democratic Party. The campaign solidified the Reagan coalition as the dominant force in American politics. The New Deal Democratic coalition had prevailed from the 1930s to the 1960s. The Reagan coalition came to power in 1980, consolidated its majority in 1984, and dominated politics for the next quarter century.

Many believe the decisive moment in the campaign came on July 19, during the Democratic National Convention in San Francisco, when Walter Mondale said in his acceptance speech, "Let me tell the truth. It must be done. Mr. Reagan will raise taxes, and so will I. He won't tell you. I just did."

It had a nice rhythm. It certainly startled Democrats and caught Republicans off guard. Was there some devious strategy here? Was Mondale trying to snooker President Reagan into categorically ruling out any tax increase, so that he could then argue that Reagan would be forced to cut Social Security and Medicare in order to reduce the deficit? If that was the strategy, it didn't work. Voters heard three words: "So will I." Mondale was making a campaign promise to raise taxes! It was an invitation for Republicans to depict him as another tax-and-spend liberal. And they did.

President Reagan's job approval ratings held steady at 55 percent to 60 percent through the whole campaign, which is to say that most Americans felt he deserved to be reelected. Reagan had two things going for him: the economy and foreign policy. Those are not small things. Democrats got exactly nowhere trying to convince people that the president had failed in either area.

Reagan did the two things he was elected to do. He curbed inflation, and he restored the nation's military security. As it happens, many people disagreed with the way he accomplished those goals. Inflation was reduced at the cost of a severe recession. We improved our military strength at the cost of a significantly higher level of international tension. Still, after four failed presidencies in a row, it was rare enough to have a president who did what he was elected to do. As Reagan was fond of saying, "You don't quarrel with success."

Democrats had done very well by campaigning on the "fairness" issue in the 1982 midterm election. The economy had gone from bad to worse. The Reagan administration and the Federal Reserve used a deep recession to squeeze inflation out of the economy. Two years later, Walter Mondale ran on the fairness issue, but his timing was off. When the economy is bad, middle-class people are receptive to the argument that something may be wrong with the system. They say, "People like me are hardworking and have the right values, and we still can't make it. The system isn't fair."

In 1984, however, it was "Morning Again in America," as the slogan from a Reagan campaign ad put it. When the economy is good, middle-class Americans say, "I'm doing okay, and so are people like me. If some people aren't making it, maybe it's their own fault. There's nothing wrong with the system." The fairness issue falls flat.

In 1980 a lot of voters were worried about Reagan's foreign policy. Democrats ran ads suggesting that Reagan was going to blow us all up. That concern remained widespread after Reagan won. No sooner did he take office than a nuclear freeze movement broke out all over the world. By 1984, however, those fears had diminished. Reagan had been president for four years, and we were still here. Polls showed that in 1984 voters were less concerned with Reagan's recklessness or his intellectual competence than they were in 1980. That is what incumbency does for you.

The Reagan campaign put to rest lingering concerns about the

candidate's recklessness by running one of the most subtle and imagina-
tive ads in American political history: the "Bear in the Woods" ad. The
ad showed a vaguely menacing bear on the prowl. The narration said,
"There is a bear in the woods. For some people, the bear is easy to see.
Others don't see it at all. Some people say the bear is tame. Others say
it's vicious. And dangerous. Since no one can really be sure who's right,
isn't it smart to be as strong as the bear? If there is a bear."

The masterstroke of the 1984 campaign turned out to be Reagan's
"feel-good" commercials, which worked because they tapped a genuine
sentiment among voters: that things were getting better under Reagan's
leadership. Those commercials would have looked ridiculous in 1982,
when things were very bad. Reality imposes limits on a campaign's ability to manipulate the public.

In 1984 you could see a new Democratic Party emerging. The 1984
election revealed marked changes in the nature of the Democratic vote
over the previous three decades. Both Walter Mondale and Adlai Stevenson were midwestern liberals, and both got about the same share
of the national vote (41 percent for Mondale in 1984; 42 percent for
Stevenson in 1956). But the sources of their support were very different.
Mondale did significantly better than Stevenson among black voters,
college graduates, women, Jews, and professionals. Stevenson's support
had been much stronger among whites, southerners, men, blue-collar
workers, union members, and Catholics.[2]

Voters were excited briefly when Mondale chose as his running
mate New York congresswoman Geraldine Ferraro, the first woman
ever nominated on a national party ticket. Just after the Democratic
convention, a *Newsweek* poll showed Mondale slightly ahead of Reagan. It was the only poll that ever showed Mondale leading. In the end,

however, both men and women went for Reagan: men by 25 points, women by 12.

My keenest recollection of the 1984 campaign was my experience on election night. I was in Los Angeles, working with the *Los Angeles Times* on its exit poll. National Public Radio had engaged me to participate in its *Morning Edition* broadcast the next morning at five o'clock West Coast time. After the newspaper shut down for the night, I went off to the NPR studio in Santa Monica.

But the NPR engineer had closed the studio and gone home. He forgot that I was scheduled to appear early that morning. There were no cell phones in those days. Nearby businesses were all closed. The only option was to find the nearest pay phone. I found an open-air telephone (no booth) on a residential street corner.

Because the telephone transmission was poor, I had to shout the entire interview—in the pitch darkness. As I spoke, I noticed lights coming on in the surrounding houses. Residents started wandering outside to see what all the commotion was. This was in Santa Monica, remember—a citadel of liberalism in the middle of Reagan country.

The good residents of Santa Monica were shouting at me—not "Pipe down, it's five o'clock in the morning!" but "He's wrong! He doesn't know what he's talking about!" They found my analysis of the Democrats' dire situation unpersuasive. In their view, the American electorate had been fooled by Ronald Reagan just as California voters had been fooled by him for the eight years of his governorship. "Reagan's a fraud!" they shouted. "Mondale speaks the truth!" Somehow Reagan had managed to fool the voters in forty-nine states—all but Mondale's home state of Minnesota and the District of Columbia.

The shouting did not end when I completed the NPR interview. The good people of Santa Monica continued to air their complaints after I hung up the telephone. I found myself conducting an impromptu election seminar with an audience of angry liberals standing in the street in their bathrobes and fuzzy slippers in the early morning darkness. Such are the passions of modern politics.

1988: Competence

"This election isn't about ideology. It's about competence." With those words, Michael Dukakis defined the theme of his campaign. The Massachusetts governor was an experienced public official thoroughly familiar with how government worked. He understood the mechanics of government, how the gears meshed and the wheels turned. Dukakis had the image of a wonk. He acknowledged that he once read a book about Swedish land-use planning while on holiday.

It might have worked if Dukakis were running against Ronald Reagan, who was anything but a policy wonk. In the Iran-contra affair, he didn't even know what was going on in the White House basement, where an unlawful plan was being organized to sell arms to Iran and divert the funds to a guerrilla group in Nicaragua. The Tower Commission, which was appointed to investigate the scandal, faulted President Reagan for "a lax managerial style and aloofness from policy detail." Michael Dukakis was never aloof from policy detail.

But Dukakis was not running against President Reagan. His opponent was George H. W. Bush. The sitting vice president had held just about every top job in Washington, including director of the Central Intelligence Agency (CIA). As for the Iran-contra affair, Bush declared publicly that he was "out of the loop—no operational role" in the scheme. Later, it was revealed that Bush had kept a diary in which he recorded, shortly after the scandal broke, "I'm one of the few people that know fully the details."[3]

How big a shock was the 1988 election for Democrats? About as big as the 1948 election had been for Republicans.

In 1948 everyone "knew" that Harry Truman could not be elected. Truman had taken office when Franklin D. Roosevelt suddenly died just eighty-two days into his fourth term. Truman was in the shadow of FDR; surely he was diminished by the comparison. Democrats had won four presidential elections in a row, all by FDR; surely it was time for a change. Republicans won control of both houses of Congress in 1946 for the first time since 1928; surely that was an omen.

Moreover, there were not one or two but three Democrats running for president in 1948. Truman (the Democratic candidate), Strom Thurmond (States' Rights Democratic candidate, or "Dixiecrat"), and former vice president Henry Wallace (Progressive Party). With the Democratic vote split three ways, surely Truman could not win. The outcome was so certain, pollsters stopped polling two weeks before the election, when Republican Thomas Dewey seemed safely ahead.

To the shock and dismay of Republicans—including the editors of the *Chicago Daily Tribune*, whose famous post–Election Day headline was "Dewey Defeats Truman"—Truman won.

In 1988 there were many reasons why Vice President George Bush could not be elected president.

1. Bush was a sitting vice president. No sitting vice president had been elected president in 152 years. Being vice president is a great way to get your party's presidential nomination. Primary voters are mostly party loyalists. Loyalty is the defining quality of a successful vice president. Party

loyalists value and reward loyalty. So Republicans nominated Richard Nixon in 1960. Democrats nominated Hubert Humphrey in 1968, Walter Mondale in 1984, and Al Gore in 2000. They all lost. In 1988 the vice presidency did to Bush what it always does to people who hold that office. It turned him into a wimp.

A vice president is never his own man. Richard Nixon was Eisenhower's man, Humphrey was LBJ's man, Mondale was Carter's man, and Gore was Clinton's man. In 1988 Bush was Reagan's man. But 1988 was the exception. If they couldn't keep President Reagan, voters wanted Reagan's man in the White House.

2. Bush was born to wealth and privilege. Republicans had not dared to nominate a well-born candidate since President William Howard Taft. They paid a price when Taft was defeated for reelection in 1912. A conservative president in a progressive era, Taft came in third with less than a quarter of the vote, behind two progressives: Democrat Woodrow Wilson and former president Theodore Roosevelt.

3. Bush ran at the wrong end of the election cycle. After a party has been in power for eight years, the voters are usually ready for a change. With no elected incumbent on the ballot, the contest is often close, and the party out of power wins. That's what happened in 1960, 1968, 1976, 2000, 2008, and 2016.

4. Bush chose Senator Dan Quayle as his running mate. Quayle's qualifications were widely in doubt. According to a 1988 exit poll conducted by CNN and the *Los Angeles*

Times, Quayle drew an astonishingly negative response from voters on Election Day: 46 percent to 32 percent unfavorable. But the Bush-Quayle ticket still won. That was strong evidence that Americans do not vote for vice president. For Democrats, losing in 1988 was worse than a defeat. "I can't tell you how humiliated I am to think of losing to Bush and Quayle," a Democratic partisan said to me just before the election.

Republicans knew from the outset that if the election turned out to be a referendum on Bush, they would lose. So they made it a referendum on Dukakis. The central issue in the campaign became Dukakis's values rather than Bush's judgment. Bush called Dukakis a Massachusetts liberal. Dukakis had a hard time denying it. He *was* a Massachusetts liberal. It just wasn't anything he'd planned on talking about during the campaign. Dukakis, like George McGovern in 1972, was an avatar of the New America. And another doomed Democrat.

The year 1988 marked the emergence of a key element of the Old America as a political force in the Republican Party: the religious right. Pat Robertson startled the political world by coming in second in the Iowa Republican caucuses. "The question that's been raised repeatedly during this campaign," Robertson said the next day, "is whether the silent and invisible army was really out there. Well, it turned out." In 1996 Robertson told the leaders of the Christian Coalition in secretly taped remarks, "We said that by the year 2000, we'd have the presidency. That's to me the next goal . . . We are going to have a profamily conservative sitting in the White House, so help us God." Robertson's prediction turned out to be true. But it was fulfilled not by the first President Bush but by his son.

When Dukakis announced his choice of Senator Lloyd Bentsen as his running mate, he evoked the image of the 1960 Kennedy-Johnson ticket: Massachusetts and Texas. Why 1960? After all, Democrats barely won the election that year. But 1960 had a larger symbolic meaning for Democrats: it was the last year before Democrats started embracing a new liberal agenda. "They thought they could make this a value-free election," a Dukakis aide said later about Democratic strategists. Dukakis discovered that it is impossible to exclude values from a presidential contest.

One question loomed over the 1988 election long after it was over: Did George H. W. Bush run a racist campaign? Critics such as Jesse Jackson and Lloyd Bentsen accused Bush of using the crime issue as a thinly veiled appeal to racism. Crime is a legitimate campaign issue, of course, especially to African Americans, who are most often victimized by crime.

In 1988 Bush did the same thing Republican candidates had been doing since Richard Nixon's Southern Strategy. He took advantage of racism. Ronald Reagan played to racial resentment when he talked about "welfare queens," a term he first used at a 1976 campaign rally: "She used eighty names, thirty addresses, fifteen telephone numbers to collect food stamps, social security, veterans' benefits, for four nondeceased veteran husbands, as well as welfare." The woman, whose racial background was not clear, was in fact convicted of defrauding the welfare system. Reagan took advantage of racism when he vetoed the 1988 civil rights bill and a bill imposing sanctions on the apartheid regime in South Africa. He resisted the extension of the Voting Rights Act of 1965 and tried to protect tax subsidies for private all-white schools.

In his 1988 campaign, George H. W. Bush allowed his supporters to run a racially explosive ad featuring a photo of Willie Horton, a black rapist and murderer who had been released on furlough from a Massachusetts prison and then went on to commit assault and rape. Lee Atwater, Bush's campaign strategist, used the Willie Horton ad to discredit Governor Dukakis as soft on crime. It was the signature Atwater strategy, exploiting racial fear and resentment without allowing his candidate to sound like an outright racist.

Twice in American history, the federal government has acted to deliver African Americans from intolerable situations: from slavery in the 1860s and from segregation in the 1960s. As a result, most African Americans do not respond to the antigovernment rhetoric of the Republican Party. They do not see the federal government as their oppressor. They are tied to the Democratic Party by racial interest and, for disadvantaged African Americans, by economic interest as well.

The race issue in this country is linked inextricably to the issue of big government. It always has been.

1996: Character

Could any Republican have defeated Bill Clinton in 1996? The answer is no. No incumbent president with a job approval rating in the high 50s loses a bid for reelection. Voters believed Clinton did what he was elected to do: turn around the economy. Just as in 1984, when voters believed Ronald Reagan did what he was elected to do. When people are happy with the incumbent's performance, there isn't much of a market for change.

Republican nominee Senator Bob Dole had another problem. He led the opposition party, but he didn't come across as a candidate of change. Not after thirty-five years in Washington. When voters were asked in 1996, "Which candidate do you think will bring needed change to government?" the answer, amazingly, was Bill Clinton—the incumbent!

The character issue was the focus of Dole's campaign. Dole's bumper stickers said, "Bob Dole. A Better Man. For a Better America."

"The slogan says it all," Governor Tom Ridge of Pennsylvania told a 1996 campaign rally where a banner with the theme was displayed behind the podium. The theme appeared, with slightly different punctuation, in Dole ads that year ("The Better Man for a Better America").

The fact is, most Americans did believe that Bob Dole was "a better man" than Bill Clinton. As early as 1992, voters expressed doubts that Clinton was "honest and trustworthy." (A majority voted for either George H. W. Bush or Ross Perot.) The first thing Americans heard about Bill Clinton in 1992 was the accusation of adultery by Gennifer Flowers, an Arkansas state employee who claimed to have had a twelve-year affair with Governor Clinton. Flowers's charges were followed by a CBS *60 Minutes* interview in which the Clintons defended their marriage. The controversy over Clinton's draft record emerged a few weeks later during the New Hampshire primary campaign. A week before the primary, a letter surfaced in which a young Bill Clinton thanked a colonel in the Reserve Officers' Training Corps for "saving me from the draft." In contrast, Dole was a wounded World War II veteran who had won two Purple Hearts and a Bronze Star for valor on the battlefield.

Voters agreed that Dole was "a better man" than Bill Clinton. Didn't character matter? Yes, it did. But performance mattered more. When Americans vote for president, they see it like hiring a plumber. In 1992 the basement was full of water, and the house was in danger of collapsing. The plumber they hired in 1988 had been in the basement for four years, but nothing seemed to get fixed. When you hire a plumber, you want to know one thing: Can he get the job done? You don't ask too many questions about his draft record or his love life. That's how voters hired Bill Clinton in 1992.

Character does count for something, of course. You want to be sure the plumber is not going to cheat you or rob the house. Did voters feel reassured about Clinton after four years? Not entirely. On Election Day 1996, the exit poll asked, "Do you think Bill Clinton is honest and trustworthy?" Again voters said no, 54 percent to 41 percent. So how in the world did he win?[4]

Clinton's campaign strategy was simply to tout his record. Particularly his centrist record after 1994, when Republicans took over Congress. "We have reduced the federal government to its smallest size in thirty years," Clinton argued. "We've reduced more regulations, eliminated more programs than my two Republican predecessors. I have worked hard for things like the Family and Medical Leave Act, the Brady Bill, the assault weapons ban, the program to put a hundred thousand police on the street . . . to help families impart values to their children . . . We're the first administration in anybody's lifetime to bring the deficit down four years in a row."

The president's carefully planned strategy of moving to the center worked. Clinton pledged to protect "the safety net." Specifically, four federal programs that, in reporters' shorthand, became "M-squared, E-squared." "I will not stand for a budget that jeopardizes these bedrock commitments to Medicare, Medicaid, education, and the environment," the president said in April 1996—and many times afterward.

President Clinton's achievement was to show Democrats how to survive at a time when the Reagan consensus still dominated US politics. Clinton's values were those of the New America. But the country wasn't quite there yet.

In the end, voters in 1996 who said character was more important than issues voted 71 percent for Dole. Those who said issues were
more important than character voted 69 percent for Clinton. Which
was more important to voters? Issues trumped character, 58 percent to
38 percent.[5]

In 1992, voters went to the polls with their eyes wide open and
their fingers crossed. They were betting that Clinton could get the job
done and that his apparent character flaws would not create a crisis. By
1996, the gamble seemed to be paying off. The economy was turning
around: unemployment had dropped from 7.4 percent to 5.2 percent.
The crisis over Clinton's personal conduct in office did occur eventually, but not until 1998. For Dole to run on the character issue was not
a bad strategy. He just did it two years too early.

Despite the complaints about the press covering the election as if it
were a horse race, one thing is clear: voters lose interest if the election
is *not* a horse race. More than two hundred public polls of the presidential race were released in 1996. Bob Dole was behind in every single
one. You can't fill the stands if everybody knows which horse is going
to win. Campaigns need excitement, thrills, tension. The press wanted
a horse race, and it did everything it could to create one: hyping Dole's
leave-taking of the Senate; swooning over his choice of conservative
idea man Jack Kemp, an influential congressman from New York, as his
running mate; dramatizing his tax cut plan; and digging up dirt about
Clinton's fund-raising operation.

But those damned polls kept coming out saying that none of it
made any difference. The voters just weren't buying Dole. Nothing
about the campaign excited them. "Where is the outrage?" Dole complained. He wanted outrage? He might have talked about the public's

racially polarized reaction a year earlier to the O. J. Simpson verdict of acquittal for double homicide.

2004: Strength

2004 was a base election: an all-out war between the core supporters of both political parties. Voter turnout jumped to 60.7 percent of the voting-eligible population, the highest level since 1968.[6] In a contest of energized bases, Republicans usually have the advantage. As noted earlier, there have long been more self-described conservatives than liberals in the US electorate.[7] In the end, George W. Bush was reelected, but only by a narrow margin (50.7 percent of the popular vote to John Kerry's 48.3 percent). The Bush campaign unleashed the dogs of political war, and President Bush's narrow victory came at the cost of bitter division.

The rhetoric was hot. "How dare the incompetent and willful members of this Bush-Cheney administration humiliate our nation and our people in the eyes of the world and in the conscience of our own people!" Al Gore fumed. "How dare they subject us to such dishonor and disgrace!"

The contempt was mutual. Vice President Dick Cheney suggested that a John Kerry victory would mean more terrorist attacks: "If we make the wrong choice, then the danger is that we'll get hit again, and we'll be hit in a way that will be devastating." Just after Kerry won the nomination in March 2004, when he didn't realize his microphone was hot, he said of the Bush campaign, "These guys are the most crooked, lying group of people I've ever seen."

Both sides were spoiling for a fight. As pollster Celinda Lake observed, "In the case of the Democratic base, and the same for the

Republican base, it's like, 'Why should we wait? We'd like to vote to-morrow. We're ready.' "

The 2004 election was the first presidential election after 9/11. The economy was just emerging from recession, and the war in Iraq had be-come controversial. But President Bush's image of strength and resolve persisted. He had defied the terrorists a few days after the attacks when he pledged retaliation. He had achieved the overthrow of the Taliban in Afghanistan.

Democrats would not get anywhere unless they put up a candidate who could match Bush's image of strength. That initially drew them to Howard Dean. In response to President Bush's Thanksgiving trip to Baghdad, Iraq, in November 2003, the former Vermont governor said, "Mr. President, if you'll pardon me, I'll teach you a little about defense." Dean was no wimpy liberal. He was tough and feisty. That's what Dem-ocrats liked about him. "We can't wait to see our guy in a debate with Bush," one of his supporters told me at a Dean meet-up in 2003. "When Bush punches him, he'll punch back. Hell, he might even punch first!"

Liberals felt bullied. They felt bullied by the Bush White House and the Republican Congress and the radio talk shows and the growing right-wing influence in the media. CBS even got bullied into cancel-ing its miniseries *The Reagans* in 2003 because conservatives protested that the portrayal of their icon was unbalanced. Liberals were looking for a candidate who would stand up to the bullies. That's what Dean promised to do.

John Kerry was not only a war hero. He was also an antiwar hero, at least to the left. Kerry initially made his national reputation when he came home from Vietnam with a Bronze Star, a Silver Star, and three Purple Hearts and became a national spokesperson for Vietnam Veter-ans Against the War. He testified before Congress in 1971, "We wish

that a merciful God could wipe away our own memories of that service." Democrats took a calculated risk when they played up Kerry's
image as a war hero. It opened him up to attacks from critics who were
still enraged, several decades later, by Kerry's antiwar activism. One
anti-Kerry ad asked, "In a time of war, can America trust a man who
betrayed his country?"

At the end of the 2004 campaign, there was a brief but intense debate over the impact of "values" on the election. After a court decision
made same-sex marriage legal in Massachusetts in 2003, conservative
activists got anti–gay marriage measures on the ballot in eleven states
in the 2004 election. All the initiatives passed, with an average of about
70 percent support. In a speech at Hamilton College a week after the
2004 election, Bill Clinton said, "With regard to the gay marriage issue,
it was an overwhelming factor in the defeat of John Kerry. There's no
question about it." Another former Democratic presidential candidate,
Michael Dukakis, had a different opinion about what happened to
Kerry, who was once his lieutenant governor. "I don't think that George
Bush won this because of gay marriage or evangelical Christianity or
any of this stuff," Dukakis said. "He won it, in my judgment, on the
national security issue."

Dukakis was right. Values issues such as gay marriage certainly mobilized both parties' bases. But the Bush campaign also undertook a
parallel and more visible effort to turn the 2004 campaign into a referendum on terrorism. Specifically, the White House moved the spotlight
away from the war in Iraq and toward the war against Al Qaeda. In
mid-September, after the party conventions, a CNN poll showed that
voters whose top concern was Iraq were voting for Kerry (56 percent
to 40 percent). Voters whose top concern was terrorism were overwhelmingly for President Bush (87 percent to 13 percent). Bush's issue,

terrorism, pushed aside Kerry's issue, the war in Iraq. The handover of authority to the Iraqis in June 2004 had exactly the effect the White House intended: it made Iraq seem like less of an American problem, at least for the time being.

The Republicans' message in 2004 was: elect Kerry, and terrorists may kill you. Democrats were outraged. Kerry's running mate, John Edwards, called the Republican charges un-American. But not unheard-of. Fear tactics often work against a largely unknown challenger—like Barry Goldwater in 1964, who was hit with the famous "daisy ad." The message was, elect Goldwater, and you could bring on a nuclear catastrophe.

Jimmy Carter had tried the same thing against Ronald Reagan in 1980. Carter charged that Reagan's "radical and irresponsible course would threaten our security and put the whole world in peril." In 1984 the Reagan reelection campaign turned the argument against the Democrats with the "Bear in the Woods" ad: "Isn't it smart to be as strong as the bear?" Fears had shifted, from Republican recklessness to Democratic weakness. The GOP exploited that fear in 1988 with an ad that made Michael Dukakis look silly riding in a tank: "Now he wants to be our commander in chief. America can't afford that risk."

Scare tactics work if they are based on real concerns about a candidate: Goldwater as trigger happy, Dukakis as weak. Were there concerns about John Kerry? When the ABC News–*Washington Post* poll asked which candidate would keep the country safer, voters preferred Bush by nearly 20 points (54 percent to 35 percent).

It was Bill Clinton who offered the best analysis of the 2004 election: "When people feel insecure, they'd rather have somebody that's strong and wrong than somebody who's weak and right." Clinton actually said that in December 2002. It turned out to be a prematurely accurate assessment, from a Democratic perspective, of what happened two years later. The lesson for Democrats in 2004 was: strong and wrong beats weak and right.

In 2004 John Kerry banked a lot on his image as a war hero. From his Iowa reunion with a man whose life he had saved in Vietnam, to the opening line of his acceptance speech—"I'm John Kerry, and I'm reporting for duty"—the senator's message was strength. It was the right message for a country still in shock after 9/11. Especially for a Democratic Party that had a lingering antimilitary image.

There was just one problem: the country already had a strong commander in chief. President Bush was famous for his resolve. He took full advantage of that early in the 2004 primary season when he made the decision to label Kerry a flip-flopper. The charge stuck, especially after Kerry explained a few days later how he had voted for a supplemental military appropriation before he voted against it.

The Swift Boat Veterans for Truth, a political committee formed in 2004 by a group of Vietnam war veterans, opposed Kerry's candidacy for president and tried to discredit his military record. The group's smear campaign landed a major blow on Kerry's image of strength. It wasn't just that they raised doubts about his war record. Kerry was unaccountably slow to respond to their charges. The Swift Boat group ran its first ad on August 5, a week after the Democratic convention. It was two weeks later that Kerry responded. In an August Pew poll, Bush led Kerry as a strong leader who was good in a crisis and who would take a stand and stick to it. President Bush professed innocence of the Swift Boat attacks. Indeed, he praised Kerry's "noble service" in Vietnam. (Bush served in the Texas Air National Guard during the Vietnam war.) When asked to denounce the Swift Boat ad, Bush condemned all "unregulated soft-money expenditures by very wealthy people." A position Democrats portrayed, justifiably, as disingenuous.

In October 2004, 65 percent of voters in a CNN poll said Kerry had changed his positions on issues for political reasons. And President Bush? No flip-flopper he. By 60 percent to 36 percent, voters in 2004 said Bush had not changed his positions for political reasons. He was Mr. Resolve.[8] Kerry made the point that there is a fine line between resolve and stubbornness, but the country did not discover it until Bush's second term.

2012: Austerity

No president in recent decades has gotten reelected with economic numbers as bad as Obama had in 2012. Most objective indicators showed that the economic recovery had stalled. Job growth was less than a hundred thousand a month, not fast enough to keep up with the growth of the labor force. At the same time, subjective indicators were improving. Consumer confidence was up. The number of voters who believed the country was headed in the right direction was the highest since 2009, according to an NBC News–*Wall Street Journal* poll. So was the number who believed the economy would get better in the next year. Most Americans said they thought the nation's economy was recovering.[9]

What drove the optimism? Politics. Optimism about the economy grew fastest among Democrats. It was their way of expressing confidence in Obama. Instead of the weak economy dragging down the president, his growing popularity pulled up economic confidence. Most forecasting models assume that the economy is the cause and the election is the effect. Sometimes that may be backwards.

The economy had been recovering in 1992, but voters refused to acknowledge it because they had lost confidence in the first President Bush. He didn't seem to be doing anything to boost the economy, and that made things look worse. He appeared hopelessly out of touch with ordinary Americans. Mitt Romney had the same problem twenty years later.

In 2012 Romney ran a sharply focused campaign that promoted a simple message: he was a turnaround artist. "All of these experiences—starting and running businesses for twenty-five years, turning around the Olympics, governing a state—have helped shape who I am and how I lead . . . Turning around a crisis takes experienced leadership and bold action." Romney had been called upon to save the scandal-ridden 2002 Winter Olympic Games in Salt Lake City, Utah. Under Romney's leadership, the games became a financial success. Romney was a business executive. Very few business executives had been elected president. (Two of them were named Bush; another was Herbert Hoover, who was president at the onset of the Great Depression.) Romney counted on his management credentials to give him credibility as someone who could do what Obama had failed to do so far: turn around the economy.

Critics called Romney a takeover artist. His private equity firm, Bain Capital, sometimes took over small companies and squeezed them for profits by cutting costs, increasing debt, and laying off workers. According to the *New York Times*, the company "made eye-popping sums of money in deal after deal."

Romney needed to revitalize his campaign. I tell students that there are ten reasons to choose a running mate. Reason number one: pick someone who will help you win. The other nine reasons don't matter. When he named Paul Ryan as his running mate in August, Romney signaled a major redefinition of his campaign. It was no longer mainly about creating jobs and turning around the economy. It was about fiscal discipline and turning around the budget. That was Ryan's calling; the congressman from Wisconsin was chairman of the House Budget Committee.

Romney's initial turnaround message wasn't resonating. After all, his experience was not in creating jobs. It was in creating wealth, for himself and for his investors. That's what private equity firms do. The polls, which had been virtually tied all year, began to show an Obama lead in late summer. Romney was under pressure to change course—fast. Hence, Paul Ryan, who came out of the world of conservative think tanks and policy wonks. Ryan had his own "road map" that offered a bracing regimen of fiscal discipline aimed at getting the nation's debt under control largely by reining in spending on entitlements—Medicare, Medicaid, and Social Security—which are the programs with the broadest public support.

The basic difference between the two major parties is this: Republicans believe economic growth is sufficient. If the economy is growing, people can solve their own problems. Government should just get out of the way. Democrats believe economic growth is necessary but not sufficient. Government has to provide a safety net for people who are economically vulnerable.

If the 2012 campaign were a debate over economic growth, Obama would have lost. Instead, Republicans turned it into a debate over the safety net. Ronald Reagan was the first president to use the term "safety net." He promised to protect it. The Romney-Ryan Republicans threatened to shred the safety net. There has never been a big market for that message.

By naming Ryan, Romney appeared to be embracing Ryan's proposed budget, which called for nearly $4 trillion in federal spending cuts over ten years. Many government services would shrink to a level not seen since the 1930s. Ryan proposed changing Medicare from a guaranteed benefit program to a private insurance program with government assistance for beneficiaries who could not afford the premiums. He proposed changing Medicaid to a block grant program where states receive federal funds for a broad social purpose—providing health care for low-income citizens—and can decide for themselves how to allocate and spend the money.

It was an austerity budget, although Ryan claimed it would "preempt austerity" by stimulating economic growth. Romney warned that the United States should not be like Europe, where big government had created a genuine debt crisis. "At some point," the candidate said, "America is going to become like Greece or like Spain or Italy—or like California." Most European countries adopted tough austerity programs to deal with debt. And what happened? Angry voters threw out governments left (Spain) and right (France). And extremist parties, especially anti-immigrant parties, started to pick up support.

In mid-September, *Mother Jones* magazine leaked a video of Romney's remarks at a Florida fund-raiser. The political impact was devastating. The Republican candidate came across as disdainful of what he called the "47 percent" of Americans who depend on the government safety net, depicting them as slackers and freeloaders. Romney's remark clinched the case: he would protect the rich while cutting services for people who depend on the government safety net because, as he put it, "My job is not to worry about those people." Romney acknowledged later that what he said was "completely wrong," but the damage persisted because he matched the stereotype of the country club conservative.

In 2012 the culture wars that began in the sixties finally seemed to shift to the advantage of liberals and Democrats, at least in presidential elections when the New America comes out to vote. The first sign of the shift came in 1998, when the public sided overwhelmingly with President Clinton in the impeachment drama. The tilt was confirmed in 2012, when voters approved of same-sex marriage in popular referendums. Before 2012, same-sex marriage had been rejected by voters thirty-two times. In 2012 it was approved by voters in all four states where it was on the ballot.

The conventional wisdom saw 2012 as a status quo election. The president was reelected. Democrats continued to have a majority in the Senate. Republicans retained control of the House of Representatives. Only two states changed their presidential votes from 2008 to 2012: North Carolina and Indiana, both of which went from Democratic in 2008 to Republican in 2012. All that sound and fury and almost nothing changed.

In 2012 the New America defeated the forces of reaction. There were some doubts about whether the 2008 majority would show up a second time. Many Democrats were disappointed in President Obama and frustrated by his inability to deliver the hope and change he had promised. But they did show up. What drove them to the polls was not hope but fear: fear that Tea Party Republicans would take over the country.

ELEVEN

2016: Populist Backlash

Nothing captures the breakdown of American politics more than the election of Donald J. Trump. Not only did most voters on Election Day 2016 see him as unqualified for the job, but they also didn't think he was honest and trustworthy. (Almost two-thirds, or 64 percent, said he was not.) They didn't even like him (60 percent unfavorable rating).

It wasn't because voters thought his Democratic opponent was worse. In each case, Trump's ratings were worse than Hillary Clinton's. Of course, Trump didn't actually win the popular vote. He got 46 percent to Hillary Clinton's 48 percent. He won the election by the rules. The rules say that the winner is chosen by the electoral college, and Trump won 306 electoral votes to Hillary Clinton's 232.

Chapter 1 raised the question, How did we get from John F. Kennedy to Donald J. Trump? The simple answer is that Trump figured out a way to turn bitter division into a political asset. It worked well for him in 2016 (with help from the Kremlin). As president, Trump tried to keep the division going by declaring war on the press ("the enemy of the American people").

Trump thrives on perpetual political war. The division he created was a variation on the country's longstanding ideological schism: liberal versus conservative. Trump added a populist dimension by fiercely attacking the cosmopolitan ruling class of both political parties. "There is nothing that the political establishment will not do, no lie that they won't tell, to hold their prestige and power at your expense," he told a rally in Florida.

Trump, like any shrewd businessman, is a consummate opportunist. The bitter division in American politics created an opportunity ripe for exploitation.

He saw his first opportunity in the 2016 Republican primaries. The rule in politics is the same as the rule in war: divide and conquer. Republicans were fragmented in 2016. No fewer than seventeen candidates ran for the Republican nomination. Trump immediately stood out from the rest of the field. He wasn't an establishment Republican; the establishment favorite was Jeb Bush. He wasn't a Tea Party conservative; the conservative favorite was Ted Cruz. He wasn't even a politician; he was a television celebrity.

Trump found a constituency that had been trending Republican for decades but had never won control of the party: working-class whites. He won them with a populist style (defiance) and a populist message (antiestablishment). Trump was described as "fluent in the native tongue of disaffected whites."[1]

In 2016 antiestablishment populism was the missing imperative. As noted in chapter 2, Trump was the whole populist package: socially conservative (immigration), progressive on some economic issues (trade, jobs), and isolationist ("America First"). I asked a pollster in 2016 what would be the best question to ask if you want to identify a Trump supporter. "Try this one," he said. "Are you a country music fan?" Trump, of midtown Manhattan, carried 68 percent of the vote in West Virginia and 61 percent in Tennessee.

Polarization enabled Trump's success. Political polarization emerged in the 1960s with a values division in the nation's upper-middle class first observed in California by James Q. Wilson and Richard Todd (see chapter 1): voters on the left and on the right who are certain of their own values and furious that the rest of the country does not respect those values. We have a liberal elite epitomized by Barack Obama and a conservative elite epitomized by Mitt Romney.

We noted in chapter 2 that both major political parties are cross-class coalitions. Democrats are an alliance that includes an educated progressive establishment, working-class economic populists, and disadvantaged minorities. Republicans are an alliance that includes a country-club conservative establishment, racial-backlash voters, and religious fundamentalists. Trump rallied his populist army to defeat both party establishments. The establishment was so bitterly divided it could not join forces to defeat him.

Breaking the Rules

Trump broke all the rules for a presidential candidate. The old rule in politics is "Democrats fall in love, and Republicans fall in line." That didn't happen in either party in 2016. Democrats' true love was Bernie

Sanders, not Hillary Clinton. But the party establishment feared that Americans would not elect a seventy-five-year-old socialist from Vermont. Republicans had a history of nominating candidates who had run for president before: Richard Nixon in 1968, Ronald Reagan in 1980, George H. W. Bush in 1988, Bob Dole in 1996, John McCain in 2008, Mitt Romney in 2012. Trump had never run for anything. He is the only president who has never served either in elected office or in the military.

Trump was born to wealth and privilege. As noted in chapter 9, that's more of a problem for a Republican candidate than for a Democratic candidate because it confirms the longstanding image of Republicans as the party of the wealthy and privileged.

Then there's the oxymoron problem. Each party has to deal with a damaging stereotype. The stereotype of a liberal Democrat is weak and indecisive. George McGovern was "a thousand percent" behind his first running mate until he dropped him from the ticket. Jimmy Carter was called wishy-washy. Walter Mondale got pushed around by the special interests. Michael Dukakis embarrassed himself by riding in a tank. John Kerry got called a flip-flopper.

The Democratic Party used to have tough liberals. Harry Truman fired General Douglas MacArthur for insubordination. John Kennedy stood up to the Soviets in the Cuban Missile Crisis. If you defied LBJ, you'd probably wake up in the morning missing an important body part.

The stereotype of liberals today is wimpy, not tough. "Tough liberal" is one of the great oxymorons in politics. For decades, Democrats longed for "another Kennedy" because Kennedyism means tough liberalism.

The stereotype of a conservative is mean and nasty. Rush Limbaugh,

Newt Gingrich, Dick Cheney, and Ted Cruz are not known for their generosity of spirit. But Ronald Reagan was. Reagan came across as a nice guy who wouldn't start a war or throw old people out in the snow despite the harsh things he sometimes said. For Republicans, the winning oxymoron is a "nice conservative."

Donald Trump is nobody's idea of a nice guy. In September 2015 Trump noticed that in a poll of Republican primary voters, he led his rivals on every issue and quality but one. "The only thing I did badly on was, 'Is he a nice person?'" Trump observed with dismay. "I was last in terms of niceness." He tried to turn that to his advantage. "We're tired of the nice," he said. "We don't need the nice. We need competent."[2] In 2017 Trump told police officers, "Please don't be too nice" in handling suspects.

Trump has the temperament of a right-wing radio talk show host. It's a style that has long been influential in the Republican Party. With Trump, it took over. What Trump has is attitude—bombastic and bullying. Crude insults are rampant on talk radio. In 2012, when a law student asked Congress to do something about the high cost of female contraceptives, Rush Limbaugh said, "What does that make her? It makes her a slut, right?" In 2015 Trump denounced John McCain, who'd been a prisoner of war in North Vietnam for five and a half years. "He was a war hero because he was captured," Trump said dismissively. "I like people who weren't captured."

"He personalizes everything," Jeb Bush complained. "If you're not in total agreement with him, you're an idiot, or stupid, or you don't have energy." Energy? Radio talk-show hosts are manic.

Donald Trump was an angry candidate. He was angry about the way things were going in the country ("a disaster"). He was angry about President Obama. He was angry about the press: "the best person in [Clinton's] campaign is the mainstream media." Angry about trade. Angry about other countries supposedly taking advantage of the United States. Angry about the Iran nuclear weapons deal. Angry about everything.

A lot of Americans shared his anger. Conservatives were infuriated that Barack Obama, the most liberal president we've ever had, got elected twice. Many working Americans were enraged that their jobs were disappearing in a globalized economy. A lot of white men felt that they had lost power with the rise of political correctness.

Even in bad times, Americans don't usually elect angry candidates. They typically go for candidates who offer hope and optimism. Things were much worse in 1932 when Franklin D. Roosevelt was elected. He promised better days ahead and a "New Deal" for the American people. In 1968 the country was gripped by an unpopular war, racial violence, and student protest. Richard Nixon said he would "bring us together." In 1980, when we had an energy crisis, hyperinflation, and hostages in Iran, Ronald Reagan talked about "a shining city on a hill." In 1992, when Americans were devastated by recession, Bill Clinton ran as "the man from Hope [Arkansas, his childhood home]." In 2008, when the country seemed to be teetering into another Great Depression, Barack Obama offered "hope" and "change"—not anger.

During the first presidential debate, Trump boasted, "I think my strongest asset, maybe by far, is my temperament. I have a winning temperament." What he really had was an angry temperament. Anger management is not something most voters want to be concerned about when they elect a president.

Trump's signature attitude is defiance. In a country originally settled by runaways from authority, defiance of authority is a deeply ingrained tradition, even when the cause is hopeless. The movie *Cool*

Hand Luke, released in 1967, celebrated that tradition. Defiance was the defining characteristic of the Trump campaign. Trump defied Washington insiders. He defied political correctness. He defied the media. He defied conventional wisdom. He defied common decency with his remarks about women. He defied George W. Bush and John McCain and Mitt Romney. He even defied the Pope!

But he still got elected.

The Un-Obama

In 2016, Donald Trump was the un-Obama. He was the first Republican candidate to try to disqualify Obama on the "birther" issue (charging, falsely, that Obama may not have been a native-born citizen). To Trump supporters, Obama was the ultimate educated snob; the candidate who was disdainful of hard-pressed small-town voters who "cling to guns and religion."

President Obama insisted on facts. "We need to know all the facts," he said after the December 2015 terrorist attack in San Bernardino, California. Trump doesn't deal in facts. The *New York Times* carried out a comprehensive analysis of every public statement made by Trump during one week in early December 2015. The conclusion? "Mr. Trump uses rhetoric to erode people's trust in facts, numbers, nuance, government and the news media."[3] He continued to claim he'd seen "thousands and thousands" of Muslims in New Jersey cheering and celebrating after the 9/11 attacks, though there was no factual basis for the claim. House Democratic leader Nancy Pelosi reported that President Trump opened his first meeting with congressional leaders by saying, "You know, I won the popular vote." (He lost by 2.9 million votes.)

Trump did nothing to hide his contempt for President Obama.

"There is something going on with him that we don't know about," he said at a campaign rally.[4] He insisted Obama wasn't smart: "How does a bad student go to Columbia and then to Harvard?" Unlike himself: "When you're really, really smart like I am—" Trump said, adding, "it's true, it's true, it's always been true."[5] What the two exhibit is different kinds of intelligence: book smarts versus money smarts. Guess which one Americans are more likely to value.

Obama is thoughtful, knowledgeable, and progressive—the ultimate NPR Democrat. The professor in chief. He's always had trouble connecting with white working-class voters. He lost them to Hillary Clinton in the 2008 Democratic primaries.

As the un-Obama candidate for president, Trump embodied change. It is hard to imagine anyone as different from Barack Obama as Donald Trump. Obama was cautious, deliberative, well informed, and politically correct. Trump is coarse, boastful, uninformed, and arrogant.

President Obama's critics saw him as ineffectual. They looked at Washington and saw gridlock. Americans expect a leader to get things done. They don't want to hear "Congress won't give me what I want." Tough leaders like Lyndon Johnson and Ronald Reagan could get what they wanted out of Congress by twisting arms and turning on the charm.

Obama couldn't stop ISIS from claiming a large swath of territory. He couldn't do anything about Vladimir Putin's aggression in Ukraine and the Middle East. Most voters didn't believe he could stop Iran from getting nuclear weapons. He couldn't bring well-paying jobs back to the United States. As for his signature achievement, health care reform, as of 2016, most Americans had never supported Obamacare.[6] Even Democrats were frustrated, which helps explain Bernie Sanders. Obama couldn't keep his pledge to shut down Guantanamo. He couldn't deliver immigration reform or gun control.

There's a reason Trump came across as someone who could get things done: he was not a politician. During the Indiana primary campaign, Ted Cruz was confronted by pro-Trump protesters. An angry young man pointed to Cruz and said, "You are the problem, politician. You are the problem." With Trump, as with Ross Perot in 1992, supporters were looking for someone who could put politics aside.

After delivering a talk on politics, I was once asked by a member of the audience, "Why can't we run government like a business? That way we could keep politics out of it." I responded, "There is a reason why we can't run government like a business. Business is not a democracy. If business were a democracy, it would look like government." The questioner nodded thoughtfully and said, "I still think we should run government like a business." I couldn't change her mind. I could only offer the audience something to think about.

The conviction that drove the Ross Perot movement in 1992 endures: politics is the enemy of problem solving. "For years," former president Bill Clinton once wrote, "politicians have treated our most vexing problems here, like crime and welfare and the budget deficit, as issues to be exploited, not problems to be solved."[7]

Trump defined himself as a tough guy. He would ignore politics and just get the job done. It was not at all clear how, but his supporters didn't care. He would just do it. It's the reason why voters have been attracted to political outsiders such as General Dwight D. Eisenhower and Ross Perot—and Trump. They can put politics aside and just fix what's wrong.

President Trump's first decisive move in foreign policy, the air strike on Syria, was seen by many observers as a move to establish a sharp contrast with his predecessor. In 2013, after the government of Syrian president Bashar al-Assad was found to be using chemical weapons against his own people, President Obama tried and failed to persuade Congress to support a military strike in Syria. In 2017, when the Assad government carried out a horrifying—and televised—chemical weapons attack, President Trump didn't bother going to Congress for authorization. Within days, he launched a retaliatory missile attack on a Syrian air base.

As noted in chapter 8, the attack appeared to signal a sudden reversal of candidate Trump's foreign-policy views. Of course, Trump takes pride in being unpredictable. By authorizing the missile attack a few days after the Assad government's atrocity, Trump sent an indisputable message: he was completely different from Barack Obama. "Our administration would never have gotten this done in forty-eight hours," a senior official of the Obama administration told *Politico*. "It's a complete indictment of Obama."[8]

For all the talk of ideological polarization, 2016 doesn't seem to fit the trend. Trump was not the first choice of conservatives, and Hillary Clinton was not the first choice of liberals. What would true ideological polarization look like? Ted Cruz versus Bernie Sanders. Trump doesn't really have an ideology. What he believes in most of all is himself. That's why many conservatives don't trust him. Conservatives such as House Speaker Paul Ryan tried to push Trump to the right. Trump's response: "This is called the Republican Party. It's not called the Conservative Party."

As we noted in chapter 1, in 2016 the Trump movement and the conservative movement used each other. Trump used conservatives to legitimize his rise to power. Conservatives needed Trump in the White House to sign whatever legislation the Republican Congress passed—and shut up.

But he won't shut up. Conservatives were shocked when the

president equated Vladimir Putin's murderous record with US policies. When an interviewer called Putin a murderer, Trump replied, "What, you think our country's so innocent?" Imagine the reaction if Barack Obama had said that.

The Education Gap

In 2016 education became a key political marker. It marks the line between the Old America (generally less well educated) and the New America (more voters with college degrees). The education gap has been growing for some time. In 2012 Republican Mitt Romney carried non-college educated whites by 25 points and whites with a college degree by 14. In 2016 Trump's margin among noncollege whites increased to 39 points, while the vote was a near tie among college-educated whites (48 percent for Trump, 45 percent for Hillary Clinton).[9]

Hillary Clinton's biggest problem was that she is a charter member of the political establishment. Voters who wanted change were reluctant to support her. She embodied the status quo. She was part of both the Obama administration and her husband's administration. Elect Clinton, most voters believed, and nothing would change.

Bill Clinton tried his best to redefine his wife as the candidate of change. Speaking at the Democratic convention in July, he called Hillary "the best darn change maker I have ever met in my entire life." It was a nice try, but Trump always had a stronger claim on the change issue, and Clinton was never in a good position to compete for it.

Trump speaks the language of the disgruntled white working class. He gleefully says "notsupposedtas": things his supporters may believe but mainstream politicians are "not supposed to" say. Like foreign trade is a rip-off, and immigration is a threat, and torture is okay. "We won with poorly educated," Trump said after the 2016 Nevada caucuses. "I love the poorly educated." [10] Meanwhile, the drift of educated voters away from the Republican Party has been continuing.

It's well established that Trump won because of a surge of support among white rural and working-class voters. What's less recognized is his weakness among affluent white suburban voters who used to be the Republican Party's base. The chairman of the Harris County, Texas (Houston), Republican Party called 2016 "an anomaly of an election" because "a lot of traditional Republicans would not vote for Trump." [11] They were appalled, not just by the fact that Trump was so uninformed but also by his coarseness and vulgarity. Trump may be rich, but he has no class.

President Trump continues to appall educated voters. They're certainly not proud of the president. They find him embarrassing and shameful. The Speaker of the British House of Commons opposed inviting Trump to address Parliament when the president makes a state visit to London, saying, "I feel very strongly that our opposition to racism and sexism and our support for equality before the law and an independent judiciary are hugely important considerations in the House of Commons." [12]

An April 2017 Quinnipiac University poll showed the president with just 36 percent approval among college-educated whites. Fifty-nine percent said they were embarrassed to have Donald Trump as president. [13] Trump is doing everything he can to drive away well-educated Americans. His disdain for facts—like his claim, with no evidence, that as many as five million fraudulent votes were cast for Clinton and his assertion that the press covers up news of terrorist attacks—generated alarm among well-informed Americans. One critic writing in the *Washington Post* called Trump a "bullshit artist"—someone for whom facts are irrelevant.[14]

A pattern has been developing in American politics, at least among nonminority voters. The wealthier you are, the more likely you are to be a Republican, while the better educated you are, the more likely you are to be a Democrat. What happens to people who are wealthy and well educated? Sociologists call them "cross-pressured." If they vote their economic interests, they'll vote Republican (like Mitt Romney). If they vote their cultural values, they'll vote Democratic (like Barack Obama). Values often prevail over interests, which is why Trump has problems with upscale voters.

As for why he does well with white working-class voters, a study by the Public Religion Research Institute and the *Atlantic* magazine found that "it was cultural anxiety that drove white working-class voters to Trump," indicated by "feeling like a stranger in America, supporting the deportation of immigrants, and hesitating about educational investment." White working-class voters who were facing economic hardship were more likely to support Hillary Clinton.[15]

A 2017 Pew Research Center poll found that views of higher education have taken on a strongly partisan cast. Among Democrats, 72 percent said that colleges and universities have a positive effect on the country. Only half as many Republicans felt that way. The share of Republicans who believe colleges and universities are bad for the country jumped from 37 percent in 2015 to 58 percent in 2017.[16]

A conference of polling professionals in 2017 found that the education effect had a lot to do with polling problems in 2016. "The education issue . . . helps explain why the state polls fared so much worse than national polls," the *New York Times* reported. "Most national polls were weighted by education, even as most state polls were not." Why not? Most state polls interview only registered voters, and state-level data on the educational composition of registered voters are hard to come by. "In the past, it hardly mattered whether a political poll was weighted by education." What was new in 2016 was "the importance of education to presidential vote choice." [17]

Resentment of education has always been stronger than resentment of wealth in the United States. Especially since the educated elite has come to embrace liberal cultural values—values that conservatives denounce as political correctness. No one in government is less politically correct than Donald Trump. He claimed that some people failed to report suspicions about the San Bernardino terrorists because of concerns about racial profiling. "We have become so politically correct that we don't know what the hell we're doing," Trump said. "We don't know what we're doing." [18]

Trump is a whole lot wealthier than Mitt Romney, but his wealth never seemed to be an issue to his supporters. "He spends his own money," one said. "He's not going to have any lobbyist or any high zillionaires that he has to do favors for." [19] If he has made all that money and wants to use it to run for president, a lot of people think that means he's committed to the public good.

Since the 1960s, educated white liberals have become a dominant force in the Democratic Party. After Trump took office, they exploded in rage. They have a deep commitment to diversity and inclusion. Trump has no respect for that commitment.

Younger, better-educated Americans tend to live in major metropolitan areas that are increasingly diverse. White working-class Americans have been fleeing those areas. Some because they can't afford to live there, others because they want a different lifestyle. In 2014 Andrew

Levison wrote in the *New Republic,* "Today two-thirds of white workers live in small towns, the urban fringes around metropolitan areas or rural areas; only a third remain in central cities or suburbs." [20]

While Trump won the electoral college, Hillary Clinton carried the national popular vote by nearly three million. Her problem was where she got those votes. The *Cook Political Report,* an online newsletter, separated thirteen battleground states from states that were not competitive. Clinton won the noncompetitive states by more than 3.7 million votes. [21] She piled up huge majorities in states where she didn't need the extra votes. For example, Clinton carried California by 4.3 million votes.

The Trump campaign focused on the battleground states, and it paid off. He carried the thirteen swing states narrowly (by about 816,000 votes out of 46 million). The closeness of the vote didn't matter as long as Trump got the electoral votes. When I gave a talk to a California audience after the 2016 election, a voter asked me what she and other California Democrats could do about that problem. My advice: "Have you considered moving to Michigan?"

Polarization Persists

In 2016 Donald Trump staged a hostile takeover of the Republican Party. There are two Republican establishments, and Trump beat both of them. One was the old Washington and Wall Street establishment. The other was the conservative counterestablishment. The story of the GOP since 1980 has been the increasing power of conservative activists. It started with the election of Ronald Reagan and culminated in the Tea Party revolt.

In 2016 the establishment candidate, former Florida governor Jeb

Bush, was humiliated and driven out of the race by Trump. The Tea Party favorite, Ted Cruz, lasted longer than Bush. But Trump ended up stealing the Tea Party base of the GOP. The mainstream Republican establishment has always regarded the Tea Party with deep suspicion. After all, outlandish Tea Party candidates kept the GOP from winning a Senate majority in 2010: Christine O'Donnell in Delaware ("I'm not a witch"), Sharron Angle in Nevada (unemployed Americans are "spoiled"), Ken Buck in Colorado (ban all abortions, including those for victims of rape and incest).

The Tea Party was at war not just with Barack Obama and the Democrats but also with the mainstream Republican Party establishment, which it claims betrayed the conservative cause for the sake of governing. (Imagine that.) Antiestablishment conservatives have always nurtured a keen sense of betrayal. In the 1950s, Senator Joseph McCarthy took on the Republican Party establishment for betraying the conservative cause. He saw Communist infiltration in Washington. Trump just sees stupidity ("Our leaders are stupid; they are stupid people"), as opposed to himself ("I'm, like, a really smart person").

The mainstream Republican establishment was committed to winning, and Trump looked like a sure loser. After Bush dropped out, the establishment found a new standard-bearer. Marco Rubio drew just enough support from wealthier, better-educated Republican voters to stay alive for a while. They are the kind of Republicans who find Trump embarrassing. Rubio ended up winning only Minnesota and the District of Columbia (shades of Walter Mondale).

Trump took over the Republican Party by forming an alliance with conservatives. The symbol of that alliance was the Trump-Pence ticket. Conservatives may have been wary of Trump, but their reservations were resolved pretty quickly: he won. The 2016 presidential race brought conservatives to a level of power they had not enjoyed even under Ronald Reagan. And if Trump falters or betrays them? Conservatives will be there to pick up the pieces.

Trump was only a few months into his presidency when his populist supporters began to complain that the president was abandoning them. Steve Bannon, President Trump's key alt-right adviser, appeared to be losing influence after he was removed from the National Security Council. Bannon returned to his position as chief executive of Breitbart News Network after seven months in the White House. Trump had staffed his administration with Wall Street executives and billionaires. His air strike on Syria threatened to involve America in another conflict where our national interests were not clear. "If you abandon populism," Patrick Howley, a former Breitbart News Network staffer warned the president in an open letter on *The American Spectator*'s website, "then you will not really have any constituency any more. Will you be an establishment Democrat? Will you be a neocon? How will people even think of you? You will be adrift." [22]

As President Trump neared his first hundred days in office, his job approval rating in the *Washington Post*–ABC News poll was at a historic low (42 percent), making him "the least popular chief executive in modern times." But his base remained loyal. His job rating among those who voted for him in 2016 was a solid 94 percent. [23]

The year 2016 also saw the Democratic Party move decisively to the left even though the party did not nominate the more liberal contender. Democrats seemed to be moving sideways, from Clinton to Clinton. But the party that nominated Hillary Clinton was considerably more liberal than the party that had nominated and elected her husband in the 1990s.

After fifty years, liberals were no longer on the defensive. Former president Bill Clinton led the Democratic Party to the center and kept it competitive through the 1990s, when the Reagan consensus still prevailed. Then in 2008 Barack Obama led a new, more liberal coalition of Democrats to power in the wake of the financial crash and the Iraq War. Obama got elected twice with a majority of the popular vote, the first Democrat to do that since Franklin D. Roosevelt.

In 2016, in an impressive show of confidence, Democrats wrote the most liberal platform in the party's history. It condemned capital punishment, called for measures to curb the "greed, recklessness, and illegal behavior" of Wall Street, pledged to expand Social Security, advocated more than doubling the minimum wage, endorsed a path to citizenship for illegal immigrants, and demanded stronger gun laws.

In her acceptance speech, Hillary Clinton promised to make college tuition free for the middle class, reform the criminal justice system, pass the biggest investment in new jobs since World War II, and make "Wall Street, corporations, and the superrich" pay their fair share of taxes. Not a word about the national debt.

California governor Jerry Brown, who opposed Bill Clinton from the left in 1992, said that Democrats in 2016 "want more interventionist government to make things more fair... No one is going to say government is the problem, not the solution."[24]

What drove the Democrats' shift to the left? Three things.

First, the country was changing, demographically and ideologically. The New America coalition that came to power with Obama has continued to grow in size and confidence. In 2016 a majority of Democrats described themselves as liberals. Hillary Clinton's defeat seemed to be less of a defeat for liberalism than for her.

Second, wrenching economic changes—globalization and the Great Recession—generated a populist backlash in both parties. Among

Democrats, the backlash came in the form of left-wing economic populism: the anger at Wall Street that fueled Bernie Sanders's campaign. Both parties saw mounting hostility to foreign trade.

"Let there be no mistake," Hillary Clinton said in June 2016. "Senator Sanders, his campaign, and the vigorous debate we've had about how to raise incomes, reduce inequality, and increase upward mobility have been very good for the Democratic Party and for America."[25] In other words, Sanders's causes were also her causes.

Sanders surprised the political world by getting 43 percent of the Democratic primary vote and winning twenty-two states to Clinton's twenty-nine. When she won the Democratic nomination, she promised a payoff that sounded like it came right out of a Sanders stump speech: "We all want an economy with more opportunity and less inequality, where Wall Street can never wreck Main Street again. We want a government that listens to the people not the power brokers, which means getting unaccountable money out of politics."[26]

Third, the election of Donald Trump exposed the ugly face of intolerance and bigotry in the Republican Party—a face that Republicans had kept largely hidden since 1968. As a result, Trump generates resistance among liberals who find him appalling. It took a few weeks for the conservative resistance to materialize after Obama took office in 2009. It began on February 19, with on-air editor Rick Santelli's call on CNBC for a "tea party in July" to protest mortgage bailouts. The liberal resistance emerged even faster. It began the day after Trump took office in January 2017, with the Women's March on Washington—the largest political demonstration since the anti–Vietnam War protests of the 1960s.

In order to build a Democratic bench, one group, Run for Something, got pledges from seven thousand young people around the country to run for state and local office. Their pitch: "Donald Trump is president. Trust us, you're qualified to run for local office."[27]

The polarization between Democrats and Republicans in Congress shows no sign of abating, especially now that the Senate filibuster rule requiring a three-fifths supermajority has been eliminated for confirming judicial and executive nominations. (The filibuster is still allowed for most legislation.) It means the Senate will operate more and more like the House of Representatives: rule by a simple partisan majority. No need any longer to build bipartisan support for presidential appointments.

Angry White Men

The Republican Party has become the party of angry white men. What are they angry about? Political correctness. White working-class men see political correctness as a way of shutting them out.

And worse. "Political correctness is killing people," Ted Cruz said in a Republican debate, meaning that it inhibited the Obama administration from going after the bad guys for fear of racial profiling. Donald Trump led the charge. "I am so tired of this politically correct crap," Trump said at a campaign rally, eliciting the biggest cheers of his appearance.

For decades, political correctness has been used to shut down debate. Activists on the left refuse to allow people to say things that might offend less privileged groups such as women, gays, African Americans, and immigrants. It has become a real issue at universities, which are supposed to be bastions of free speech.

President Obama became the symbol of political correctness. He knew it. And he was not unsympathetic to his critics. Speaking about white blue-collar men, Obama said on National Public Radio, "I may represent change that worries them."

White working-class men seethe whenever political correctness denigrates them as "privileged." They certainly don't feel "privileged," not after the economic devastation of the past decade. Their response? Defiance.

When Latino protesters showed up at a Trump rally, a Trump supporter shouted, "Somebody press one for English!"[28] Here's how Trump described negotiating with the Japanese and Chinese: "When these people walk into the room, they don't say, 'Oh, hello! How's the weather? How are the Yankees doing?' They say, 'We want deal.'"[29] Trump bragged about having "a great relationship with the blacks."[30] Trump is not just politically incorrect. He's proud of it. A psychologist described Trump as "the walking id of the Republican base."[31]

The backlash to political correctness has deep roots in the Republican Party. Racists were one of the earliest constituencies in the new Republican coalition. They were almost all Barry Goldwater had in 1964, and they were the target of Richard Nixon's Southern Strategy in 1972. Republicans such as Goldwater, Nixon, Reagan, and the Bushes perfected the art of appealing to racial resentment without sounding like racists.

Political correctness turns conflicts of interest into conflicts of values. That immediately escalates the stakes. There are no two sides to an issue if one of them is labeled politically incorrect. The rules of political correctness say that if you are incorrect, you don't get to speak. Trump's response to that is "Phooey!"

In 1960 the great sociologist Seymour Martin Lipset shocked the left by writing about "working-class authoritarianism": the predisposition to intolerant, extreme, and undemocratic attitudes among "lower-class persons."[32] In 2016 Trump played on those sentiments when he expressed admiration for Russian president Vladimir Putin. "He's running his country, and at least he's a leader, unlike what we have in this country," Trump said. As for Putin's methods, "I think our country does plenty of killing also."[33]

There is an element of economic populism in Trump's appeal to working-class voters. He defies conservative orthodoxy by criticizing free trade and promising to protect entitlements. Conservatives have long aimed to reduce spending on Social Security and Medicare, the two biggest government spending programs. But they are the two most popular government programs. Trump doesn't talk about cuts because he doesn't want to anger his populist base. Nor does he talk about another cause dear to the right: reducing the national debt. "The man doesn't have a limited-government bone in his body," a conservative blogger complained during the campaign.[34] It is estimated that the 2017 Republican tax law, which Trump endorsed, will add at least $1.5 trillion to the national debt in the first ten years.

The seventeenth-century philosopher Montesquieu once said, "Great events have great causes." The election of Donald Trump can be seen as part of a great populist wave roiling politics in the United States and Europe after 2010. The causes? One was the Great Recession of 2008–09 that devastated the economic security of working people and created a massive backlash against the increasingly globalized economy. The backlash is captured by Trump's message of economic nationalism: "America First."

Another great cause was the refugee crisis that resulted from turmoil in the Middle East. The flood of refugees into Europe—and the threat of refugees coming to the United States—generated a right-wing populist backlash. In Britain, it was a major factor behind Brexit, the vote in June 2016 to leave the European community. "I think Brexit is going to be a wonderful thing for your country," President Trump said at a press conference with British prime minister Theresa May in January 2017. "I think when it irons out, you're going to have your own identity, and you're going to have the people that you want in your country."[35] The "America First" slogan captures the same cultural backlash.

Donald Trump is a builder. The first thing he pledged to do in his election night victory speech was to "begin the urgent task of rebuilding our nation." The president-elect promised, "We are going to fix our inner cities and rebuild our highways, bridges, tunnels, airports, schools, hospitals. We're going to rebuild our infrastructure, which will become, by the way, second to none."[36]

That kind of talk thrills the working-class voters who put him over the top. What they hear is "jobs." It also piques the interest of progressive Democrats. Massachusetts senator Elizabeth Warren told the AFL-CIO (American Federation of Labor and Congress of Industrial Organizations) executive council, "[Trump] spoke to the very real sense of millions of Americans that their government and their economy have abandoned them. And he promised to rebuild our economy for working people."[37] What some progressives hear is "economic stimulus plan." What conservatives hear is "big government." If a policy sounds like big government, conservatives are instinctively against it. Developers like Trump don't care how things get done as long as they get done.

To Tea Party conservatives, all government spending is evil. But not to American voters. They see a difference between spending on public works, which is what Trump proposed, and spending on social welfare programs, which is what Democrats favor. Public works spending involves benefits that are available to everyone and that people cannot provide for themselves, such as good schools, fast highways, and gleaming new airports. Social welfare spending is targeted by need. It helps disadvantaged people get things that others are able to provide for themselves, such as housing, food, and medical care. Middle-class voters are okay with that as long as they are convinced that the benefits are going to the "truly needy" and that no one is taking advantage of the system.

Franklin D. Roosevelt's New Deal was not a social welfare program. The Great Depression of the 1930s was like a natural disaster that affected everybody, the just and the unjust alike. When the Democrats took over in 1933, they came up with an ambitious program of public works. Trump's soon-to-be chief political strategist Steve Bannon told the *Hollywood Reporter*, "We're going to build an entirely new political movement. It's everything related to jobs. The conservatives are going to go crazy. I'm the guy pushing a trillion-dollar infrastructure plan. With negative interest rates throughout the world, it's the greatest opportunity to rebuild everything."[38]

That sounds like big-government conservatism—the exact opposite of the austerity plans that small government conservatives in the United States and Europe have been pushing since the Great Recession. Trump's plan, like the New Deal, would be driven not by ideology but by experimentation. "We're just going to throw it up against the wall and see if it sticks," Bannon said. "It will be as exciting as the 1930s; greater than the Reagan Revolution." Bannon called it "an economic nationalist movement" driven by opposition to globalization. Totally different from the kind of austerity plan House Speaker Paul Ryan and Tea Party conservatives were pushing.

Builders do not think small. Trump's plan sounds like the sort of thing populist demagogues have done since the Roman Empire: massive public works projects to put people to work and display national greatness, sometimes with dangerous consequences.

Carnage?

In his inaugural address on January 20, 2017, President Trump offered a harrowing picture of the United States: "Mothers and children trapped in poverty in our inner cities. Rusted-out factories scattered like tombstones across the landscape of our nation . . . The crime and the gangs and the drugs that have stolen too many lives and robbed our country of so much unrealized potential. This American carnage stops right here and stops right now." [39]

At his first press conference, the forty-fifth president said, "Our administration inherited many problems across government and across the economy. To be honest, I inherited a mess. It's a mess, at home and abroad. A mess." [40] At his first address to a joint session of Congress, the president painted another bleak picture: "We have the worst financial recovery in sixty-five years . . . Overseas we have inherited a series of tragic foreign-policy disasters." [41]

Did Americans believe the country was in such terrible shape? A CNN poll taken at the time of Trump's inauguration showed the country evenly divided. Exactly half said things were going well in the country, and half said things were going badly. (Only 15 percent said "very badly.") Voters gave the departing President Obama a 60 percent job approval rating. [42]

Want to see bleak? That was when Ronald Reagan took office in 1981, and 74 percent of Americans said things were bad. Or when Barack Obama was elected during the financial crisis in 2008, when 83 percent said things were bad. Of course, 50 percent positive in 2017 was well below the euphoria people felt in 1984 when it was "Morning in America" and 74 percent thought things were going well. Or at the peak of the Clinton boom in 2000, when 79 percent were happy.[43]

Trump needed a crisis. So he went about trying to declare one. A crisis would give him the sweeping mandate he craved. Trump repeatedly exaggerates the size of his victory, calling it "a massive landslide . . . in the electoral college" and "one of the biggest electoral college victories in history." It wasn't. In 43 out of 54 presidential contests since 1804, the winner received a larger percentage of electoral votes than Trump did in 2016.

Republicans did manage to keep their losses to a minimum and preserve their majorities in Congress, with net Republican losses of six seats in the House of Representatives and two in the Senate. If there was any sense of a mandate, it was created by the fact that both the presidential and congressional results defied expectations. Trump was not expected to win, and it was supposed to be a close call for Republicans to maintain their majority in the Senate, where they had twenty-four seats at risk compared with ten for the Democrats.

Every election includes a phantom candidate called "expected." It's not enough to win the election. You have to do "better than expected." If you do "about as well as expected," it's no big deal. If you do "worse than expected," you lose, even if you win.

I once figured out a way to formalize the expectations game. It was during the 1998 midterm election, at the peak of the Monica Lewinsky scandal, and President Clinton was facing impeachment. I decided to canvass about fifty columnists, pundits, political reporters, and talking heads. They are the people who set expectations. With the help of CNN's staff, I asked each of them one question: What do you expect to happen on Tuesday night?

The people we canvassed live in a bubble. They read one another's columns and watch one another's commentary. We discovered after a handful of calls that everyone was saying the same thing: they expected the Democrats to lose between five and ten House seats in the election. All of them knew that the president's party loses House seats in a midterm. That had been true since 1934. With Clinton in disgrace, it was bound to happen again.

At the beginning of the evening, I announced, more or less officially, what the chattering class "expected" to happen that night. The final result would be measured against those expectations. Would the Democrats do better than expected, worse than expected, or about as well as expected? "Stay tuned."

At the end of a long evening, the network announced that Democrats had made a net gain of five House seats. For the first time in more than sixty years, the president's party had gained House seats in a midterm election. It wasn't a big gain, but Democrats did better than expected. The election result amounted to a rebuke of congressional Republicans who were determined to defy public opinion and impeach President Clinton. The unexpected result shocked the political establishment. So what happened? Within a few days, Newt Gingrich resigned as Speaker of the House, the victim of the expectations game.

In 2016 Donald Trump and the Republican Party were beneficiaries of the expectations game. They both did better than expected. Their performance was driven by a high turnout of conservatives and populists, particularly in rust belt states. Conservatives were enraged by President Obama's regime of political correctness and claimed a mandate to end it. Blue-collar whites were angry over job losses and their declining influence in the culture.

There was no overwhelming crisis driving the election. Most voters cited the economy as the most important issue—far more important than immigration or terrorism or foreign policy. Voters who were concerned about the economy gave the edge to Hillary Clinton.

The result was that President Trump did not have a "honeymoon." For a president, as for most newlyweds, a honeymoon is a once-in-a-lifetime opportunity. A newly inaugurated president has a fresh reserve of political capital. His popularity rating is likely to be extremely high. That is a president's principal source of power in Washington. The president's job approval rating is the Dow Jones Industrial Average of Washington.

When a president is popular, he can be bold. Franklin D. Roosevelt had his first "Hundred Days," when he demanded and got much of the legislation defining the New Deal. Dwight D. Eisenhower went to Korea. John F. Kennedy used his honeymoon to establish the Peace Corps and the Alliance for Progress, a multibillion-dollar aid program to promote economic growth and democracy in Latin America, as well as to allow an ill-fated invasion of Cuba known as the Bay of Pigs to proceed. Lyndon Johnson called for the Great Society; he also started bombing North Vietnam. Ronald Reagan "hit the ground running" with a radical program of tax cuts, military expansion, and domestic retrenchment. Barack Obama got a $787 billion economic stimulus plan through Congress.

Donald Trump hit the ground stumbling. The effort to repeal Obamacare faltered in Congress. His executive orders on immigration were struck down by federal courts. His job approval ratings fell to record lows for a newly elected president: below 40 percent in the Gallup poll.

I argued in chapter 1 that the US Constitution was written not to create a strong government but to limit government power. That's why we have such an elaborate system of checks and balances and separation of powers. In the United States, it is much easier to stop things than to get things done. For government to work, there has to be a crisis—an overwhelming sense of public urgency that can break down blockages and lubricate the system. Abraham Lincoln had a secession crisis. Franklin Roosevelt had the Great Depression and, later, World War II. Ronald Reagan had hyperinflation and a tax revolt. Bill Clinton had a recession. Barack Obama had a financial crash.

No doubt the working-class whites who came out in unexpected numbers for Donald Trump and Republican candidates in 2016 were driven by a sense of crisis. They wanted "change." For some that meant jobs. For others it meant respect for traditional American values and restoring national "greatness" ("Make America Great Again!"). The "change" Trump supporters wanted was the opposite of the "hope and change" Barack Obama campaigned for in 2008.

The last president who got elected with a dubious mandate was George W. Bush in 2000. He got his mandate eight months after he took office, on September 11, 2001. After he was reelected in 2004, Bush said, "I earned political capital, and I intend to spend it." He did spend it—all of it—on the war in Iraq. No one would dare want to see another tragedy like 9/11, but a crisis that came anywhere close to that magnitude could give President Trump the authority he craves.

Contempt Versus Defiance

If you declare war on the establishment, you shouldn't be surprised if the establishment fights back. President Trump exploits division—most often in his attacks on the "fake news" press—in order to keep his populist army mobilized. But if he does not deliver what he promised them—jobs—his supporters may not be there for him, either.

Unlike his four predecessors, each of whom tried and failed to unite the country, Donald Trump made no promise to bring the country together. He promised confrontation, not reconciliation. He exploited the division and continues to exploit it as president with his attacks on the press. "That's how dictators get started," Senator John McCain warned.

As president, Trump has found that the press is a more inviting target than the political establishment. Journalists are professionals. They are supposed to adhere to professional standards of accuracy and news judgment. A professional is someone who knows more than you do. You go to a professional doctor or lawyer or accountant because he or she knows more than you do about medicine or divorce law or tax policy.

Professionalism implies elitism. And that makes the media a good foil for populists. Trump found the perfect tool for challenging the authority of the news media: Twitter. The internet has no professional standards. It's full of "fake news," questionable sources, and extreme rhetoric. On the internet, information can be weaponized. Trump uses Twitter to evade the authority of the professional news media and communicate directly with his followers. "It's my voice," he told the *New York Times*. "They want to take away my voice . . . They're not going to take away my social media."[44] An academic critic wrote that for the Trump campaign, "It was more important to swamp the communications environment than it was to advocate for a particular belief or fight for the truth of a particular story."[45]

Resentment of professionals, intellectuals, and educated elites is an old theme in US politics going all the way back to Andrew Jackson.

Trump exploits it relentlessly. The cultural elite's response to Trump? Contempt. Actress Meryl Streep denounced Trump as a "bully" for his "instinct to humiliate" the less fortunate. Trump's response? Defiance. He called the three-time Oscar winner "one of the most overrated actresses in Hollywood" and "a Hillary flunky who lost big." Contempt versus defiance. That is likely to be the prevailing mode of political discourse as long as Trump is in office.

Donald Trump may be secure as long as Republicans maintain their majority in Congress and as long as his supporters stand by him. They can threaten to "Cantor" any Republican officeholder who opposes or even criticizes the president, just as the Tea Party brought down House Majority Leader Eric Cantor in 2014.

Trump is anything but a healer. He represents a dramatically different idea: a strongman who offers "winning." We will see whether President Trump can really solve problems or whether he will end up trapped in the standoff like his predecessors. In the meantime, Democrats have to console themselves with the idea that sooner or later, the country will demand an un-Trump, just as they went for the un-Bush in 2008 and the un-Obama in 2016.

Abandonment and Triangulation

By the middle of Trump's first year in office, it became clear that the alliance between Trump and the Republican establishment was not working. After the Senate's failure to repeal the Affordable Care Act in July 2017, Trump started launching (or tweeting) attacks on Republican leaders of Congress. At the same time, many Republican senators became openly critical of the president. Having won control of both the White House and Congress, the Republican Party started to come apart.

Intraparty tensions are not unusual in American politics. When Bill Clinton took office in 1993, Democrats held solid majorities in Congress. But Congress refused to deliver Clinton's number one priority, health care reform. As noted in chapter 2, American politicians are independent political entrepreneurs. Unlike legislators in a parliamentary system, members of Congress are not foot soldiers in a party army.

What was unusual in 2017 was the harsh tone of the recriminations. "Can you believe that [Senate Majority Leader] Mitch McConnell, who has screamed 'repeal and replace' for 7 years, couldn't get it done?" Trump tweeted. "Mitch, get back to work." Asked whether McConnell should resign as majority leader, Trump replied, "If he doesn't get repeal and replace done, and he doesn't get taxes done, and if he doesn't get a very easy one to get done—infrastructure—if he doesn't get them done, then you can ask me that question." [46] The president was bullying McConnell as if the senator was an underling in his employ, not a leader of a separate and equal branch of government.

After Senator Lindsey Graham criticized Trump for his initial failure to condemn white supremacist violence in Charlottesville, Virginia, Trump tweeted, "Such a disgusting lie. He just can't forget his election trouncing [in the 2016 Republican presidential primaries]. The people of South Carolina will remember!" [47]

When Senator Lisa Murkowski voted against the Republican health care bill, Trump put her in the line of fire. "Sen. Murkowski of the great state of Alaska really let the Republicans and our country down yesterday. Too bad," he tweeted. At a political rally, he said, "Any senator who votes against repeal and replace is telling America that they are fine with the Obamacare nightmare, and I predict they'll have a lot of problems." [48]

Arizona senator Jeff Flake published a polemic attacking President

Trump's leadership, *Conscience of a Conservative: A Rejection of Destructive Politics and a Return to Principle.* Flake argued that the conservative decision to embrace Trump in order to gain power has "put at risk our institutions and our values," warning, "If this was our Faustian bargain, then it was not worth it."[49]

In return, Trump praised Flake's 2018 Republican primary opponent, tweeting "Great to see Dr. Kelli Ward is running against 'Flake Jeff Flake,' who is WEAK on borders, crime, and a non-factor in Senate. He's toxic."[50]

Republican senators balked when President Trump urged them to keep trying to repeal Obamacare. Trump taunted them as "total quitters" if they gave up the effort. Senator Roy Blunt's response: "It's time to move on."[51] "We've got other things to do," Senator John Thune said. "It's important that Congress assert its authorities under the Constitution and be an equal branch of the government."[52] Meaning, we don't work for Trump.

Congressional Republicans could not fail to notice that, in a trial heat for the 2018 congressional election, Americans in July 2017 said they preferred a Democratic Congress over a Republican Congress by seven points (44 to 37 percent).[53] To paraphrase Samuel Johnson, the eighteenth-century English lexicographer, the prospect of electoral disaster, like the prospect of being hanged, concentrates the mind wonderfully.

Presidents like Lyndon Johnson have been known to bully and threaten members of Congress from their own party. But never in such a public and abusive manner. The conflict appears to portend a split in the Republican Party between Trump supporters and the party establishment. The division appeared mostly at the elite level. During his first year, rank-and-file Republicans remained loyal to President Trump. The president was solid on their issues: abortion, taxes, trade, immigration, education, guns, police accountability, affirmative action. The problem was that most of those conservative positions were unpopular beyond the Republican Party base.

An August 2017 Quinnipiac poll showed Trump's approval rating at 35 percent among the public at large. Among Republicans, it was more than twice as high (77 percent). That is consistent with the finding reported in chapter 3, that since 1980, party bases are stronger than they were in the past, at least in modern times. "Just as Reagan converted the GOP into a conservative party, Trump has converted the GOP into a populist working-class party," Stephen Moore, distinguished visiting fellow at the Heritage Foundation, told a meeting of congressional Republicans.[54] *New York* magazine described the party's new ideology as "Trump First."[55]

Two things are happening in the Republican Party. The Republican establishment, which saw Trump as a useful idiot, is abandoning the president. They increasingly see him as a threat to the conservative agenda and a menace to the country. "Ever since we've been here, we've really been following our [own] lead," Tennessee Republican senator Bob Corker told the *Washington Post*. After describing major Republican initiatives, Corker said, "Almost every bit of this has been 100 percent internal to Congress."[56] Meaning, Trump does not know how to work with Congress, even a Congress controlled by his own party.

The tax bill that passed Congress in December 2017 on a party-line vote was less a tribute to Trump's leadership than to the skill of House Speaker Paul Ryan and Senate majority leader Mitch McConnell in holding their Republican majorities together. Tax cuts are a core principle of Republican ideology. Presidents Ronald Reagan and George W. Bush achieved major tax cuts during the summer of their first year in office. Republicans can't resist tax cuts any more than Democrats could resist a civil rights bill. Moreover, after a year in which Republicans enjoyed total control of Congress and the White House, it would have been shameful if Republicans had no major legislation to show for it.

Congress also passed a bipartisan bill toughening sanctions on Russia as punishment for its interference in the 2016 election. After reluctantly signing the bill, Trump blamed Congress for "bringing relations with Russia to an all-time and very dangerous low."[57] A bipartisan group of senators worked to produce a bill that would protect Robert Mueller, the special counsel investigating ties between the 2016 Trump campaign and Russia, from being fired by President Trump.[58]

At the same time, Trump seemed to be "triangulating"—attempting to establish a political identity separate from both Democrats and Republicans. That's what President Clinton did after Republicans won control of Congress in 1994. As noted in Chapter 9, Clinton embraced positions that Republicans could accept on trade, crime, a balanced budget, welfare reform, and deregulation of Wall Street.

Triangulation may not work for Trump as well as it did for Clinton. For one thing, Trump did not embrace many positions favored by Democrats. Moreover, the political situation for Republicans in 2017 was totally different from that of Democrats in 1995. Democrats were deeply demoralized after they got their brains beaten out in the 1994 midterm. President Clinton represented their only access to power. Republicans were supposed to be triumphant after their sweeping victories in 2016. They controlled every branch of the federal government and most state governments. They were not desperate to follow a leader who wanted to "triangulate."

The showdown between the Republican establishment and President Trump will come in the 2018 and 2020 elections, when loyalty to President Trump is likely to be the central issue. Trump has encouraged his supporters to challenge Republican incumbents who were critical of him or insufficiently supportive. While Trump's base may be strong enough to win Republican primaries, the real test will be whether Trump's people can get elected. Or will they end up losing the way many out-of-the-mainstream Tea Party Republicans did in 2010?

Reagan succeeded in turning the Republican Party into a conservative party by proving that a conservative party could win. Trump will have to do the same thing if he wants to remake the Republican Party in his own image. He has to prove that a populist white working-class party can win.

Democrats have an opportunity to emerge Phoenix-like from the ruins of the Trump presidency. How? By doing what successful political parties have always done in this country: create a coalition. A coalition is made up of diverse interests that join together to pursue a shared objective: "If you want to stop Trump—for whatever reason—you're one of us. No further questions." Democrats need to welcome the growing number of voters who want to stop Trump, including a lot of mainstream Republicans. And not look for reasons to say, "Sorry, you're not one of us."

The Great Divider

As this book has shown, the polarization of American politics did not begin with Trump. It has been going on for at least fifty years. The difference between Trump and his predecessors is that Trump deliberately foments division. He uses every issue, every policy, every tweet, to set one group of Americans against another. He thrives on political confrontation. The result is a level of bitterness and resentment the United States has not seen since the Civil War.

Trump is committed to one thing above all—winning. It doesn't much matter what he wins as long as he is perceived as coming out on top. He promised his supporters in 2016, "You're going to win so much, you're going to be so sick and tired of winning." How do you win by dividing people? Especially if there are more people against you than for you?

The answer is, the same way he won the election—not by convincing the majority but by outmaneuvering them. In 2016, Trump identified a key constituency—working-class white voters in major swing states (Pennsylvania, Michigan, Ohio, Wisconsin)—and targeted them with a culturally populist message. It was Trump and them against the political and media elite. His populist base enabled Trump to win those states with bare majorities while losing California by more than four million votes.

What if he doesn't win? Then it's somebody else's fault. Trump said to his cabinet in October 2017, "We're not getting the job done. I'm not going to blame myself, I'll be honest. They [the lawmakers] are not getting the job done. . . . I'm not happy about it." But government is not business. He can't fire Congress.

Trump is betting that, through sheer force of personality, he will get things done and break the gridlock in Washington. He loses no opportunity to boast about how much he has achieved as president, declaring in June 2017 that rare is the president "who's passed more legislation, who's done more things than what we've done, between the executive orders and the job-killing regulations that have been terminated." Politifact rated his claim as "mostly false."

As long as Republicans control Congress, Trump may win on some issues like taxes with purely partisan majorities. But as was the case with Obamacare, a partisan policy is vulnerable to political sabotage. Instead of policymaking by compromise, our political future may be cycles of lurching political revenge. As Connecticut governor Dannel Malloy, a Democrat, put it, "If [Trump] had followed Lincoln, he'd have tried to reinstate slavery."

The Benefits of Weak Government

When you have a mentally unstable president with a fragile ego, ungovernability can be a blessing. It was noted in Chapter 1 that the US system was designed to be difficult to govern. The framers of the Constitution had just waged a revolution against a king. The king's abuses of authority were delineated in the Declaration of Independence. To the founders, strong government meant despotism. A system of weak government always had popular support because so many American settlers, with the important exception of slaves, were runaways from authority. They came to America to escape the authority of abusive governments, established churches, and economic monopolies. They had an inherent distrust of government and wanted it to interfere with their lives as little as possible.

The constitutional system limits President Trump's ability to abuse power. In a divided country, the constitutional system of checks and balances and separation of powers kicks into place. It raises barriers to action even when one party controls all the major branches of government. The most lasting damage Trump can do is likely to come from his nominations of federal judges, at least while a Republican majority in the Senate is in place to confirm his nominees. Federal judgeships are lifetime appointments.

In Trump's case, gridlock is sustained by public opposition to much of the president's agenda, like building a wall on the Mexican border. Public opinion remains a controlling factor in American politics. Even pro-Trump conservatives in Congress are reluctant to support policies that could generate voter backlash.

A system of limited government is particularly important when the country has a president with the temperament of a megalomaniac. In Trump's case, the signs are unmistakable. In July 2017, when Joshua Green published a book calling Steve Bannon the chief architect of Trump's election victory (*Devil's Bargain: Steve Bannon, Donald Trump, and the Storming of the Presidency*), Trump was annoyed that Bannon was getting too much credit. The president tweeted, "I love reading about all the 'geniuses' who were so instrumental in my election success. Problem is, most don't exist. #Fake News!" A month later, Bannon was out.[59]

The most alarming sign of megalomania occurred at a bizarre televised cabinet meeting in June 2017 when Trump called on each cabinet member, one by one, to lavish praise on himself. Like this from his chief of staff at the time: "Mr. President, we thank you for the opportunity and the blessing that you've given us to serve your agenda and the American people." It was a moment worthy of North Korea's "Dear Leader" Kim Jong-un. President Trump joined in the self-adulation, saying, "Never has there been a president . . . with few exceptions . . . who's passed more legislation, who's done more things than I have." At the time, Trump had no major legislative accomplishments, other than the confirmation of Supreme Court Justice Neil Gorsuch to replace conservative Justice Antonin Scalia.

A new president's first six months are typically a honeymoon period when he can achieve his most ambitious objectives. After nine months, Trump's proposals for infrastructure spending, tax reform, and a border wall with Mexico had not gotten anywhere. With polls showing the public skeptical of the prospects for "victory" in Afghanistan, Trump risked facing resistance from Republicans as well as Democrats to increasing the US troop commitment.

Trump rose in defiance of the political establishment. The political establishment, horrified by his conduct in office, quickly abandoned him. He has to rely on the loyalty of his populist army. They admire and celebrate his defiance of the establishment. But they, too, may abandon the president the moment they feel he is betraying them. As some believe he did in Afghanistan. Trump got elected on an isolationist platform. In November 2013, he tweeted, "We have wasted an enormous amount of blood and treasure in Afghanistan. Their government has zero appreciation. Let's get out!" [60]

Despite the constitutional limits on a president's power, there is always a risk. The risk arises if the country faces a crisis—a military conflict with North Korea or Iran, a terrorist incident, a natural disaster. Events like those are unpredictable. They can rally public urgency and turn an otherwise ungovernable system into one where the president becomes immensely powerful. The constitutional barriers break down. A crisis can transform the political situation and define a presidency. Exactly the way 9/11 did for President George W. Bush.

So far, Trump's plans have been thwarted by Congress (repeal of Obamacare), the federal courts (the travel ban), and hostile state governments (climate change). The system of checks and balances is working exactly as intended. The US constitutional system, which was designed in the 1770s to protect the country from a tyrant, can also protect the country from a megalomaniac.

Acknowledgments

I am grateful to the Schar School of Policy and Government at George Mason University and to Third Way in Washington, DC, for their generous support.

Over the years, I have benefited from the guidance of wonderful editors: Tim Rutten and the late Art Seidenbaum at the *Los Angeles Times*; John Fox Sullivan and the late Dick Frank at *National Journal*; Jack Beatty at *The Atlantic*; and, on this book, the wisdom and patience of Alice Mayhew. And especially to my longtime editor, Allison Silver at the *Los Angeles Times* and elsewhere, who has been a true friend and trusted adviser. Thanks also to my agent, Rick Broadhead, who came up with the idea for this project and stood by me for years. And Seymour Martin Lipset, who taught me how to think about politics.

My thanks also to the many great producers and colleagues I worked with at CNN—Paul Steinhauser, Shirley Zilberstein, Susan Steele, Sasha Johnson, Matt Hoye, Tom Hannon, Keating Holland, and Rob Yoon. And to friends who offered support and inspiration: Xandra Kayden; Douglas and Sherry Jeffe; Arnon Adar; and the late Alan Baron, who was one of a kind.

Notes

Chapter 1. Old America Versus New America

1. Rahm Emanuel, "Rahm Emanuel: You Never Want a Serious Crisis to Go to Waste," *Wall Street Journal* video, 0:10, posted by Jim Swift, February 9, 2009, www.youtube.com/watch?v=1yeA_kHHLow.
2. The best analysis of the US tradition of weak government is John W. Kingdon, *America the Unusual* (New York: Worth, 1999), especially ch. 2.
3. Frank Newport, "The Terry Schiavo Case in Review," Gallup News online, last modified April 1, 2005, www.gallup.com/poll/15475/terri-schiavo-case-review.aspx.
4. "Trust in Government," Gallup News online, accessed September 21, 2017, www.gallup.com/poll/5392/trust-government.aspx.
5. William Schneider, "Public Opinion and Foreign Policy: The Beginning of Ideology," *Foreign Policy* 17 (Winter 1974–75): 88–120.
6. Salena Zito, "Taking Trump Seriously, Not Literally," *Atlantic*, September 23, 2016, www.theatlantic.com/politics/archive/2016/09/trump-makes-his-case-in-pittsburgh/501335.
7. James Q. Wilson, "A Guide to Reagan County: The Political Culture of Southern California," *Commentary*, May 1967, 37–45.

8. Richard Todd, "Turned-On and Super-Sincere in California," *Harper's*, January 1967, 42–47.
9. Noel Sheppard, "David Brooks: 'Sometimes Obama Governs Like a Visitor from a Morally Superior Civilization," *mrcNewsBusters* (blog), December 30, 2012 http://newsbusters.org/blogs/noel-sheppard/2012/12/30 /david-brooks-sometimes-obama-governs-visitor-morally-superior-civiliz.

Chapter 2. Populism

1. Edward R. Schmitt, *President of the Other America: Robert Kennedy and the Politics of Poverty* (Amherst: University of Massachusetts Press, 2011), 210–11; Mark Stricherz, "The Death of the Bobby Kennedy Coalition," *Crisis*, February 21, 2008.
2. "New Hampshire Exit Polls (D)," CNN online, last modified February 9, 2016, www.cnn.com/election/primaries/polls/nh/Dem.
3. White House, "Remarks by the President on the Economy in Osawatomie, Kansas," news release, last modified December 6, 2011, https://obama whitehouse.archives.gov/the-press-office/2011/12/06/remarks-president -economy-osawatomie-kansas.
4. Phil Gailey, "Reagan, at Prayer Breakfast, Calls Politics and Religion Inseparable," *New York Times* online, August 24, 1984, www.nytimes.com /1984/08/24/us/reagan-at-prayer-breakfast-calls-politics-and-religion-in separable.html.
5. William Schneider, "The Republicans in '88," *Atlantic*, July 1987, www .theatlantic.com/past/docs/politics/policamp/repub88.htm.
6. Marie Diane, undated, comment on Erick Erickson quote from @EWErickson, saved from dailykos.com, www.pinterest.com/pin/16987 0217169850826.
7. Marjorie Connelly, "The 1994 Elections: Portrait of the Electorate: Who Voted for Whom in the House," *New York Times* online, November 13, 1994, www.nytimes.com/1994/11/13/us/the-1994-elections-portrait-of -the-electorate-who-voted-for-whom-in-the-house.html.
8. CNN Political Unit, "New CNN Poll: GOP Divided Over Tea Party Movement," CNN online, last modified September 15, 2011, http:// politcalticker.blogs.cnn.com/2011/09/15/new-cnn-poll-gop-divided-over -tea-party-movement.

9. Tara Golshan, "Donald Trump on Brexit: 'I Hope America Is Watching,' " Vox, last modified June 24, 2016, www.vox.com/2016/6/24/12023518 /donald-trump-brexit.

10. Nikki Casey, "Was Donald Trump's Speech His Bar Mitzvah Moment?" *Forward* online, last modified March 1, 2017, http://forward.com/opin ion/364614/was-donald-trumps-speech-his-bar-mitzvah-moment.

11. Alec Tyson and Shavia Maniam, "Behind Trump's Victory: Divisions by Race, Gender, Education," Pew Research Center, last modified November 9, 2016, www.pewresearch.org/fact-tank/2016/11/09/behind-trumps -victory-divisions-by-race-gender-education/.

12. "Exit Polls," CNN online, last modified November 23, 2016, http://edi tion.cnn.com/election/results/exit-polls.

Chapter 3. Polarization

1. "First Night: Clinton Takes To the Stage for the Ultimate Sell," *Independent* (UK) online, last modified June 4, 2004, www.independent.co.uk /news/world/americas/first-night-clinton-takes-to-the-stage-for-the-ulti mate-sell-731119.html.

2. Kingdon, *America the Unusual*, ch. 4.

3. "Exit Polls," CNN online, last modified November 23, 2016, www.cnn .com/election/results/exit-polls.

4. Kevin Phillips, *The Emerging Republican Majority* updated ed. (Princeton, NJ: Princeton University Press, 2014).

5. Barack Obama, *The Audacity of Hope: Thoughts on Reclaiming the American Dream* (New York: Vintage Books, 2008), ch. 1.

6. Bill Bishop with Robert G. Cushing, *The Big Sort: Why the Clustering of Like-Minded America Is Tearing Us Apart*, with new afterword (Boston: Mariner Books, 2009).

7. Jeffrey M. Jones, "Obama's Fourth Year in Office Ties as Most Polarized Ever," Gallup News online, last modified January 24, 2013, www.gallup .com/poll/160097/obama-fourth-year-office-ties-polarized-ever.aspx.

8. Jeffrey M. Jones, "Obama's Approval Most Polarized for First-Year President," Gallup News online, last modified January 25, 2010, www .gallup.com/poll/125345/obama-approval-polarized-first-year-president .aspx.

Chapter 4. Political Separation

1. Bishop with Cushing, *The Big Sort*.
2. "Political Polarization in the American Republic: How Increasing Ideological Uniformity and Partisan Antipathy Affect Politics, Compromise and Everyday Life," Pew Research Center, last modified June 12, 2014, www.people-press.org/2014/06/12/political-polarization-in-the-american-public.
3. Harry J. Enten, "How Polarisation in Washington Affects a Growing Feeling of Partisanship," *Guardian*, last modified December 28, 2012, www.theguardian.com/commentisfree/2012/dec/28/democrats-republicans-polarisation-congress.
4. "State Government Trifectas," Ballotpedia, accessed on September 23, 2017, https://ballotpedia.org/State_government_trifectas.
5. David Hawkings, "The Incredible Shrinking Split Tickets," *Roll Call* online, February 1, 2017, www.rollcall.com/news/hawkings/polarized-politics-split-tickets-midterms.
6. "Vital Statistics on Congress," Brookings Institution online, last modified April 7, 2014, www.brookings.edu/wp-content/uploads/2016/06/Vital-Statistics-Chapter-2-Congressional-Elections.pdf.
7. Nate Silver, "As Swing Districts Dwindle, Can a Divided House Stand?," *New York Times* online, December 27, 2012, http://fivethirtyeight.blogs.nytimes.com/2012/12/27/as-swing-districts-dwindle-can-a-divided-house-stand/?_r=0.
8. Enten, "Polarisation in Washington."
9. Emily Eakin, "Study Finds a Nation of Polarized Readers," *New York Times* online, March 13, 2004, www.nytimes.com/2004/03/13/books/study-finds-a-nation-of-polarized-readers.html; Husna Haq, "Conservative Books Are Leaping Off the Shelves, Say Amazon. Liberal Titles, Not So Much," *Christian Science Monitor*, August 22, 2012.
10. John Wagner, "Trump Plus 'Reasons to Vote for Democrats' Book Filled with Blank Pages," *Washington Post* online, April 17, 2017, www.washingtonpost.com/news/post-politics/wp/2017/04/17/trump-plugs-reasons-to-vote-for-democrats-book-filled-with-blank-pages/?utm_term=.e2b18013ae50.

11. "President Clinton: Scandals and Investigations, Continued," PollingReport.com, accessed September 23, 2017, http://www.pollingreport.com /scandal2.htm; Terry Neal and Richard Morin, "For Voters, It's Back Toward the Middle," *Washington Post* online, November 5, 1998, www .washingtonpost.com/wp-srv/politics/campaigns/keyraces98/stories/ poll110598.htm.

12. "Portrait of the Electorate: Table of Detailed Results," *New York Times* online, November 6, 2010, www.nytimes.com/interactive/2010/11/07 /weekinreview/20101107-detailed-exitpolls.html.

Chapter 5. The Great Reversal

1. On the relationship between progressives and New Deal Democrats, see Richard Hofstadter, *The Age of Reform: From Bryan to F.D.R.* (New York: Vintage Books, 1955), ch. 7; also David Plotke, *Building a Democratic Political Order: Reshaping American Liberalism in the 1930s and 1940s* (Cambridge: Cambridge University Press, 1996), ch. 4, 5, and 6.

2. Seymour Martin Lipset and Earl Raab, *The Politics of Unreason: Right-Wing Extremism in America, 1790–1970* (New York: Harper & Row, 1970).

3. Robert J. Blendon et al., "Americans' Views of Health Care Costs, Access, and Quality," *Milbank Quarterly* 84 no. 4 (2006): 623–57, www.ncbi.nlm .nih.gov/pmc/articles/PMC2690297.

4. David W. Moore, "Universal Vs. Government Health Insurance," Gallup News online, last modified December 9, 2003, www.gallup.com/poll /9943/universal-vs-government-health-insurance.aspx.

5. "Tracking Health Care Costs: A Slowing Down of the Rate of Increase," Center for Studying Health System Change, Issue Brief, no. 6, January 1997: www.hschange.org/CONTENT/75/75.pdf; "Real GDP Growth of the United States from 1990 to 2016," Statista, www.statista.com/statis tics/188165/annual-gdp-growth-of-the-united-states-since-1990.

6. Lydia Saad, "Public Is of Two Minds About Health Care Reform, Poll Shows," *St. Louis Post-Dispatch* online, August 2, 1994, www.questia .com/newspaper/1P2-32889631/public-is-of-two-minds-about-health -care-reform-poll.

7. Paul Steinhauser, "Poll: Health Care Costs Too Expensive, Americans Say," CNN online, last modified March 19, 2009, www.cnn.com/2009/POLITICS/03/19/health.care.poll/index.html?eref=ib_us.

8. "The *New York Times*-CBS News Poll," *New York Times*, July 24–28, 2009, http://graphics8.nytimes.com/packages/images/nytint/docs/new-york-times-cbs-news-poll-health-care-overhaul/original.pdf.

9. Ashley Kirzinger et al., "Kaiser Health Tracking Poll—July 2017: What's Next for Republican ACA Repeal and Replacement Plan Efforts?," Kaiser Family Foundation, July 14, 2017, www.kff.org/health-reform/poll-finding/kaiser-health-tracking-poll-july-2017-whats-next-for-republican-aca-repeal-and-replacement-plan-efforts.

10. Ashley Kirzinger, Bryan Wu, and Mollyann Brodie, "Kaiser Health Tracking Poll: Health Care Priorities for 2017," Kaiser Family Foundation, January 6, 2017, http://kff.org/health-costs/poll-finding/kaiser-health-tracking-poll-health-care-priorities-for-2017.

11. Mollyann Brodie et al., "Kaiser Health Tracking Poll," Kaiser Family Foundation, March 2012, https://kaiserfamilyfoundation.files.wordpress.com/2013/01/8285-f.pdf.

12. Liz Hamel et al., "Kaiser Health Tracking Poll: October 2014," Kaiser Family Foundation, October 21, 2014, http://kff.org/health-reform/poll-finding/kaiser-health-tracking-poll-october-2014.

13. Elise Vieback, Paul Kane, and Ed O'Keefe, "McCain Returns to Senate For Health-Care Vote to Emotional Applause from Colleagues," *Washington Post* online, July 25, 2017, www.washingtonpost.com/powerpost/mccain-returns-to-senate-with-health-care-debate-still-up-in-the-air/2017/07/25/cfc77534-7146-11e7-8839-ec48ec4cae25_story.html?utm_term=.e339ea40c17c.

14. Ashley Kirzinger et al., "Kaiser Health Tracking Poll—June 2017: ACA, Replacement Plan, and Medicaid," Kaiser Family Foundation, June 23, 2017, www.kff.org/health-reform/poll-finding/kaiser-health-tracking-poll-june-2017-aca-replacement-plan-and-medicaid.

15. Jacob Pramuk, "Rough Series of Polls Show Americans Broadly Disapprove of GOP Health Care Plan," CNBC online, last modified June 28, 2017, www.cnbc.com/2017/06/28/senate-gop-health-care-bill-has-dismal-approval-rating-poll.html.

Notes

Chapter 6. The Intensity Factor

1. Michael E. Miller, "S.F. Middle School Delays Election Results Because Winners Not Diverse Enough," *Washington Post* online, October 20, 2015, www.washingtonpost.com/news/morning-mix/wp/2015/10/20/s-f-middle-school-delays-election-results-because-winners-not-diverse-enough.

2. Jeffrey M. Jones, "On Social Ideology, the Left Catches Up to the Right," Gallup News online, last modified May 22, 2015, www.gallup.com/poll/183386/social-ideology-left-catches-right.aspx.

3. Nate Silver, "As Swing Districts Dwindle, Can a Divided House Stand?," *New York Times* online, December 27, 2012, https://fivethirtyeight.blogs.nytimes.com/2012/12/27/as-swing-districts-dwindle-can-a-divided-house-stand.

4. *The General Social Survey: Chronicling Changes in American Society*, Associated Press–NORC Center for Public Affairs Research, March 2015, www.apnorc.org/PDFs/GSS/GSSOverviewReport_FINAL.pdf.

5. *Washington Post*–ABC News national poll March 3–6, 2016, *Washington Post* online, March 2016, www.washingtonpost.com/apps/g/page/politics/washington-post-abc-news-national-poll-march-3-6-2016/1982.

6. Todd S. Purdum, "California G.O.P. Faces a Crisis as Hispanic Voters Turn Away," *New York Times* online, December 9, 1997, www.nytimes.com/1997/12/09/us/california-gop-faces-a-crisis-as-hispanic-voters-turn-away.html.

Chapter 7. The Power of Definition

1. "Americans' Response to the Nomination of Clarence Thomas," *Public Perspective*, November/December 1991, https://ropercenter.cornell.edu/public-perspective/ppscan/31/31012.pdf.

2. Ibid.

3. Robert C. Smith and Richard Seltzer, *Contemporary Controversies and the American Racial Divide* (Lanham, MD: Rowman & Littlefield, 2000), 72.

4. Tom W. Smith and Jaesok Son, *General Social Survey 2012 Final Report: Trends in Public Attitudes Towards Abortion*," NORC at the University of

Chicago, May 2013, www.norc.org/PDFs/GSS%20Reports/Trends%20 in%20Attitudes%20About%20Abortion_Final.pdf.

5. "Abortion," Gallup News online, May 3–7, 2017, www.gallup.com/poll /1576/Abortion.aspx.

6. Lydia Saad, "Americans Agree with Banning "Partial-Birth Abortion," Gallup News online, last modified November 6, 2003, www.gallup.com /poll/9658/Americans-Agree-Banning-PartialBirth-Abortion.aspx.

7. Moises F. Salinas, *The Politics of Stereotype: Psychology and Affirmative Action* (Santa Barbara, CA: Greenwood, 2003), 38.

8. "Public Backs Affirmative Action, but Not Minority Preferences," Pew Research Center, June 2, 2009, www.pewresearch.org/2009/06/02/public -backs-affirmative-action-but-not-minority-preferences/.

9. Jeffrey M. Jones, "In U.S., Most Reject Considering Race in College Admissions," Gallup News online, last modified July 24, 2013, www.gallup .com/poll/163655/reject-considering-race-college-admissions.aspx.

10. Bruce Drake, "Public Strongly Backs Affirmative Action Programs on Campus," Pew Research Center, April 22, 2014, www.pewresearch.org /fact-tank/2014/04/22/public-strongly-backs-affirmative-action-pro grams-on-campus.

11. "Trends in American Values: 1987–2012; Partisan Polarization Surges in Bush, Obama Years," Pew Research Center, June 4, 2012, www.people -press.org/files/legacy-pdf/06-04-12%20Values%20Release.pdf.

12. "Support for Same-Sex Marriage at Record High, but Key Segments Remain Opposed," Pew Research Center, June 8, 2015, www.people-press .org/2015/06/08/support-for-same-sex-marriage-at-record-high-but-key -segments-remain-opposed.

Chapter 8. The Burden of Indispensability

1. Henry A. Kissinger, *Does America Need a Foreign Policy? Toward a Diplomacy for the 21st Century* (New York: Simon & Schuster, 2001).

2. "Americans' Views on the Issues," *New York Times*–CBS News Poll, June 6, 2013, www.nytimes.com/interactive/2013/06/06/us/new-york-times -cbs-news-poll-june-2013.html?_r=0.

3. "CNN Poll: Cutting Biggest Govt. Spending Programs off the Table," CNN

online, January 25, 2011, http://politicalticker.blogs.cnn.com/2011/01/25
/cnn-poll-cutting-biggest-govt-spending-programs-off-the-table.

4. "President Bush Delivers Graduation Speech at West Point," WhiteHouse
.gov, June 2002, http://georgewbush-whitehouse.archives.gov/news/re
leases/2002/06/20020601-3.html.

5. Brad Knickerbocker, "Gates, Clinton: Libya Not a 'Vital Interest,' but
US Could Be There for Months," *Christian Science Monitor* online,
March 27, 2011, www.csmonitor.com/USA/Military/2011/0327/Gates
-Clinton-Libya-not-a-vital-interest-but-US-could-be-there-for-months.

6. Robert S. McNamara, *In Retrospect: The Tragedy and Lessons of Vietnam* (New York: Vintage Books, 1995).

7. Darren K. Carlson, "Public Convinced Saddam Is a Terrorist," Gallup
News online, last modified March 25, 2003, www.gallup.com/poll/8041
/Public-Convinced-Saddam-Terrorist.aspx?g_source=mn2-us.

8. "Bush Delivers Graduation Speech at West Point," WhiteHouse.gov.

9. John Mueller, "The Iraq Syndrome," *Foreign Affairs*, November/Decem-
ber 2005, www.foreignaffairs.com/articles/north-korea/2005-10-01/iraq
-syndrome.

10. "CNN Opinion Research Poll," CNN online, January 12, 2007, www.cnn
.com/2009/POLITICS/02/26/us.troops.poll/index.html?iref=topnews.

11. "Iraq," Polling Report, accessed September 29, 2017, www.pollingreport
.com/iraq3.htm.

12. "CNN Opinion Research Poll," CNN online, May 8, 2007, http://i.a.cnn
.net/cnn/2007/images/05/08/rel6d.pdf.

13. Paul Steinhauser, "CNN Poll: Afghanistan War Opposition at All-Time
High," CNN online, last modified September 1, 2009, http://political
ticker.blogs.cnn.com/2009/09/01/cnn-poll-afghanistan-war-opposition
-at-all-time-high.

14. "ISAF Commander's Counterinsurgency Guidance," Scribd, August 2009,
www.scribd.com/doc/19075680/COMISAF-COIN-GUIDANCE.

15. "Presidential Job Approval Center," Gallup News online, accessed September 29, 2017, www.gallup.com/interactives/185273/presidential-job
-approval-center.aspx.

16. "Text of President Obama's May 23 Speech on National Security
(Full Transcript)," *Washington Post* online, May 23, 2013, www.wash

ingtonpost.com/politics/president-obamas-may-23-speech-on-national
-security-as-prepared-for-delivery/2013/05/23/02c35e30-c3b8-11e2-9fe2
-6ee52d0eb7c1_story.html?utm_term=.6aa8d9e7cf09.

17. "Terrorism," Gallup News online, accessed September 29, 2017, www
.gallup.com/poll/4909/Terrorism-United-States.aspx.

18. "The President, Social Security and Iraq," CBS News–*New York Times*
Poll, June 10–15, 2005, www.cbsnews.com/htdocs/CBSNews_polls/bush
616.pdf.

19. "Bush Campaign to Base Ad on Kerry Terror Quote," CNN online, October 11, 2004, www.cnn.com/2004/ALLPOLITICS/10/10/bush.kerry.terror.

20. White House Office of the Press Secretary, "Remarks by the President at
the National Defense University," news release, May 23, 2013, https://
obamawhitehouse.archives.gov/the-press-office/2013/05/23/remarks
-president-national-defense-university.

21. Alyssa Brown and Frank Newport, "In U.S., 65% Support Drone Attacks
on Terrorists Abroad," Gallup News online, last modified March 25, 2013,
www.gallup.com/poll/161474/support-drone-attacks-terrorists-abroad
.aspx.

22. Scott Clement, "What Explains the Public's Support for Air Strikes Against
ISIS? The Terrorism Nerve," *Washington Post* online, September 9, 2014,
www.washingtonpost.com/news/the-fix/wp/2014/09/09/what-explains
-the-publics-support- for-air-strikes-against-isis-the-terrorism-nerve/?utm
_term=.4e485abf7f2f.

23. Peter Baker, "White House Looks to Syria Vote as Rudder for Rest of
Term," *New York Times* online, September 5, 2013, www.nytimes.com
/2013/09/06/world/europe/obama-arrives-in-russia-for-g20-summit.html
?pagewanted=all.

24. "Public Sees U.S. Power Declining as Support for Global Engagement
Slips," Pew Research Center, December 3, 2003, www.people-press
.org/files/legacy-pdf/12-3-2013%20APW%20VI.pdf.

25. White House Office of the Press Secretary, "Remarks by President Trump
to the People of Poland," news release, July 6, 2017, www.whitehouse.gov
/the-press-office/2017/07/06/remarks-president-trump-people-poland
-july-6-2017.

26. Peter Beinart, "The Racial and Religious Paranoia of Trump's Warsaw
Speech," *Atlantic*, July 6, 2017, www.theatlantic.com/international

/archive/2017/07/trump-speech-poland/532866; also see Stephen Wertheim, "Donald Trump's Plan to Save Western Civilization," *New York Times* online, July 22, 2017, www.nytimes.com/2017/07/22/opinion/sunday/donald-trumps-plan-to-save-western-civilization.html.

Chapter 9. Successful Challenges

1. Theodore Roosevelt was younger, forty-two, when he took office, but Vice President Roosevelt became president in 1901 after President William McKinley was assassinated. Roosevelt got elected three years later.
2. *Howard K. Smith*, "The Political Obituary of Richard M. Nixon," November 11, 1962, IMDb.com, www.imdb.com/title/tt1188135/?ref_=ttep_ep9.
3. Joe McGinnis, *The Selling of the President 1968: The Classic Account of the Packaging of a Candidate* (New York: Simon & Schuster, 1969).
4. Satya Nagendra Padala, "Recessions Since Great Depression," *International Business Times*, February 11, 2011, www/ibtimes.com/recessions-great-depression-265903.
5. Jon Cohen, "Reagan's 'Comeback,'" *Washington Post* online, October 13, 2008, http://voices.washingtonpost.com/behind-the-numbers/2008/10/reagans_comeback.html.
6. Martin Plissner, *The Control Room: How Television Calls the Shots in Presidential Elections* (New York: Simon & Schuster, 1999), 120–21.
7. "Election Results 2008," *New York Times* online, November 5, 2008, http://elections.nytimes.com/2008/results/president/national-exit-polls.html.
8. Tim Hibbitts, "The Man Who Supposedly Cost George H. W. Bush the Presidency," Polling Report, January 30, 2012, www.pollingreport.com/hibbitts1202.htm.
9. Thomas E. Patterson, "Voter Participation in Presidential Primaries and Caucuses," accessed October 1, 2017, http://journalistsresource.org/wp-content/uploads/2011/12/Voter-Turnout-in-Presidential-Primaries-and-Caucuses_Patterson.pdf.
10. Arthur Schlesinger Jr., *Kennedy or Nixon: Does It Make Any Difference?* (New York: Macmillan, 1960).
11. "Election Results 2008," *New York Times* online, November 5, 2008, http://elections.nytimes.com/2008/results/president/national-exit-polls.html.

12. In 2011, women comprised 6.7 percent of the state and federal prison population. E. Ann Carson and Elizabeth Anderson, *Bulletin: Prisoners in 2015*, US Bureau of Justice Statistics, December 2016, www.bjs.gov/content/pub/pdf/p15.pdf.

13. Samuel J. Best and Brian S. Krueger, *Exit Polls: Surveying the Electorate, 1972–2010* (Washington, DC: CQ Press, 2012), 107.

14. "Exit Polls: Pennsylvania," CNN online, accessed October 1, 2017, www.cnn.com/ELECTION/2008/primaries/results/epolls/#PADEM.

15. Juhem Navarro-Rivera, "Change and Continuity Among White Voters with No College Degrees," PRRI, September 27, 2012, http://publicreligion.org/2012/09/change-and-continuity-among-white-voters-with-no-college-degrees; Ruy Teixeira and John Halpin, "The Obama Coalition in the 2012 Election and Beyond," *American Progress*, December 2012, http://cdn.americanprogress.org/wp-content/uploads/2012/12/Obama Coalition-5.pdf; Ryan Morris, Voting Preferences of the American Electorate, 1980–2008, *National Journal*, August 24, 2012; "Exit Polls," CNN online, accessed October 1, 2017, www.cnn.com/ELECTION/2008/results/polls/#val=USP00p1; Nate Cohn, "Obama's Problem with White, Non-College Educated Voters Is Getting Worse," *New Republic*, June 11, 2012, www.newrepublic.com/article/103969/obamas-problem-white-non-college-educated-voters-getting-worse.

16. "2008 Presidential Democratic Primary Election Results," ElectionAtlas.org, accessed October 1, 2017, http://uselectionatlas.org/RESULTS/national.php?year=2008&elect=1.

17. Paul Steinhauser, "CNN Poll: Majority Think Country Headed for Depression," CNN online, October 6, 2008, http://politicalticker.blogs.cnn.com/2008/10/06/cnn-poll-majority-think-us-headed-for-depression (crosstabulations by author).

18. "Exit Polls," CNN online, accessed October 1, 2017, www.cnn.com/ELECTION/2008/results/polls/#val=USP00p6.

19. "Exit Polls," CNN online, accessed October 1, 2017, www.cnn.com/ELECTION/2008/results/polls/#val=USP00p1.

20. Joe Concha, "Gallup: Obama Approval Ratings Most Polarized in US History," *The Hill*, January 25, 2017, http://thehill.com/homenews/media/316024-gallup-obama-approval-ratings-most-polarized-in-us-history.

Chapter 10. Failed Challenges

1. Godfrey Sperling, "Nixon's 'Secret Plan' That Never Was," *Christian Science Monitor* online, December 9, 1997, www.csmonitor.com/1997/1209/120997.opin.column.1.html.

2. "Election Polls—Vote by Groups, 1952–1956," Gallup News online, accessed October 1, 2017, www.gallup.com/poll/9451/election-polls-vote-groups-19521956.aspx; "Election Polls—Vote by Groups, 1985–1988," Gallup News online, accessed October 1, 2017, www.gallup.com/poll/9463/election-polls-vote-groups-19841988.aspx.

3. Lawrence E. Walsh, *Final Report of the Independent Counsel for Iran/Contra Matters* vol. 1: Investigations and Prosecutions (Washington, DC: United States Court of Appeals for the District of Columbia Circuit 1993), ch. 28, http://fas.org/irp/offdocs/walsh/chap_28.htm.

4. "The Vote '96: Presidential Election Exit Poll Results—Part 1," CNN online, last modified November 6, 1996, www.cnn.com/ALLPOLITICS/1996/elections/natl.exit.poll/index2.html.

5. "The Vote '96: Presidential Election Exit Poll Results—Part 1," CNN online, last modified November 6, 1996, www.cnn.com/ALLPOLITICS/1996/elections/natl.exit.poll/index2.html.

6. Brian Faler, "Election Turnout in 2004 Was Highest Since 1968," *Washington Post* online, January 15, 2005, www.washingtonpost.com/wp-dyn/articles/A10492-2005Jan14.html.

7. Lydia Saad, "Conservatives Remain the Largest Ideological Group in the U.S.," Gallup News online, last modified January 12, 2012, www.gallup.com/poll/152021/conservatives-remain-largest-ideological-group.aspx.

8. Frank Newport, "Questions and Answers with the Editor in Chief," Gallup News online, last modified October 5, 2004, www.gallup.com/poll/13294/questions-answers-editor-chief.aspx.

9. "Direction of the Country," Polling Report, accessed October 1, 2017, www.pollingreport.com/right.htm; "Economic Outlook," Polling Report, accessed October 1, 2017, www.pollingreport.com/consumer2.htm; "NBC News/*Wall Street Journal* Survey," *Wall Street Journal* online, July 17–21, 2013, http://online.wsj.com/public/resources/documents/wsjnbcpoll_july2013.pdf.

Notes

Chapter 11. 2016: Populist Backlash

1. Peter Holley and Sarah Larimer, "How America's Dying White Supremacist Movement Is Seizing on Donald Trump's Appeal," *Washington Post*, February 29, 2016, www.washingtonpost.com/news/morning-mix/wp/2015/12/21/how-donald-trump-is-breathing-life-into-americas-dying-white-supremacist-movement; sh?utm_term=.6380fe1cf273.

2. James Hohmann, "Trump: Maybe America Should Try Making a Jerk President," *Washington Post* online, August 27, 2015, www.washingtonpost.com/news/post-politics/wp/2015/08/27/trump-maybe-america-should-try-making-a-jerk-president/?utm_term=.983f4449 56af.

3. Patrick Healy and Maggie Haberman, "95,000 Words, Many of Them Ominous, from Donald Trump's Tongue," *New York Times* online, December 5, 2015, www.nytimes.com/2015/12/06/us/politics/95000-words-many-of-them-ominous-from-donald-trumps-tongue.html?_r=0.

4. Noah Bierman, "Donald Trump on Obama: 'Something Going On with Him That We Don't Know About,'" *Los Angeles Times* online, December 3, 2015, www.latimes.com/politics/la-na-donald-trump-jewish-group-20151203-story.html.

5. Maggie Haberman, "Trump: How'd Obama Get into Ivies?," *Politico*, last modified April 26, 2011, www.politico.com/story/2011/04/trump-howd-obama-get-into-ivies-053694.

6. Ashley Kirzinger, Elise Sugarman, and Mollyann Brodie, "Kaiser Health Tracking Poll: November 2016," Kaiser Family Foundation, December 1, 2016, www.kff.org/health-costs/poll-finding/kaiser-health-tracking-poll-november-2016.

7. *Public Papers of the Presidents of the United States: William J. Clinton*, Book 2, July 1 to December 31, 1996 (Washington, DC: Office of the Federal Register, 1998), accessed October 1, 2017, https://books.google.com/books?id=EiXhAwAAQBAJ&pg=PA2186&1pg=PA2186&dq=Bill+Clinton+for+years+politicians+have+treated+our+most+vexing+problems+like+crime&source=bl&ots=Ee8Qf8ia0b&sig=NAPiqH9WRr4dARofv5en5Xa7Z0Y&hl=en&sa=X&ved=0ahUKEwiG8_H_wrnTAhWnJMAKHb2-Di8Q6AEIMjAD#v=onepage&q=Bill%20Clinton%20for%20years%20politicians%20have%20treated%20our%20most%20vexing%20probl ems%20like%20crime&f=false.

8. Susan B. Glasser, "President Not-Obama: How Trump's Syria Strike Got Even Some Key Obama Advisers Cheering," *Politico*, April 7, 2017, www.politico.com/magazine/story/2017/04/trump-syria-attack-doctrine-foreign-policy-theory-214999.

9. Ruy Teixeira and John Halpin, *The Obama Coalition in the 2012 Election and Beyond* (Washington, DC: Center for American Progress, December 2012), http://cdn.americanprogress.org/wp-content/uploads/2012/12/ObamaCoalition-5.pdf; "Exit Polls," CNN online, last modified November 23, 2016, www.cnn.com/election/results/exit-polls.

10. Josh Hafner, "Donald Trump Loves the 'Poorly Educated'—and They Love Him," *USA Today* online, last modified February 24, 2016, www.usatoday.com/story/news/politics/onpolitics/2016/02/24/donald-trump-nevada-poorly-educated/80860078.

11. David Weigel, "Democrats' Trump-Era House Map Starts in Diverse South," *Washington Post* online, January 28, 2017, www.washingtonpost.com/powerpost/democrats-trump-era-house-map-starts-in-diverse-south/2017/01/28/ff26302c-e4dd-11c6-a547-5fb9411d332c_s tory.html?utm_term=.0518a9b18c2b.

12. Paul Waugh, "Commons Speaker John Bercow Slams Trump 'Racism, Sexism' and Vows to Block Westminster Invite," *Huffington Post*, February 7, 2017, www.huffingtonpost.co.uk/entry/racist-sexist-donald-trump-john-bercow-westminster-hall-state-visit_uk_5898aafee4b076856216dee7; Toby Helm, "We Will Boycott Trump Speech, Say Labour's Female MPs," *Guardian*, last modified February 4, 2017, www.theguardian.com/us-news/2017/feb/04/labour-female-mps-trump-speech-boycott.

13. Quinnipiac University Poll, "Trump Slump Continues as He Drops Below Obama, Quinnipiac University National Poll Finds; Republicans in Congress Drop to More Than 3–1 Negative," news release, April 4, 2017, https://poll.qu.edu/national/release-detail?ReleaseID=2448.

14. Quinta Jurecic, "Can a President Who Disregards the Truth Uphold His Oath of Office?," *Washington Post* online, January 27, 2017, www.washingtonpost.com/posteverything/wp/2017/01/27/can-a-president-who-disregards-the-truth-uphold-his-oath-of-office/?utm_term=.583bfc25406f.

15. Emma Green, "It Was Cultural Anxiety That Drove White, Working-Class Voters to Trump," *Atlantic*, May 9, 2017, www.theatlantic.com/politics/archive/2017/05/white-working-class-trump-cultural-anxiety/525771.

16. Hannah Fingerhut, "Republicans Skeptical of Colleges' Impact on U.S., but Most See Benefits for Workforce Preparation," Pew Research Center, July 20, 2017, www.pewresearch.org/fact-tank/2017/07/20/repub licans-skeptical-of-colleges-impact-on-u-s-but-most-see-benefits-for -workforce-preparation.

17. Nate Cohn, "A 2016 Review: Why Key State Polls Were Wrong About Trump," *New York Times* online, May 31, 2017, www.nytimes.com/2017 /05/31/upshot/a-2016-review-why-key-state-polls-were-wrong-about -trump.html?_r=0.

18. Healy and Haberman, "95,000 Words."

19. Adam Wren, "Trump County, USA: America's Most Reliable Bellwether County Has Fallen for the Wild Man from New York," *Politico*, December 4, 2015, www.politico.com/magazine/story/2015/12/2016-indiana -county-predicts-every-election-trump-fever-213411.

20. Andrew Levison, "Democrats Have a White Working Class Problem—and Not Just in the South," *New Republic*, August 5, 2014, https://newrepub lic.com/article/118960/democrats-white-working-class-problem-isnt-just -south.

21. David Wasserman, "2016 National Popular Vote Tracker," *Cook Political Report*, accessed October 2, 2017, https://docs.google.com/spreadsheets /d/133Eb4qQmOxNvtesw2hdVns073R68EZx4SfCnP4IGQf8/htmlview ?sle=true#gid=19.

22. Peter Baker, "As Trump Drifts Away from Populism, His Supporters Grow Watchful," *New York Times* online, April 18, 2017, www.nytimes .com/2017/04/18/us/politics/populism-donald-trump-administration .html.

23. Dan Balz and Scott Clement, "Nearing 100 Days, Trump's Approval at Record Lows but His Base Is Holding, *Washington Post* online, April 23, 2017, www.washingtonpost.com/politics/nearing-100-days -trumps-approval-at-record-lows-but-his-base-is-holding/2017/04/22 /a513a466-26b4-11e7-b503-9d616bd5a305_story.html?hpid=hp_rhp -top-table-main_poll-1202am%3Ahomepage%2Fstory&utm_term=.5ab 73666e171.

24. Dan Balz, "Bill Clinton: Once Again in the Spotlight, but Before a Different Party," *Washington Post* online, July 26, 2016, www.washington post.com/politics/bill-clinton-once-again-in-the-spotlight-but-before-a

-different-party/2016/07/26/82837bd8-534c-11e6-b7de-dfe509430c39
_story.html?utm_term=.2b1352da1c36.

25. "Presidential Candidate Clinton Primary Night Speech," C-Span, June 7, 2016, www.c-span.org/video/?410728-1/hillary-clinton-clinches-demo cratic-nomination.

26. Kate Reilly, "Read Hillary Clinton's Historic Victory Speech as Presumptive Democratic Nominee," *Time*, June 8, 2016, http://time.com/4361099 /hillary-clinton-nominee-speech-transcript.

27. Run for something, "Donald Trump Is President. Trust Us, You're Qualified to Run for Local Office," Twitter, February 18, 2017, https://twitter .com/runforsomething/status/833077889411248132.

28. Ben Schreckinger, "Donald Trump, Protesters Go Big in Texas," *Politico*, last modified September 15, 2015, www.politico.com/story/2015/09/don ald-trump-2016-dallas-megarally-213625.

29. "30 of Donald Trump's Wildest Quotes," CBS News online, accessed on October 2, 2017, www.cbsnews.com/pictures/wild-donald-trump-quotes/11.

30. Garance Frank-Ruta, "Donald Trump: 'I Have a Great Relationship with the Blacks,'" *Atlantic*, April 14, 2011, www.theatlantic.com/politics/ar chive/2011/04/donald-trump-i-have-a-great-relationship-with-the-blacks /237332.

31. Max Ehrenfreund, "What Social Science Tells Us About Racism in the Republican Party," *Washington Post* online, December 11, 2015, www .washingtonpost.com/news/wonk/wp/2015/12/11/what-social-science -tells-us-about-racism-in-the-republican-party/?utm_term=.09fc110 d35c0.

32. Seymour Martin Lipset, *Political Man: The Social Bases of Politics* (New York: Doubleday, 1960), ch. 4, "Working Class Authoritarianism."

33. Nick Gass, "Trump on Putin's Alleged Killing of Journalists: 'At Least He's a Leader,'" *Politico*, last modified December 18, 2015, www.politico .com/story/2015/12/trump-praises-putin-216929.

34. Meus Renaissance, "Excellent Article: Trump Proves Republican Obama Hate Was Never About Obama's Ideas," *NeoGAF* (blog), November 17, 2016, www.neogaf.com/forum/showthread.php?p=224756838.

35. Aidan Quigley, "Trump Praises Brexit During Theresa May Press Conference," *Politico*, January 27, 2017, www.politico.com/story/2017/01 /trump-praises-brexit-theresa-may-press-conference-234277.

36. "Transcript: Donald Trump's Victory Speech," *New York Times* online, November 9, 2016, www.nytimes.com/2016/11/10/us/politics/trump-speech-transcript.html?_r=0.

37. "Read: Elizabeth Warren's Post-Election Speech," *Boston Globe* online, November 10, 2016, www.bostonglobe.com/news/politics/2016/11/10/read-warren-post-election-speech/dW4AAapP7REzDNoFrpLfNI/story.html.

38. Michael Wolff, "Ringside with Steve Bannon at Trump Tower as the President-Elect's Strategist Plots 'An Entirely New Political Movement' (Exclusive)," *Hollywood Reporter* online, November 18, 2016, www.hollywoodreporter.com/news/steve-bannon-trump-tower-interview-trumps-strategist-plots-new-political-movement-948747.

39. "The Inaugural Address," White House, January 20, 2017, www.whitehouse.gov/inaugural-address.

40. "Full Transcript and Video: Trump News Conference," *New York Times* online, February 16, 2017, www.nytimes.com/2017/02/16/us/politics/donald-trump-press-conference-transcript.html.

41. White House Office of the Press Secretary, "Remarks by President Trump in Joint Address to Congress," news release, February 28, 2017, www.whitehouse.gov/the-press-office/2017/02/28/remarks-president-trump-joint-address-congress.

42. "Direction of the Country," Polling Report, accessed October 2, 2017, www.pollingreport.com/right.htm; "President Obama: Job Ratings," Polling Report, accessed October 2, 2017, www.pollingreport.com/obama_job2.htm#CNN.

43. "CNN Poll," CNN online, November 22, 2017, http://i2.cdn.turner.com/cnn/2016/images/11/22/rel20a.-.trump.expectations.pdf.

44. Mark Leibovich, "This Town Melts Down," *New York Times Magazine*, July 11, 2017, www.nytimes.com/2017/07/11/magazine/washington-dc-politics-trump-this-town-melts-down.html?_r=1.

45. Dan Batz, "A Scholar Asks, 'Can Democracy Survive the Internet?,'" *Washington Post* online, April 22, 2017, https://law.stanford.edu/press/scholar-asks-can-democracy-survive-internet.

46. Matt Flegenheimer, "Deepening Rift, Trump Won't Say If Mitch McConnell Should Step Down," *New York Times* online, August 10, 2017, www

.nytimes.com/2017/08/10/us/politics/president-trump-escalates-criticism-of-mitch-mcconnell-as-majority-leader.html?mcubz=1.

47. Eugene Scott and Miranda Green, "Trump, Graham Feud over President's Charlottesville Response," CNN online, last modified August 17, 2017, www.cnn.com/2017/08/16/politics/lindsey-graham-donald-trump-charlottesville/index.html.

48. Eugene Scott, "Trump Calls Out Murkowski over Health Care Vote," CNN online, last modified July 26, 2017, www.cnn.com/2017/07/26/politics/twitter-trump-murkowski-health-care/index.html.

49. Jeff Flake, "My Party Is in Denial About Donald Trump," *Politico*, last modified July 31, 2017, www.politico.com/magazine/story/2017/07/31/my-party-is-in-denial-about-donald-trump-215442.

50. David Wright, "Trump: Flake 'Toxic,' Boosts His Primary Opponent," CNN online, last modified August 17, 2017, www.cnn.com/2017/08/17/politics/trump-tweet-jeff-flake-kelli-ward-arizona-republican-primary/index.html.

51. Sean Sullivan, "GOP Leaders Say It's Time for Senate to Move On from Health Care," *Washington Post* online, July 31, 2017, www.washingtonpost.com/powerpost/gop-leaders-say-its-time-for-senate-to-move-on-from-health-care/2017/07/31/d6000d3c-760d-11e7-9eac-d56bd5568db8_story.html?utm_term=.48b25704829f.

52. Elana Schor and Seung Min Kim, "GOP Lawmakers Square Off Against Trump," *Politico*, August 4, 2017, www.politico.com/story/2017/08/04/senate-struggles-to-rein-trump-241302.

53. Cameron Easley, "Health Care Failure Takes a Political Toll on Trump, GOP Lawmakers," *Morning Consult*, last modified August 2, 2017, https://morningconsult.com/2017/08/02/health-care-failure-takes-political-toll-trump-hill-republicans.

54. Jonathan Swan, "Trump Adviser Tells House Republicans: You're No Longer Reagan's Party," *The Hill*, November 23, 2016, http://thehill.com/homenews/campaign/307462-trump-adviser-tells-house-republicans-youre-no-longer-reagans-party.

55. Eric Levitz, "Trump Has Converted the GOP Base to His Ideology: Trump First," *New York* online, August 22, 2017, http://nymag.com/daily/intelligencer/2017/08/trump-converted-gop-base-to-his-ideology-trump-first.html.

56. Sean Sullivan, "Can This Marriage Be Saved? Relationship Between Trump, Senate GOP Hits New Skids," *Washington Post* online, August 1, 2017, www.washingtonpost.com/powerpost/can-this-marriage-be-saved-rela tionship-between-trump-senate-gop-hits-new-skids/2017/08/01/cb93eb1a -76d1-11e7-9eac-d56bd5568db8_story.html?utm_term=.e0acab03a682.

57. "Trump Slams Congress for Bringing Russia Relations to 'Dangerous Low,'" Fox News online, last modified August 3, 2017, www.foxnews .com/politics/2017/08/03/trump-slams-congress-for-bringing-russia-rela tions-to-dangerous-low.html.

58. Darren Samuelsohn, "Bipartisan Bills Unveiled to Protect Mueller," *Politico*, last modified August 3, 2017, www.politico.com/story/2017/08/03 /robert-mueller-senate-bills-protection-241296.

59. Mandy Mayfield, "Trump on 'Geniuses' Who Were Instrumental in Election Success: They 'Don't Exist,'" *Washington Examiner*, July 29, 2017, www.washingtonexaminer.com/trump-on-geniuses-who-were-instrumen tal-in-election-success-they-dont-exist/article/2630117.

60. Jennifer Martinez, "'Time to come home!': Trump's Tweets Reveal a Strong Opinion on the Afghanistan War Before He Became President," *Business Insider*, last modified August 21, 2017, www.businessinsider .com/trump-tweets-afghanistan-opposition-2017-8.

Index

Index

antiwar activism
  and intensity factor, 121
  and Kerry, 232–33
  in 1960s and 1970s, 14, 20, 67, 186, 216, 217, 259
  and Obama, 175–76
  and populism, 32
  and US role in world affairs, 166
Arab-Israeli War (1973), 32
Assad, Bashar al-, 163, 249, 250
Aurora, Colorado: shooting in, 127
austerity: as theme for 2012 election, 236–40
authoritarian nationalism, 181

Bachmann, Michele, 37, 112
Bannon, Steve, 257, 264, 279
Baron, Alan, 183–84
"Bear in the Woods" (Reagan ad), 220, 234
Bennett, Bill, 87, 131
Bethesda, Maryland, 80–82
Biden, Joe, 122, 168
bipartisanship, 76–77, 107, 206, 207–8, 260. See also partisanship
Bishop, Bill, 73–74
Black Lives Matter, 118
Bloomberg, Michael, 30, 125
Blunt, Roy, 273
Boehner, John, 91
books: and political separation, 78–79
border wall, Mexican, 65, 279, 280
Bork, Robert, 139–40
Bosnia, 157, 160, 161
Bradley, Bill, 35, 208
Bradley, Tom, 12
Brady Handgun Violence Prevention Act (1991, 1993), 122, 123, 229
Brandeis University: mock Republican convention at, 53–55
Breitbart News Network, 257
Brexit, 262–63
Brooks, David, 27, 81, 82
Brown, Jerry, 188, 258
Brown, Scott, 105
Brown v. Board of Education (1954), 59
Brown, Willie, 150–51
Bryan, William Jennings, 51
Buchanan, Patrick, 195, 196, 199
budget. See economy; taxes
Burwell v. Hobby Lobby Stores, Inc. (2014), 40

Bush, George H. W.
  approval ratings for, 66–67, 172, 194
  as business executive, 237
  and conservatives, 192
  and economy, 156, 194, 195, 237
  election of 1988 and, 32, 193, 199, 222–25, 226–27, 244
  election of 1992 and, 3, 33, 193, 195, 196, 210, 228
  and foreign policy, 194, 195
  and Iran-contra scandal, 222–23
  and Iraq, 203
  and New versus Old America, 3
  and Persian Gulf War, 193, 194
  and polarization, 66–67, 70
  and populism, 32, 33, 39
  and race, 210, 226–27, 261
  and Republican image, 193, 200
  and taxes, 196
  wealth of, 193, 194, 224
  and world affairs, 156, 159, 160–61, 165, 166, 172
Bush, George W.
  and abortion, 201
  and affirmative action, 201
  approval rating for, 67, 68, 172
  books about, 78
  as business executive, 237
  character of, 205
  as compassionate conservative, 201
  convention speech of, 202
  and death penalty, 31
  and economy, 194, 203
  election of 2000 and, 5, 12–13, 20, 123, 172, 197, 198, 200, 202, 203, 205, 225, 269
  election of 2004 and, 175, 231, 232, 233–34, 235–36, 269
  election of 2008 and, 271
  and gay issues, 152, 201
  and immigration, 130–31, 132, 133
  inaugural speeches of, 171
  and intensity factor, 130–31, 132, 133
  and Iraq, 20, 70, 203, 232, 233, 234, 269
  likability of, 198
  mandate for, 269
  and New versus Old America, 5, 12–13, 20
  and 1960s culture, 206
  and polarization, 53, 67, 68, 70
  and political separation, 76, 78, 82

Index

Index

Index

Index

economy (*cont.*)
  and political separation, 79
  and populism, 30, 31–34, 36, 37–38, 64, 65, 243, 259, 262
  and progressives, 263
  public opinion about, 236
  and race, 227
  and Republican conservatism, 189, 196
  and role of government, 92–93, 94–95, 96, 238
  and single issue voting, 127
  and values/interests, 24, 26
  See also specific person or election
education, 229, 251–55, 258, 274
Edwards, John, 168, 207, 234
Eisenhower, Dwight D., 59, 66, 185, 193, 214, 224, 249, 268
elections
  close votes in, 198–99
  congressional, 7, 15
  expectations in, 266–67
  as horse races, 230
  and Law of Missing Imperative, 184
  and party stereotypes, 244
  scare tactics in, 233–35
  for state and local government, 7, 15–16
  television coverage of, 15
  "wave," 75
  See also specific election or candidate
election of 1912, 196, 224
election of 1932, 246
election of 1946, 223
election of 1948, 223
election of 1956, 220
election of 1960, 74, 185, 198, 199, 224, 226
election of 1964
  and change, 214, 215
  choice as theme of, 213–15
  and civil rights, 189, 214, 215
  and communism, 214
  and economy, 214
  election of 1972 compared with, 215–16
  failed challenges in, 213–15
  and Law of the Missing Imperative, 183–84
  and moderates, 190
  and New versus Old America, 2, 22, 189
  and polarization, 55, 59, 61
  and political separation, 76
  and populism, 38
  and taxes, 215

truck campaign in, 183–84
  and Vietnam, 214
  See also specific candidate
election of 1968
  anger during, 246
  and antiwar activism, 186, 216
  challengers in, 196
  and change, 187
  and civil rights, 195
  Democratic convention for, 216
  and economy, 195
  failed challenges in, 224
  and Law of the Missing Imperative, 186–87
  and New versus Old America, 19–20
  order as theme of, 186–87
  and polarization, 59, 61, 67, 69
  and populism, 32, 34, 35, 36, 39
  and race, 186, 208
  and Vietnam, 19–20, 32, 61, 69, 186, 195, 217
  See also specific candidate
election of 1972
  and abortion, 69, 216
  and antiwar activism, 216, 217
  and Cold War, 189
  election of 1964 compared with, 215–16
  failed challenges in, 215–17
  and moderates, 190
  and New versus Old America, 2, 3, 4, 20, 22, 189, 225
  peace as theme for, 215–17
  and polarization, 59, 61–62, 69
  and populism, 32, 35, 36, 39
  and race, 189, 208
  and taxes, 61–62
  and Vietnam, 20, 32, 62, 216, 217
  See also specific candidate
election of 1976
  challengers in, 195–96
  and civil rights, 188
  failed challenges in, 224
  and Law of the Missing Imperative, 187–88
  morality as theme of, 187–88
  and New versus Old America, 2
  and polarization, 62
  and populism, 32–33
  and race, 188, 226
  See also specific candidate
election of 1980
  and abortion, 141, 191, 192
  anger during, 246

Index

Index

Index

and political separation, 74, 76
and populism, 27, 37, 38, 43
public opinion about, 236, 238
and race, 210
and role of government, 92, 238
and same-sex marriage, 240
as status quo election, 240
and Tea Party, 240
and wealth image, 194
See also specific candidate
election of 2014, 2, 15, 23, 75, 108,
   111–12, 134, 210, 271
election of 2016
   as antiestablishment revolt, 196
   books about, 78
   and breakdown of American politics, 241
   and change, 189, 248, 251, 258, 269
   and coalitions, 22
   and conservatives, 250–51
   and crisis, 267–68, 269
   and Democratic party shift to left,
      258–59
   demographics and, 6
   and economy, 253, 258–59, 268
   and education, 251–55, 258
   and electoral college, 6–7, 241, 255, 266
   expectations for, 267
   failed challenges in, 224
   and gay rights, 154
   and gridlock, 6–7, 189
   and gun laws, 258
   and health care, 115, 248
   and immigration, 129, 133, 134, 258, 268
   and intensity factor, 117, 118–19, 133,
      134
   and jobs, 246, 258, 263, 264
   and middle class, 258
   and New versus Old America, 1, 4, 5,
      6–7, 10, 22, 25, 26
   and Obama, 211–12, 271
   and polarization, 57, 63, 64, 68, 69, 71,
      189, 211–12, 250, 255–56
   and political separation, 74, 75, 76, 78,
      80–81
   popular vote in, 241, 247, 255
   and populism, 4–5, 23, 27, 30, 31,
      34, 36, 38, 43–44, 49–52, 63, 196,
      241–80
   primaries for, 242, 272
   and public opinion, 6–7
   and race, 210
   and religion, 43–44, 57

and role of government, 258
Russian role in, 23
and Russian sanctions, 275
slogans/theme for, 2, 10, 50, 58, 117,
   269
and taxes, 258, 268
and Tea Party, 242, 256
and terrorism, 268
and Trump as breaking the rules, 243–47
and Trump as nonpolitician, 196
Trump rebellion in, 196
and Trump-Republican relationship,
   252, 255, 256–57, 275
Trump views about, 266
and unification, 212
and US role in world affairs, 176–77,
   178–82, 268
voting "fraud" in, 252
and working-class whites, 242, 251, 252,
   253, 267, 269
See also Clinton, Hillary; Trump, Donald
election of 2018, 273, 275–76
election of 2020, 276
electoral college, 6–7, 12–13, 23, 241, 255,
   266
elites, 30, 31–38, 243, 270–71
Emanuel, Rahm, 8
environment, 229, 280
Equal Rights Amendment (ERA), 191–92

fairness
   election of 1982 and, 219
   as theme for 1984 election, 217–22
Family and Medical Leave Act, 229
Fantasy Decade, 155–58, 162
federal judgeships: and Trump, 278, 279
Feinstein, Dianne, 17, 146
financial crisis of 2008, 4, 9, 63, 210, 258,
   265, 269
Flake, Jeff, 272–73
Flowers, Gennifer, 228
Ford, Gerald, 33, 55, 62, 187, 192, 195–96
foreign policy. *See* world affairs; *specific
   election or issue*
Frey, William, 129

Gallup Polls, 16, 85, 88, 99, 100, 102, 120,
   137, 139, 145, 148, 166, 172, 174,
   211, 268
Gates, Robert, 162
gay rights, 14–15, 87, 122. *See also* same-
   sex marriage

Index

gender
  election of 1984 and, 220–21
  election of 2000 and, 201–2
  See also affirmative action; civil rights;
    gay rights
Gephardt, Richard, 35, 159
Gingrich, Newt, 37, 41–42, 46, 84, 200,
  201, 245, 267
Goldberg, Arthur, 55
Goldwater, Barry
  and communism, 214
  election of 1964 and, 2, 38, 54, 55, 59,
    189, 213, 214, 215–16, 234, 261
  and Law of the Missing Imperative, 184
  and New versus Old America, 2, 26
  and polarization, 54, 55, 59, 60, 61
  and populism, 38, 39
  and race, 261
  and taxes, 215
Gonzalez, Elian, 16, 135, 136–37, 157
Gore, Al
  and class issues, 209
  Clinton (Bill) relationship with, 204
  and Clinton scandals, 17
  election of 1992 and, 3
  election of 2000 and, 4, 5, 12–13, 35,
    80, 123, 172, 197, 198, 199, 202, 203,
    204, 205, 224
  election of 2004 and, 231
  and gun laws, 123, 124
  and intensity factor, 123, 124
  and New versus Old America, 3, 4, 5,
    12–13, 17
  and populism, 35
  and Social Security, 203
  and taxes, 203
  and world affairs, 172
government
  business compared with, 249
  distrust of, 278
  shutdown of, 5, 45–46, 110, 115, 200
  See also Constitution, US; government,
    role of
government, role of
  and abortion, 140–47
  and benefits of weak government,
    278–80
  and change, 94
  and Constitution, 268–69
  and crisis, 269
  debate about, 91–97
  and definition of issues, 135–40

Democrat views about, 258
and economy, 238
election of 2012 and, 92, 238
election of 2016 and, 258
and funding for government, 93–94
and government as instrument of justice,
  96
and health care, 97–116
and infrastructure, 263–64
and New versus Old America, 10
and party government, 105–8, 113
public opinion about, 136, 137
and race, 227
and Tea Party, 263
Graham, Lindsey, 272
Great Depression, 237, 246, 258, 262, 264,
  269
gridlock, 6–10, 189, 248, 277, 279
gun laws
  debate about, 140
  election of 1994 and, 123, 229
  election of 2008 and, 209
  election of 2016 and, 258
  and intensity factor, 120–21, 122–27, 132
  and political separation, 79–80, 81
  public opinion about, 125, 126
  and role of government, 140
  and Trump as un-Obama, 248
  and Trump-Republican party
    relationship, 274

Hagel, Chuck, 163, 169
Hannity, Sean, 78
Hart, Gary, 35, 36, 208
health care
  as complicated, 116
  costs of, 100
  debate about, 97–116
  and economy, 100, 103
  and middle class, 98–99, 100, 102, 103,
    104
  and partisanship, 278
  and party government, 113
  and political separation, 77, 89
  and popular opinion, 99–100
  and preexisting conditions, 114–15
  public opinion about, 98, 99–100, 102,
    103–4, 106, 107–8, 112, 114
  and role of government, 97–116
  universal, 98, 99
  See also Affordable Care Act; Medicaid;
    Medicare; *specific person or election*

Index

Hill, Anita, 14, 138–39
Himmelfarb, Milton, 26
Hofstadter, Richard, 197
Hollywood, 13, 87
Horton, Willie, 226–27
House of Representatives, US. *See* Congress, US; *specific person or election*
Huckabee, Mike, 37
Humphrey, Hubert, 34, 35, 36, 55, 61, 187, 215, 216, 224
Hussein, Saddam, 159, 160, 161, 165, 166, 167, 169

immigration
    election of 2016 and, 129, 133, 134, 258, 268
    and intensity factor, 118, 119, 120, 121, 128–34
    and path to legalization and citizenship, 129–30, 132, 133
    Proposition 187 and, 133–34
    public opinion about, 21, 129–30, 132
    and religion, 133
    and role of government, 95
    and taxes, 130, 132
    and Trump, 248, 253, 268, 274, 280
infrastructure, 64, 65, 263–65, 272, 280
intensity factor
    and abortion, 119, 120, 121, 124, 143
    and economy, 119
    election of 2016 and, 117, 118–19, 133, 134
    and gun laws, 120–21, 122–27, 132
    and immigration, 118, 120, 121, 128–34
    importance of, 120–22
    and New versus Old America, 118, 119
    of public opinion, 21, 120–22
    and social issues, 119, 120, 121
interests
    and New versus Old America, 24–27
    and political separation, 74
Iran, 173, 188, 248, 280
Iran-contra scandal, 67, 68, 87, 222–23
Iraq
    antiwar sentiment about, 112
    and intensity factor, 112, 121
    and Obama, 207
    and polarization, 66, 69, 70
    and power of public opinion, 19, 20

and US role in world affairs, 159, 161, 163, 164, 165–70, 171, 172, 174, 176, 177, 179
    See also ISIS; Persian Gulf War; *specific person or election*
ISIS (Islamic State of Iraq and Syria), 176–77, 178, 248
isolationism, 156, 157, 158–60, 178, 180, 181, 243, 280
Israel, 160

Jackson, Andrew, 49, 92–93, 95, 270
Jackson, Henry "Scoop," 62, 187
Jackson, Jesse, 33, 205, 226
Javits, Jacob, 61
Jefferson, Thomas, 92, 97
Jeffords, Jim, 61, 68
Jewish voters, 25–26
Jindal, Bobby, 117
jobs
    and affirmative action, 148, 149
    and angry white men, 263, 264
    and economic populism, 65
    and economy, 194
    and health insurance, 102
    and political separation, 73
    and role of government, 95
    and values of NASCAR nation, 48
    See also specific person or election
Johansson, Scarlett, 11
Johnson, Lyndon B. "LBJ"
    and civil rights, 55, 60, 195
    and communism, 214
    Congress relationship with, 273
    conservative reaction to, 214
    and economy, 195
    election of 1960 and, 226
    election of 1964 and, 22, 183, 184, 215
    election of 1968 and, 19–20, 195, 196
    "honeymoon" period for, 268
    Humphrey as vice president for, 224
    and New versus Old America, 4, 19–20, 22
    and polarization, 55, 59, 60, 61, 67, 192
    and political separation, 76
    popular vote for, 4
    toughness of, 244, 248
    and Vietnam, 195, 268
Johnson, Samuel, 273
Justice Department, US, 122

Index

Index

and Law of the Missing Imperative, 184
and New versus Old America, 2, 3, 4,
    20, 22, 24, 189, 225
and polarization, 58, 59, 61, 62, 69
and populism, 35, 36
McNamara, Robert S., 164–65
media
    and political separation, 77–78
    and populism, 270
    Trump views about, 242, 245–46, 247,
        252, 270, 277, 279
Medicaid, 45, 64, 115, 201, 229, 238, 239
Medicare
    and Clinton (Bill), 200, 229
    election of 1984 and, 218
    election of 1994 and, 45
    election of 2000 and, 203
    election of 2012 and, 238, 239
    as entitlement program, 112, 113
    funding for, 65
    and health care reform, 101, 107, 112,
        113
    passage of, 98, 107
    and polarization, 65
    and political separation, 77
    and populism, 45
    Trump and, 65, 262
Meet the Press (NBC-TV), 125
meritocracy: and political separation, 82
metric system, 31
Mexico: border wall with, 65, 279, 280
middle class
    election of 1984 and, 219
    election of 2016 and, 258
    and entitlement programs, 112
    and health care, 98–99, 100, 102, 103,
        104
    and polarization, 243
    and social welfare spending, 264
    and US as NASCAR nation, 47
    and values, 243
Military Academy, US (West Point):
    Bush (George W.) speech at, 161, 167,
        182
moderates
    and Bush (George W.) as compassionate
        conservative, 201
    disappearance of, 75–79
    election of 1964 and, 190
    election of 1972 and, 190
    election of 1980 and, 190, 192
    and political separation, 75–79

Mondale, Walter, 35, 36, 209, 218, 219,
    220–21, 224, 244, 256
Moore, Roy, 80
Moore, Stephen, 274
morality: as theme of 1976 election, 187–88
movements
    and New versus Old America, 21–24
    See also specific movement
Moynihan, Daniel Patrick, 8
Mueller, Robert, 275
Murkowski, Lisa, 69, 272

NASCAR Nation: and populism, 47–49
nation building, 170–72
National Defense Education Act (1958),
    9, 215
National Institutes of Health, US, 81
National Opinion Research Center
    (NORC), 126, 144, 145
National Public Radio (NPR), 13, 221
National Rifle Association (NRA), 124, 125
national security. *See* terrorism; world
    affairs; *specific person, election, or
    issue*
National Security Council, 165, 257
NATO (North American Treaty
    Organization), 162, 178, 179
NBC News, 125, 236
Netanyahu, Benjamin, 26
New America
    characteristics of, 1–2, 11, 22, 97
    and coalitions, 21–24
    and Constitution, 6, 7, 8, 9
    Democrats as party of, 52
    and Democrats shift to left, 258
    and education, 251
    emergence of, 1–2
    and gridlock, 6–10
    and health care, 97, 104
    and knowing the times, 11–15
    and movements, 21–24
    Old America versus, 1–27
    and politics as national, 15–16
    and populism, 18–19, 50
    and public opinion, 6–10, 16–21
    Republicans resistance to, 118, 153
    and same-sex marriage, 153
    and showdowns, 10–11
    and values, 24–27, 57
    See also specific person or election
New Deal, 25, 33, 60, 63, 96, 128, 192,
    246, 264, 268

Index

Index

Obama, Barack—and elections
  election of 2008 and, 4, 12, 23, 24, 26,
    35, 36, 62–63, 205–12, 258, 269
  election of 2012 and, 4, 10–11, 23, 26,
    27, 74, 76, 122, 124, 236–37, 238,
    240, 258
  election of 2014 and, 15
  election of 2016 and, 211–12, 271
Obamacare. *See* Affordable Care Act
Occupy movement, 38
O'Donnell, Christine, 256
Oklahoma City bombing (1995), 5, 31,
  157
Old America
  characteristics of, 2, 11, 117
  and coalitions, 21–24
  and Constitution, 6, 7, 8, 9
  and education, 251
  emergence of, 1–2
  and gridlock, 6–10
  and intensity factor, 119
  and interests, 24–27
  and knowing the times, 11–15
  and movements, 21–24
  New America versus, 1–27
  and polarization, 58
  and politics as national, 15–16
  and populism, 18–19, 50
  and public opinion, 6–10, 16–21
  and religion, 154
  and same-sex marriage, 153, 154
  and showdowns, 10–11
  and values, 24–27, 57
  See also specific person or election
O'Neill, Thomas P., Jr., "Tip," 14
Operation Desert Storm. *See* Persian Gulf
  War
order: as theme of 1968 election, 186–87
The O'Reilly Factor (Fox TV), 78
Osawatomie, Kansas
  Obama speech at, 95
  Roosevelt (Theodore) speech at, 94–95

Pakistan, 173
Palin, Sarah, 37, 127, 211
parallel universes: and political separation,
  79–82
Parks, Rosa, 14
Partial Birth Abortion Ban Act (2003),
  145–46
partisanship, 74, 85, 119, 151, 278. *See
  also* bipartisanship

Patriot Act, 9, 107
peace: as theme for 1972 election,
  215–17
Peace Corps, 268
Pelosi, Nancy, 107, 168, 247
Perot, Ross, 3, 4, 30, 89, 195, 196–97, 228,
  249
Persian Gulf War (1991), 33, 156, 159,
  160–61, 164, 165, 167, 168, 172, 193,
  194
Pew Research Center
  affirmative action studies by, 148–49,
    151
  education poll by, 253
  polarization study by, 74
  and same-sex marriage, 152
  and US role in world affairs, 177
Phillips, Kevin, 61
Planet America (TV show), 126–27
Planned Parenthood, 127
*Planned Parenthood of Southeastern
  Pennsylvania v. Casey* (1992), 144
Pledge of Allegiance, 32, 69
polarization
  beginning of, 53–58
  and class politics, 63
  in Congress, 260
  and cultural revolution of 1960s, 53–56,
    57, 62
  in Democratic party, 257–60
  emergence of political, 243
  and hardening of party bases, 66–71
  institutionalization of, 65
  and middle class, 243
  and Old America, 58
  Pew study about, 74
  and political parties, 58–63, 66–71,
    192
  and populism, 60, 61, 63, 64, 65
  and public opinion, 67, 71
  and race, 59, 60, 61
  from Reagan to Trump, 63–65
  and religion, 56–57, 69
  in Republican party, 256–57, 271–74
  and tribal politics, 65–66
  and values, 57, 63, 243
  *See also specific person, election, or
    issue*
political correctness, 65–66, 118, 119, 246,
  247, 248, 254, 260–61, 267
The Political Obituary of Richard Nixon
  (documentary), 186

Index

Index

and Constitution, 8
election of 1984 and, 219
election of 2008 and, 211–12
importance of, 18, 21, 29, 116, 279
intensity of, 21, 120–22
and knowing the times, 11
and New versus Old America, 6–10, 11, 16–21
and phony poll of 1980, 191
and polarization, 67, 71
and political separation, 84–85
and populism, 29, 116
power of, 16–21
and role of government, 136, 137
See also New York Times newspaper/poll;
Pew Research Center; *specific topics*
Public Religion Research Institute, 253
Putin, Vladimir, 181, 248, 251, 262

Qaddafi, Mu'ammar, 160, 162
Quayle, Dan, 224–25
Quinnipiac University, 252, 274

race
and anger/defiance of white men, 260–65
and crime, 226
and economy, 227
and judicial confirmation hearings, 139–40
and New versus Old America, 14
and partisanship, 151
and polarization, 59, 60, 61
and political correctness, 260
and political parties, 227, 243
and political separation, 74, 87, 88
and populism, 38–39, 261
and role of government, 227
Supreme Court decisions about, 59
and terrorism, 254
See also affirmative action; civil rights;
working-class whites; *specific person or election*
radio talk show hosts, 245
Rainbow Coalition, 33
Reagan, Ronald
and abortion, 141
approval ratings for, 67, 199, 218
and bipartisanship, 107
and bleakness of US, 265
Bush (George H. W.) as vice president for, 224

and change, 188
and civil rights, 226
Clinton (Bill) compared with, 17, 87
and coalitions/movements, 22, 26, 218
competence of, 222
conservatism of, 200
and conservatism of Republican party, 255, 257, 274, 276
crisis for, 269
and culture war of 1960s, 55
and economy, 218–19, 269
"Eleventh Commandment" of, 141
and gun laws, 123
as Hollywood celebrity, 13
"honeymoon" period for, 268
inaugural address of, 91
influence in 1990s of, 258
and intensity factor, 123
and Iran-contra scandal, 222
legacy of, 229
likability of, 198
and national security, 234
and New versus Old America, 2, 13, 17, 22, 26
and polarization, 55, 60, 61, 62, 66, 67, 68, 69, 70
and political separation, 76, 87
and populism, 32, 34, 39
and race, 226, 261
and religion, 189
and Republican image, 194
and role of government, 91, 94
and "safety net," 238
and Social Security, 189
stereotype image of, 245, 248
and taxes, 218, 226, 268, 269, 274–75
and world affairs, 156, 159, 219
Reagan, Ronald—and elections
election of 1964 and, 215
election of 1968 and, 187
election of 1976 and, 195–96, 226
election of 1980 and, 22, 69, 188–93, 217, 234, 244, 246
election of 1984 and, 2, 39, 69, 217–21, 227, 234
election of 1988 and, 193, 222
election of 2000 and, 55
The Reagans (CBS miniseries), 232
Reed, Ralph, 42
Reform Party, 196–97
refugee crisis, 262–63
Reid, Harry, 52, 125, 131

319

Index

Index

sex
  and New versus Old America, 14, 16–17
  and role of government, 137
  See also gay rights; same-sex marriage;
    women's rights; *specific person or*
    scandal
Sharpton, Al, 205
Shepard, Matthew, 14
showdowns: and New versus Old America,
  10–11
Silver, Nate, 76, 125
Sixteenth Amendment, 93
60 Minutes (CBS-TV), 228
social issues
  election of 1980 and, 191–92
  and intensity factor, 119, 120, 121
  See also specific issue
Social Security
  and bipartisanship, 77
  and Clinton (Bill), 98–99, 101
  election of 1980 and, 189
  election of 1984 and, 218
  election of 2000 and, 203
  election of 2012 and, 238
  election of 2016 and, 258
  as entitlement program, 112, 113
  passage of, 98, 107
  and Trump, 65, 262
social welfare: and Tea Party, 263, 264
Somalia, 157, 161, 163, 164
Sotomayor, Sonia, 150
South Korea, 178
Soviet Union. *See* Russia
Specter, Arlen, 68, 130
standoff
  for Trump, 271
  and uniting the country, 212
Starr, Kenneth, 84
The Starr Report, 83, 84, 87
Stevenson, Adlai, 35, 184, 220
stock car racing: and populism, 47–49
Streep, Meryl, 271
Streisand, Barbra, 17
strength: as theme for 2004 election,
  231–36
Supreme Court, Alabama, 80
Supreme Court, US
  and abortion, 141–44, 145–46, 147
  and affirmative action, 149–50
  and Affordable Care Act, 109–10, 112,
    115
  and Bork confirmation hearings, 139–40

  and gun laws, 124
  and intensity factor, 119, 124
  nominations to, 119
  and polarization, 58, 59
  and race issues, 59, 147
  religious right's views about, 40
  and role of government, 136, 141–44
  and same-sex marriage, 58, 153
  and Schiavo case, 136
  and Thomas confirmation hearings, 14,
    137–38, 140
Swift Boat Veterans for Truth, 235–36
Syria, 159, 163–64, 177, 180, 181, 249–50,
  257. *See also* ISIS

Taft, William Howard, 196, 224
Taliban, 160, 170, 171, 232
taxes
  and bipartisanship, 107
  and class issues, 99
  and class politics, 35
  and coalitions/movements, 22, 23
  and crises, 9
  and funding for government, 93–94
  and gridlock, 9
  and immigration, 130, 132
  income, 93
  in 1970s, 9
  and Obamacare mandate as tax, 108–10,
    112, 113
  and political separation, 81
  and populism, 30
  public opinion and, 19, 21
  and Trump-Republican party
    relationship, 274–75
  See also specific person or election
Tea Party
  and abortion, 256
  and Cantor, 271
  and change, 46
  as coalition, 23
  formation of, 2
  and health care, 104, 105, 106
  and infrastructure, 263–64
  and New versus Old America, 2, 4, 5, 6,
    23, 24
  and Obama, 2, 4, 6, 44–45, 46, 70, 106
  and polarization, 70, 256
  and political separation, 76
  and politics, 44–46
  and populism, 38, 44–46
  and Republican conservatism, 255

Index

Index

and populism, 4–5, 19, 23, 27, 30, 33, 34, 38, 43–44, 49–52, 63, 64, 65, 96, 242, 243, 257, 262, 264–65, 276, 277, 280
and pragmatism, 9–10
and progressivism, 243, 263
and race, 210, 254, 272
and religion, 43–44
Republican relationship with, 252, 255, 256–57, 259, 271–76
and role of government, 96, 263, 264
and Russia/Putin, 181, 262, 275
and Social Security, 262
standoff for, 271
and taxes, 262, 272, 274–75, 278, 280
and terrorism, 181, 252, 254
and trade issues, 96, 119
"triangulation" of, 275–76
on Twitter, 270, 271, 272, 273, 279, 280
as un-Obama, 247–51
and US role in world affairs, 177–82, 243, 249–50, 257, 280
Warsaw speech of, 181–82
wealth of, 244, 254
and winning, 277–78
and working-class whites, 251, 252, 253, 262, 263, 269, 274, 276, 277
See also election of 2016
Tsongas, Paul, 35, 208
Twitter: Trump on, 270, 271, 272, 273, 279, 280

Udall, Morris, 62, 187
Ukraine, 248
unification: election of 2016 and, 212
United Nations, 215
United States
bleak picture of, 265–69
See also specific person, election, or topic
uniter: as theme of 2008 election, 205–12
University of California, Berkeley, 26–27

valence issues, 57–58
values
case study about, 83–89
and Clinton administration, 203, 204
and economy, 24, 26
and education, 252, 254
and Flake criticism of Trump, 272
and intensity factor, 119
and middle class, 243
and New versus Old America, 24–27, 57

and polarization, 57, 63, 243
and political correctness, 261
and political separation, 83–89
and politics, 74
and populism, 30, 32, 35, 37, 46, 49
and role of government, 94
See also specific person or election
Values Voter Summit, 40
Vietnam War
and Democratic party, 60
and intensity of issues, 121
and Johnson, 268
and Kerry, 232–33, 235–36
and polarization, 55, 60, 61, 62
and political separation, 86–87
public opinion about, 19–20
and US role in world affairs, 159, 163, 164–65, 168, 169, 171, 177
See also specific election
Vietnam Veterans Against the War, 232–33
voting
and Latino population, 128–29
single-issue, 121
split-ticket, 75
by suburban voters, 252
See also working-class whites; specific election
Voting Rights Act (1965), 107, 226

Waco, Texas, 5, 157
Wall Street Journal, 143, 236
Wallace, George, 34, 39, 61, 62, 187
war
getting out of, 168–70
and ISIS, 176–77
limited, 162–64
and new Cold War, 172–76
political, 164–65, 171
preemptive, 165–68, 176
and US role in world affairs, 162–70
See also specific war
War Powers Act, 9
Warren, Earl, 59
Warren, Elizabeth, 263
Warsaw, Poland: Trump speech in, 181–82
Washington Post newspaper, 125, 130, 178, 180, 234, 253, 257, 274
Watergate, 187, 188
wealth, 244, 252, 254. See also specific person
Webster v. Reproductive Health Services (1989), 141–43, 144

323

Index

About the Author

BILL SCHNEIDER is a professor at the Schar School of Policy and Government at George Mason University. He is also a visiting professor at the Luskin School of Public Affairs at UCLA. He is a contributor to Al Jazeera English. He was the Cable News Network's senior political analyst from 1990 to 2009.

Schneider has covered every US presidential and midterm election since 1976 for the *Los Angeles Times*, the *Atlantic Monthly*, CNN, and Al Jazeera. Schneider has been labeled "the nation's electionmeister" by the *Washington Times* and "the Aristotle of American politics" by the *Boston Globe. Campaigns & Elections* magazine called him "the most consistently intelligent analyst on television." He was a member of the CNN political team that won an Emmy for its 2006 election coverage and a Peabody for its 2008 coverage.

In 2003, the Graduate School of Arts and Sciences at Harvard University awarded Schneider its Centennial Medal for contributions to society. He was also the recipient of an honorary doctorate of humane letters from Brandeis University in 2008.

Bill Schneider is coauthor, with Seymour Martin Lipset, of *The Confidence Gap: Business, Labor, and Government in the Public Mind*. He has also written extensively on politics and public opinion for the *Los Angeles Times*, the *New Republic*, the *Atlantic*, the *Washington Post, Politico*, Reuters, *National Journal*, the *Huffington Post*, and NBC News's *Think*.

Printed in the United States
By Bookmasters